A STUDY OF THE GREEK LOVE-NAMES

This is a volume in the Arno Press collection

MORALS AND LAW IN ANCIENT GREECE

Advisory Editor
Gregory Vlastos

Editorial Board
Kenneth Dover
M. I. Finley
Arnaldo Momigliano

See last pages of this volume for a complete list of titles

A STUDY OF THE GREEK LOVE-NAMES

DAVID M. ROBINSON
AND
EDWARD J. FLUCK

ARNO PRESS
A New York Times Company
New York • 1979

Editorial Supervision: MARIE STARECK

Reprint Edition 1979 by Arno Press Inc.

Copyright 1937, The Johns Hopkins Press
Copyright renewed 1965 by Equitable Trust Company as
    Executor of David M. Robinson

Reprinted by arrangement with Harvard University and
    Trustees under deed Helen Tudor Robinson, c/o
    Maryland National Bank
Reprinted from a copy in The University of Illinois
    Library

MORALS AND LAW IN ANCIENT GREECE
ISBN for complete set: 0-405-11529-6
See last pages of this volume for titles.

Manufactured in the United States of America

Library of Congress Cataloging in Publication Data

Robinson, David Moore, 1880-1958.
    A study of Greek love-names.

    (Morals and law in ancient Greece)
    Reprint of the ed. published by the Johns Hopkins
Press, Baltimore, which was issued as no. 23 of the Johns
Hopkins University studies in archaeology.
    Originally issued in part as E. J. Fluck's thesis,
Johns Hopkins University, under title: A study of the
Greek love-names.
    Bibliography: p.
    1. Civilization, Greek. 2. Love names--Greece.
3. Homosexuality, Male--Greece. 4. Greek language--
Terms and phrases. 5. Vases, Greek. I. Fluck, Edward
James, 1909-   joint author. II. Title. III. Series.
IV. Series: The Johns Hopkins University studies in
archaeology ; no. 23.
DF93.R6 1979   938'.09   78-19375
ISBN 0-405-11569-5

A STUDY OF THE GREEK LOVE-NAMES

INCLUDING A DISCUSSION OF PAEDERASTY
AND A PROSOPOGRAPHIA

PLATE I

1. *Erasts* and *Eromenoi* on Kylix by Peithinos in Berlin. A δύσερως ἀνήρ looks on from left. Inscription: ὁ παῖς ναίχι καλὸς καλός. See p. 13.

2. Interior of Kylix in Athens by the Brygos Painter. The Reclining Man is singing: ὦ παίδων κάλλιστε. See p. 31.

3. Kylix by Euphronios in Munich. Leagros in Thracian Costume, Inscription: Λέαγρος καλός. See p. 4.

THE JOHNS HOPKINS UNIVERSITY
STUDIES IN ARCHAEOLOGY, NO. 23

A STUDY OF THE GREEK LOVE-NAMES

INCLUDING A DISCUSSION OF PAEDERASTY AND
A PROSOPOGRAPHIA

BY

DAVID M. ROBINSON, PH. D., LITT. D.
PROFESSOR OF ARCHAEOLOGY AND EPIGRAPHY

AND

EDWARD J. FLUCK, PH. D.
FORMERLY FELLOW OF THE ARCHAEOLOGICAL INSTITUTE OF AMERICA AT THE
AMERICAN SCHOOL OF CLASSICAL STUDIES IN ATHENS AND VOGELER
FELLOW IN ARCHAEOLOGY AT THE JOHNS HOPKINS
UNIVERSITY, INSTRUCTOR IN CLASSICS
AT MUHLENBERG COLLEGE

ὅ τι καλὸν φίλον ἀεί

BALTIMORE
THE JOHNS HOPKINS PRESS
1937

Copyright 1937, The Johns Hopkins Press

Printed in the United States of America
By J. H. Furst Company, Baltimore, Maryland

PREFACE

The *kalos* inscriptions, or so-called "love-names," on Attic vases are derived from the usual phrase *ho pais kalos*[1] on these vases and in Greek literature. There are countless instances of the writing of the formula *ho pais kalos* and fewer of the feminine *he pais kale*. The love-names are formed by the addition of the adjective *kalos* to a proper-name (which can often be identified with some historical person of the period). Sometimes the bare adjective is strengthened by a ναίχι, or a κάρτα (Klein, *Die Griechischen Vasen mit Lieblingsinschriften,* p. 37, no. 1), or νὴ Δία (cf. Theognis kalos, Chapter IV, no. 265 below), or it is put in the superlative κάλλιστος (cf. Chapter IV, nos. 22 and 118 below). The expression ὁ δεῖνα καλὸς δοκεῖ is sometimes found (cf. Andokides kalos *sub* Meletos, Chapter IV, no. 169). There is a variation on this form of "So-and-so seemed fair to So-and-so" in the inscription ὁ δεῖνα καλὸς βένεται = φαίνεται (Graef-Langlotz, *Die Antiken Vasen von der Akropolis,* II, 1, p. 21, no. 256). This last form suggests that *ho pais kalos* often is equal to *eromenos* for the *erastes* who either wrote it himself or had it written; i. e. that the "beloved" seemed "fair" to the "lover." From this connotation, which will be developed later, and from the German word *Lieblingsnamen* for these inscriptions comes our English "love-name." Several times the patronymic, or father's name, is added to the love-name (cf. Glaukon kalos and Diphilos, nos. 104 and 72 in Chapter IV).

The material on the subject is divided in the following fashion. Chapter I contains an account of the *kalos* inscriptions on vases, their position, significance, and value to archaeology. Chapter II covers the lexicography of *kalos,*

---

[1] "The boy is beautiful." A score of labels in the Metropolitan Museum (1936) wrongly translated this as "the handsome youth." That would require ὁ καλὸς παις or ὁ παις ὁ καλός.

v

especially where it relates to the vases in helping to interpret and understand the conditions which led to the use of the inscription on those vases. From this point onwards the monograph lists and tries to suggest identifications, wherever possible, for all names found in connection with *kalos*. Chapter III discusses all these names known through literature or other arts, and Chapter IV attempts a comprehensive cataloguing of all the names on Attic vases. A brief appendix is added, containing the few *kalos* inscriptions which occur on non-Attic vases, principally Boeotian.

DAVID M. ROBINSON
EDWARD J. FLUCK

The Johns Hopkins University,
    April 15, 1937

CONTENTS

CHAPTER	PAGE
I. The Love-Names on Attic Vases	1
II. The Love-Names in Greek Literature	15
III. Prosopographia of Love-Names in Literature and Art other than Vases	46
IV. Prosopographia of Love-Names on Attic Vases	66
APPENDIX. Love-Names on Non-Attic Vases	192
SELECTED BIBLIOGRAPHY	197
ABBREVIATIONS	199
INDEX	201

A STUDY OF THE GREEK LOVE-NAMES
INCLUDING A DISCUSSION OF PAEDERASTY AND A PROSOPOGRAPHIA

CHAPTER I

THE LOVE-NAMES ON ATTIC VASES

In 1898 when Klein's work, *Die Griechischen Vasen mit Lieblingsinschriften,* appeared, there were five hundred and fifty-eight vases known with *kalos* inscriptions. The author counted two hundred and twenty proper-names used with *kalos* or *kale* on these vases, which he distributed among twenty-three known painters and an indefinite number of unknown artists. He also noticed that on vases of the black-figured style "love-names" fall far behind artists' signatures in frequency. This would not be so apparent, however, if the exact opposite were not true for the red-figured period, when the *kalos* inscription begins to occupy the field, and is much more common than the artist's signature.

The vases with this type of inscription extend from the period of Taleides[1] and Exekias,[2] who first, probably under the influence of certain popular and contemporary poets, transferred this formula, *ho pais kalos,* to vases, through to the last quarter of the fifth century. Since only thirty of the two hundred and twenty names which Klein counted are those of women, and these are always names of *hetairai* and coined

---
[1] Taleides, Timagoras, Exekias, and Amasis, whose earliest work dated from the middle of the sixth century, all use love-names. Taleides uses those of Neokleides and Kleitarchos, both of which were known to Klein.

[2] Exekias praised Stesias on his earliest vases (Hoppin, *Handb. B. F. Vases*, pp. 100, 108), and changed his affection to Onetorides on his later and better vases (Hoppin, *op. cit.*, pp. 92, 106, 109, 111; Furtwaengler-Reichhold, *Gr. Vasenmalerei*, pls. 131-132). Cf. Beazley, *Attic Black-Figure*, pp. 17-21, 29-31; Technau, *Exekias*, pp. 8, 15.

to refer to the trade (as Pantoxena, Xenodoke, etc.), our studies in identification will be mostly confined to the names of males, these being the more significant historically. Then, too, *ho pais kalos* and not *he pais kale* is really the *raison d'être* of the movement; this will be made clear later.

Several of Klein's names are questionably included in a list of this type, and a few have been proved definitely out of place. Such are *prosagoreuo* (which is now correctly understood not as a proper name, but as a *Schlagwort* or "catchword," like the frequent "χαῖρε," and so meaning "greetings") and *Paidikos,* which has been interpreted as the name of a "favourite," the name of a painter, or even as equivalent to the plural *paidika,* relative to the amatory habits of youths. But Pottier [3] has published an alabastron in the Louvre [4] with the inscription Παιδικὸς ἐποίησεν, and this proves that, though the name is to be stricken out of Klein's list of *Lieblingsnamen,* it is not a general expression for *eromenos* or *paidika* as Studniczka suggested,[5] but must be considered as a potter's signature (its adjectival quality is no more astonishing than that of the names of two other known painters, Smikros and Olympikos).

The love-name has come to be of great importance in classifying the work of anonymous painters, who, not having signed their vases, are known only by their styles and by the names of the boys with which they adorned their output. Such are, for instance, Beazley's Aischines-Painter (meaning the painter who thought that Aischines was "fair"), the Lysis-Painter, the Diogenes-Painter, the Epeleios-Master, etc. The names are most numerous on red-figured ware, for the history of which they are indispensable, as a whole group of vases is unsigned and says nothing about masters' identities, but a good deal about the boys who were pleasing these masters and in vogue with the people at the time.

The problem of whether we are to regard a love-name as

---

[3] *Rev. Ét. Gr.,* VI, 1893, p. 40.
[4] Hoppin, *Handb. R. F.,* II, p. 272.
[5] *Jahrb.,* II, 1887, p. 159, note 109.

belonging to a person who was a particular and private favourite of the painter, or to some youth whose reputation was city-wide, is much-disputed. In only a few cases can we be positive about the first theory: a black-figured hydria of Timagoras in praise of Andokides (see Meletos kalos, Chapter IV); a red-figured alabastron in the British Museum (p. 85) with the inscription: Ἀφροδισία καλή. τὼς (for οὕτως) δοκεῖ Εὐχ[ε]ίρῳ; and a tile from some building in Athens (see Hippeos, p. 57, no. 45, also p. 74, no. 7; p. 76, no. 12). In these cases the inscription reads that " so-and-so seemed fair to so-and-so-else," and the name of the *erastes* is that of a known potter. Furtwaengler, however, criticizes Hauser for assuming that this is the case with all the other love-names on Attic-vases, and says:[6] " Hauser betont besonders das persönliche Element bei den Lieblingsinschriften; er möchte die ' παῖδες ' am liebsten als rein private Liebschaften der Vasenmaler ansehen. Er geht darin zu weit. Der Fall, dass ein Liebling bei mehreren Malern erscheint, ist doch zu oft bezeugt. Die ' παῖδες ' werden gewiss die jeweils in der Palästra besonders bewunderten und beliebten Knaben gewesen sein, die in der Mode waren, und die jeder pries; die einzelnen Maler trafen unter diesen natürlich eine ihrem oder vielleicht auch ihrer Kunden Geschmack entsprechende Auswahl." That the admiration for a beautiful youth must often have been city-wide and not merely the personal feeling of a single individual is also attested by the multitude of his admirers in many cases, to which the *kalos* inscriptions bear witness.

Sometimes, it is true, the painters praised their own associates and professional competitors with a *kalos* inscription on their vases (see Epilykos kalos, Chapter IV, e. g.), but Studniczka[7] believes that generally these inscriptions are nothing less than expressions of the private feelings of their authors for their " etwaigen obscuren ' paidika ' " or of the popularity which the bearers of those names enjoyed in Athens of the time. He continues: " Über den Kreis, aus welchem

---

[6] *Berl. Phil. Woch.*, XIV, 1894, p. 109: Review of Hartwig.
[7] *Jahrb.*, II, 1887, p. 150.

diese Namen vorwiegend gewählt wurden, lässt uns der hocharistokratische Klang von vielen sowie Darstellungen, wie die des schmucken jungen Hippeus Leagros in der Geryoneusschale des Euphronios, nicht im Zweifel [see plate I, 3]. . . . Im Kerameikos wurde 'allerhand Skandal an die Wände geschrieben.'" The Kerameikos was a show-place for all the mad pranks of Athens' *jeunesse dorée*,[8] and there is no doubt that many of the names on vases are those of the scions of high families, who sported about the potters' quarter. Identifications, perfectly agreeable in point of time, have been made to this effect of many of the names. Hoppin [9] thinks that many of these names may have been put on the vase to fill the order of the purchaser; in speaking of the Baltimore kylix with Χαιρίας καλός and a scene of an ephebe purchasing vases in a shop in the Kerameikos, he says: "that the name may have had something to do with the actual purchaser of the vase." He says further:[10] "Anyone who has examined a large number of Attic vases must have been struck by the fact that these names form no part of the original design or subject of the vase, and are added wherever the space permits, in a singularly haphazard fashion. Therefore it is by no means a fantastic theory if the inscriptions, especially those with *kalos,* were added to the vase after it was finished, to suit the individual taste of the purchaser." Miss Richter, *Red-Figured Athenian Vases in the Metropolitan Museum,* p. xxx, well says: "the boy called 'handsome' was a favorite of the client or of the artist or was a universally acknowledged beauty." Apart from the obvious objection that Leagros, for instance, could never have ordered for himself or received, as gifts from others, all the vases (Klein counted 45) with his name, the second half of Hoppin's theory can also be criticized. Miss Richter [11] has thoroughly established the fact that "instead of the two, three, or four firings often assumed

---

[8] Meursius, *Ceramicus Geminus,* cap. 18, in Gronovs' Thesaurus, IV.
[9] *Euthymides and His Fellows,* p. 100.
[10] *Op. cit.,* p. 102.
[11] *The Craft of Athenian Pottery,* p. 108.

by archaeologists, the evidence points to only one fire, after total completion of the vase." This would invalidate the theory that painted inscriptions were added to suit the taste of the purchaser, unless, of course, he had confided that taste to the vase-maker before the vase was made. In the case of a vase with a popular name like Leagros or Glaukon or Memnon, it is probable that the vase-painters simply added the inscription themselves to the vase before its firing, knowing full well that the name of so popular a character about the city would make a " best seller " out of the vase. In the case of less renowned persons, we can assume that a vase with an inscription praising their beauty was made at the express order of a client. Incised inscriptions could have been put on either by the purchaser himself or, at his order, by the artisan for the boy he wanted to please. Miss Richter's belief, that the great majority of Athenian vases was made for actual use, not for votive, decorative, or funeral purposes, would also favor the theory that, when the love-names are not those of popular or well-known characters of the day, they must have been put on the vase at the command of the one ordering the vase (for his own, private " pretty boy "). When the inscription simply reads *ho pais kalos,* the problem disappears, and only the matter of the purpose of the inscription remains; for this we agree with Symonds' explanation [12]: "Another attention ... from a lover to a boy was to have a vase or drinking-cup of baked clay made with a portrait of the youth depicted on its surface, attended by winged genii of health and love. The word 'fair' was inscribed beneath." [13] " C'est la porte ouverte au caprice," says Pottier neatly.[14]

The general purposes of these inscriptions have been summarized by Jahn,[15] who finds that a *kalos* inscription is either

---

[12] *A Problem in Greek Ethics,* 1901, p. 41.

[13] For vase illustrations of this, cf. Harrison, *Prolegomena,* figs. 171 and 172, pp. 636-637.

[14] *Mon. Piot,* IX, 1902, p. 168.

[15] *Die Vasensammlung zu Muenchen,* p. cxxvi. Cf. now Miss Richter, *Red-Figured Athenian Vases in the Metropolitan Museum of Art,* pp. xxix-xxv.

spoken by a person in the scene, or designates a person in the scene, or is an expression of the painter's own *paidika,* or was put on the vase to fill the order of a client who had a boy to please somewhere. *Kalos* inscriptions can and do sometimes refer to people represented on vases.[16] This is obvious on many vases with mythological subjects, for if a god or a hero is identifiable only through his attributes and *kalos* stands near, it must be taken as referring to him (*e. g.* Eros,[17] Perses,[18] Gelos,[19] Hektor,[20] Dionysos,[21] and Nestor [22]). The next step is one in which *kalos* can refer to unknown men on vases, as, for instance, when it is a jest on the picture of a Seilenos.[23] Often nothing interferes with the connection between picture and inscription, as on the unsigned Euphronios vase on which all the athletes are given names,[24] and on the red-figured bell-krater by the Kleophon Painter in Boston [25] with a sacrificial scene performed by a priest and three youths with another man watching. Beazley identifies the three youths and the man: Aresias, the man watching, as one of the Thirty Tyrants; Kallias as the son of Telokles and prosecuted for mutilating the herms; Mantitheos as one of the Hermokopids banished in 415; the name of the third youth Beazley restores tentatively as Hippokles and connects the name with that of one of the Ten. He finally puts the question: "Is it not possible that the Aresias, the Mantitheos, the Kallias, and the Hippokles are those who played a part in the politics of Athens during the last two decades of the fifth century?" (See further p. 122 *s. v.* Kallias). If so, they could no longer

---

[16] Langlotz, *Zeitbestimmung,* p. 45.
[17] Gerhard, *Ant. Bildw.,* 57.
[18] Panofka, *Mus. Blacas,* XI, 1.
[19] De Witte, *Cab. Durand,* nr. 65.
[20] Gerhard, *Auserl. Vasenb.,* III, 189.
[21] F. R., pl. 7.
[22] *Rev. Arch.,* II, pl. 40.
[23] *Arch. Zeit.,* XLIII, 1885, pl. 10; Beazley, *Attic Red-Figured Vases in American Museums,* p. 82, fig. 50 bis.
[24] Hoppin, *Euthymides,* pl. 20. "Leagros kalos" infibulates himself.
[25] Beazley, *op. cit.,* p. 182; *A. J. A.,* XXXIII, 1929, p. 366, no. 11.

have been so very young by the time of the vase, which dates in the fourth quarter of the century, but, as we shall shortly see, *kalos* inscriptions are not confined only to the youths and boys of Athens, though ὁ παῖς καλός without the mention of a name is very common. Sometimes ναί or ναίχι or κάρτα ("very") is added. Cf. index of Miss Richter, *Red-Figured Athenian Vases in the Metropolitan Museum of Art*, p. 241

That the inscriptions can relate to persons pictured on Attic vases is further to be seen in many inscriptions such as the καλὸς εἶ on an amphora in Wuerzburg;[26] this vase has a scene from heroic legend, of Phoinix, Talthybios, Aias and Hektor, and the inscription is certainly, as Langlotz suggests, "kaum anders zu verstehen, denn als Begeisterung über die heroische Haltung der Beiden." Vases with "courting scenes" also lend themselves to the strengthening of this theory, as, for instance, an amphora[27] with a scene between a bearded man and an ephebe and the inscription, καλὸς εἶ, which the man is almost certainly speaking to the ephebe. The next step is to be found on a kylix in the Louvre,[28] on which the painter, the Eucharides-Painter, has written beside the hoplitodromos and the youth playing flutes, 'Αριστείδες εἶ σὺ κα[λός; here there is no reason for doubting that an identification between the person in the scene and the one named in the inscription was intentional. The case is the same with the Σώστρατος καλός εἰμι (see Sostratos kalus, Chapter IV) on another vase. Hence, there need be no reason for doubting that a *kalos* name was meant to identify a character, pictured in some favourite pastime, in the scene on a Greek vase, whether the portraiture is accurate in its attempt or not (see Langlotz sub Leagros kalos, Chapter IV).

---

[26] Langlotz, *Gr. Vas. Wuerzburg*, no. 508.

[27] Philippart, *Colls. de Céramique Grecque en Italie*, II, p. 97, no. 2.

[28] G 136; Hoppin, *Handb. R. F.*, I, p. 358, no. 16. Cf. two cases of καλὸς εἶ on vases in the Metropolitan Museum, a calyx-krater of Epiktetos II (the Kleophrades Painter, about 490 B. C.) and an amphora dating about 480 B. C., where with reference to Apollo we have καλὸς εἶ, cf. Richter, *Red-Figured Athenian Vases in the Metropolitan Museum*, pp. 34-37.

Strictly speaking, a discussion of love-names ought to include those only which are preceded or followed by the adjective, but, as a certain amount of laxity always existed in the use of the formula, of which we are aware because of the intermittent occurrences of two ways of writing the same name (now with, now without *kalos*),—all names, whether followed by *kalos* or not, excepting those of mythological, heroic, or artistic persons, are generally included in the lists. So, in scenes of a mythological or Bacchic nature, where the figures are identified by name or by attributes, *kalos* is clearly superficial to the requirements of the representation. Genre scenes, especially of the palaestra, are eminently suited to the use of the love-name. It is frequently found as an impersonal glorification in its common form, *ho pais kalos*. In other cases its mention is frequently divorced from any relation to the scene, and it is futile to attempt a connection between scene and inscription.

On the assumption that the ephebes called *kalos* could scarcely retain their good-looks for more than a decade, Hartwig summarized his conclusions as follows:[29]

1. All vases of a master with identical names belong to a definite period of about ten years during that master's activity.

2. All vases of different masters with similar names are approximately contemporary within ten years.

3. Appearance of two or more names on the same vase shows contemporaneity of the named persons (the most extreme difference in age being about a decade).

So it was, and still is, believed by many that all the names on vases are those of youths, and that all the vases with the name of a certain youth must have appeared within a ten year period; "so handelt es sich bei allen diesen Namen um . . . Jünglinge, deren Schönheitsblüte jeder Kenner des

---

[29] *Meisterschalen*, p. 8.

Südens auf allerhöchstens zehn Jahre taxiren wird."[30] But Studniczka[31] had doubted this, and believed that these inscriptions referred not only to attractive youths, but to worthy and popular men as well. Certainly throughout Greek literature it is not merely the ephebes who are called *kalos*. Langglotz (*Zeitbestimmung*, pp. 43 ff.) also has shown that occasionally older men are called *kalos*.

That the adjective *kalos* could be and was used for males at almost any stage of their lives, if they deserved it, we learn from Xenophon,[32] who has Kritoboulos say: Ἐπεὶ ὥσπερ γε παῖς γίγνεται καλός, οὕτω καὶ μειράκιον, καὶ ἀνήρ, καὶ πρεσβύτης. Τεκμήριον δέ· θαλλοφόρους γὰρ τῇ Ἀθηνᾷ τοὺς καλοὺς γέροντας ἐκλέγονται. Earlier the same speaker says: μαίνονται δὲ καὶ οἱ μὴ τοὺς καλοὺς στρατηγοὺς αἱρούμενοι. Ἐγὼ οὖν μετὰ Κλεινίου κἂν διὰ πυρὸς ἰοίην. Likewise Protagoras calls the bearded, ripened Alkibiades[33] καλὸς ἀνήρ. *Kalos*, then, can also refer to mature men. Only when *ho pais* is added can we be sure what period of his life is meant, as a male over twenty years of age would scarcely be called a boy.[34]

Perrot and Chipiez[35] think that it may be a mistake to attribute too precise a meaning to this epithet, and indeed we know that in Athens it was also a sort of vague acclamation, as is clearly seen in two passages of Aristophanes,[36] where allusion is made to the custom of using the word at every occasion as a demonstration of respect and affection for

---

[30] Hauser, *Jahrb.*, X, 1895, p. 111. Miss Richter, *Red-Figured Athenian Vases in the Metropolitan Museum*, p. xxx, note 32 says: "the frequent combination of the word παῖς with καλός on the vases would seem to indicate that the vase-painters as a rule had boys in mind." Miss Swindler, *Ancient Painting*, p. 177, calls them "débutants."

[31] *Jahrb.*, II, 1887, p. 160.

[32] *Symposion*, IV, 17.

[33] Plato, *Protag.* 1.

[34] Bluemner, *Privataltertümer*, p. 323.

[35] *Histoire de l'Art*, IX, p. 362.

[36] The Thracian chieftain in *Acharnians*, 144, is so attached to the Athenians that he writes on walls: Ἀθηναίοι καλοί.

a person, an institution, or even a people.[37] A mosaic (c. 420 B. C.) from Olynthos [38] reads: Εὐτυχία καλή, which, interpreted as "Success is fair," is an instance of this glorification of abstractions. In the same room with this mosaic was found another, Ἀφροδίτη καλή, which may be taken to mean "Love is beautiful," or as referring to the Goddess herself, or even to a girl in the house named Aphrodite. In the Agora and Pnyx on every side was heard this word, when a person beloved by the populace appeared, when an orator whose opinions were shared finished speaking—like the French *vive*. But they also certainly refer to fair ephebes, who, after inspiring the liveliest feelings in the palaistra, later were held favourites for the elegance of their appearance and the perfections of their bodies; indeed they were much more popular than the most promiscuous courtesans at the time. Wherever there is opportunity and available material, it is a human impulse to scratch the name or initials of one's beloved (see Philokles kalos, no. 70, Chapter III) on a tree or wall or the like. Columns, shields, wash-basins, foot-stools, altars, chests, wine-skins and diskoi, as well as vases were made more precious by the presence of a beloved's name (cf. the distribution of *kalos* inscriptions among the furnishings in the scenes on Greek vases).

The paederastic nature of these inscriptions, shown by abundant literary references later, is also to be noted in the very character of many of the scenes accompanying the inscriptions, and, perhaps, by simple inference from analogy: as, when the inscriptions are in praise of a woman,

---

[37] Aristoph. *Knights*, 1341, where Agorakritos calls himself an ἐραστής of Demos. In *Wasps*, 98, Xanthias says that, if his master ever saw Δῆμος καλός, he changed it to κημὸς καλός. Cf. also καλῶς τῶι κυβιστητῶι ("bravo, tumbler") in *C. V. A., Bibl. Nat., Paris*, fasc. 2, III h e, pl. 88, 1-4.

[38] These are the only *kalos* names on mosaics. Cf. Robinson, *A. J. A.*, XXXVIII, 1934, pp. 503 ff., fig. 2. As suggested, *loc. cit.*, p. 505, n. 2, Ἀφροδίτη καλή may be the name for the best throw of dice, Lucian, *Erotes*, 16. Cf. also Sallustius, Περὶ Θεῶν, ch. 4 (Mullach, *F. Ph. G.*, 1881, III, p. 32): καλήν τε φανῆναι τὴν Ἀφροδίτην.

she is always known to have been an hetaira. While many of the *paides kaloi* of the vases are aristocratic, at the same time homoerotic habits are reflected in scenes of *erastes* and *eromenoi,* gifts of rabbits, cocks, and flowers (the usual love-tokens) passing between them, and many pictures of ephebes muffled in mysterious mantles as though awaiting an assignation or keeping some secret rendezvous. Both "Achilles" and "Ganymede" are to be found in these inscriptions: the aristocratic identifications of many of the names speak for the higher reputations of the "Achilles" of the lot, whereas, when there is a scene of "conversational" couples of males, it seems we may rightly suspect innuendos to Ganymede. Feminine inflections [39] given to the adjective with the name (cf. *kale* with Hippodamas kale; see Hippodamas, Euphiletos, and elsewhere in Chapter IV), and inscriptions themselves sometimes reveal a bit of the character of the *kalos,* especially those erotically phrased. The name Hermogenes on the Memnon cup by Douris, read by Duemmler [40] ἐν ἐμὲ κνē[ι] [ἐ] ρίνε Ἑρμογένες καλός, if correctly interpreted, tells a good bit about the dark side of some of these inscriptions (cf. also Agathon kalos, Chapter IV). Duemmler writes at length about the erotic significance of κυννον on vases,[41] but Beazley [42] contests this. *Kalos* is, in its largest sense, a passionate approval of

---

[39] The inscription ἡ παῖς καλός (Graef-Langlotz, *Akrop. Vas.,* II, 2, no. 676) is on a vase with no painted scene, and seems to be deliberate, as there is small chance that a Greek would not have been familiar with the inflections of his own language. Cf. with this many inscriptions of the type of the καλή on a vase (*C. V. A., Oxford-Ashmolean,* fasc. 2, pl. 52, 5) with a scene of two youths only; and the καλέ καλά on another vase (*C. V. A., Musée Scheurleer,* fasc. 2, III I b and c, pl. 7, nos. 1, 2, and 3) with only ephebes in the scene. Unless in his illiteracy the artisan inscribing *HE* thought he was writing *HO,* or in writing *kale* pronounced it *kalos,* it is likely that here too, as in the *kale* with Hippodamas, Euphiletos, and Pithon in Chapter IV below, it must have been the intention of his perverse affections or the butt of his derision.

[40] *Berl. Phil. Woch.,* XI, 1891, col. 469; the vase is Louvre, G 115. Cf. Hoppin, *R. F.,* I, p. 244.

[41] *Kleine Schriften,* III, p. 359.   [42] *J. H. S.,* LII, 1932, pp. 171-172.

life in all its moods and occupations, as can be seen from the favourite types of scenes on vases from the time of the *kalos* inscription. Philippart [43] mentions some of these favourite themes: " Nous voyons ici le bambin espiègle, le jeune garçon réservé, docile, ou vicieux; le palestrite agile et vigoureux, l'éphèbe noble d'allures et de sentiments ou entouré de compagnons pervers; l'homme mûr, sérieux ou sensuel; le bon vivant, le bavard, l'ivrogne, le débauché." In short, Attic vases show forth the unbounded joie-de-vivre of the time, so occupied with its youths, its physical culture, its emotional adventures, its banquets and revels, and excluding that only which is not MAN.

Beazley [44] notices that the group of a man and a boy " is a favourite in Attic black-figure from the second quarter of the sixth century onwards." To illustrate the varying degrees of intimacy he cites as " good examples " a lip-cup in Berlin, 1773 (the scene is of a bearded man embracing a youth, who has his own arms around the man); a fragment of a Little-Master cup in the Louvre, F 85; a cup in Athens (Licht, *Sittengeschichte Griechenlands, Ergänzungsband,* p. 208); a tripod at Yale, 122 (Baur, pl. 4); an amphora in Wuerzburg (Langlotz, *op. cit.,* 1932, no. 241, pls. 64 and 65), dating c. 530 B. C. The scenes on both sides of this last vase are practically identical: a man, bearded and naked and with a red tainia over his arm, touches a naked boy in the customary fashion for courting (on the chin and genitals); the boy was originally intended to retaliate with the also customary gesture of defense, for his right arm is ready to turn away the man's advances on his chin—but then the painter put a spear in his hand, and so (on plate 65 at any rate) he seems completely submissive to the man's overtures. The gesture for courting, seen commonly on vases at this time, recalls the epigram (*Anth. Pal.*, X, 20):

Ἤν τινα καλὸν ἴδῃς, εὐθὺς τὸ πρῆγμα κροτείσθω.
βάζ' ἃ φρονεῖς. ὄρχεων δράσσεο χερσὶν ὅλαις.

---

[43] *Colls. de Cer. Gr. en Italie,* tome II, 1933, p. 134.
[44] *J. H. S.,* XLIX, 1929, p. 260.

In red-figured ware, though here the group is not so common, an excellent example is the kylix by Peithinos in Berlin.[45] The scenes on the exterior suggest the double nature of love, expounded in Plato's *Symposion,* 191, 192: on the one side there are three couples of youths and maidens conducting themselves in mixed company; on the other there are four couples of homoerotics, youths courting boys and offering them gifts, and in addition to these party-groups, there is an odd, unattached man looking wistfully on. Hartwig[46] says: "Durch die Gegenüberstellung dieser verschiedenen Arten des Eros erhält die Darstellung der Aussenseite der Schale geradezu den Charakter einer epigrammatischen Antithese (*Anth. Pal.,* XII, 17 and 86). Ein eigenartiges, man möchte sagen culturelles Interesse bietet die Figur des einsam bei Seite stehenden Liebhabers neben den Gruppen der Jünglinge und Knaben. Dieser später häufig wiederholte δύσερως ἀνήρ erscheint als die erste sentimentale Figur der griechischen Vasenmalerei und erinnert uns daran, dass Werke, wie unsere Schale, zu einer Zeit entstanden sind, wo die Lieder der grossen griechischen Lyriker im Bewusstsein des hellenischen Volkes lebendig waren." Furtwaengler[47] calls it a balance between the "Eros Parthenios" and "Eros Paidikos," and says that Peithinos leaves little doubt which of the two he himself prefers; the former he has represented respectably but insipidly, the latter in lively colors! The inscriptions read simply: ὁ παῖς ναίχι καλὸς καλός. See plate I, 1.

Hieron and Makron repeat *ad infinitum* the "conversational" formula. A few illustrations (Hoppin, *Handb. R. F.,* II) are: men and youths giving boys rabbits, wreaths, et cetera (p. 64, 16) on a kylix in Munich; man with a hare on a leash hands a flower to a youth (p. 71, 20), Louvre; bearded man handing a flower to a seated youth and three pairs of erasts giving rabbits to their eromenoi (p. 72, 21);

---

[45] No. 2270; illustrated by Hartwig, *Meisterschalen,* pls. XXIV, 1, and XXV; Hoppin, *Handb. R. F.,* II, p. 335; Neugebauer, *Führer durch das Antiquarium,* II, Berlin, p. 86.

[46] *Op. cit.,* p. 239.   [47] F. R., Series III, p. 21.

etc. It is worth noting that all these scenes are preliminary overtures to an end not depicted, and that on vases with scenes of ultimate obscenity the subjects are practically exclusively heterosexual. Hartwig,[48] in describing certain scenes of sexual obscenity between men and women, says: "It is remarkable that even in these scenes the *ho pais kalos* is not missing from the field; only one of these cups shows remains of a *kale*." And this "higher love" of Plato, he believes, found its way even to the Parthenon (Brit. Mus., *Sculptures of the Parthenon,* pl. 37, VI, 43-46), on the east frieze of which he [49] sees "what is probably to be understood as a group of erasts and an eromenos."

The contrast between the two opposing ideal-images of masculine beauty in Greek art of the period is most patent in a comparison of the type of the Triptolemos on the Eleusinian relief with that on a hydria in Munich.[50] On the relief he is a boy, still immature and lean of limb, but the vase-painter shows us a luxurious creature with long hair and ornamental, feminine garments—this latter anyone, not cognizant of the myth, would easily take for a woman. These contrasting conceptions refute each other not only in these two works, but almost everywhere in this period:[51] the youth pleases some because he is, as they think, almost as lovely as a maiden; others he pleases because he is represented, as on the relief, to be what he is, a boy, and so something entirely different from a woman.

---

[48] *Meisterschalen*, p. 348.

[49] Hartwig, *op. cit.*, p. 238, note.

[50] F. R., II, p. 233.

[51] Cf. the athletic types in fifth century sculpture with the fancy ephebes on the Peithinos kylix in Berlin (cf. note 45 above) and on other vases with scenes of "couples in procession."

CHAPTER II

THE LOVE-NAMES IN GREEK LITERATURE

Suidas defines *kalos* by drawing a neat distinction between it and the *agathos* of the compound expression, which was the ultimate praise of a popular Athenian, " καλὸς κἀγαθός ": τὸ μὲν καλὸς ἐπὶ τῆς ἐν σώματι ὥρας, τὸ δὲ ἀγαθὸς ἐπὶ τῆς ἐν ψυχῇ.
The Lexicon to Xenophon says, sub καλὸς κἀγαθός: " 'ἀγαθός' ad animi virtutem et probitatem pertineat, ' καλός ' autem ad actiones externas, etiam ad generis nobilitatem, diuitias, valetudinem, et alia talia referatur." Generally τὸ καλόν is *pulchritudo corporis,* but, as in Xenophon, *Sym.,* VIII, 17, τὰ τοῦ παιδὸς καλά, its plural, means " animi virtutes." Xenophon, *Sym.,* VIII, 11, καλῷ τε ἀγαθῷ ἐραστῇ, is the highest type of lover, " qui non corpus amat." Ἐμπνεῖν τι ἡμᾶς τοὺς καλοὺς τοῖς ἐρωτικοῖς (Xenophon, *Sym.,* IV, 15) shows again that it was no abstract emotion that beauty inspired in a Greek.

Ast's *Lexicon Platonicum* gives numerous references to the usages of *kalos* in Plato. In the *Charmides,* 153 ff. we have a radiant picture of attractive boys (also Xen., *Sym.,* I, 8 ff.). In *Charmides* 154 A Kritias tells Sokrates of the " new beauties," περὶ τῶν καλῶν. *Protagoras* 315 d qualifies a youth as " fair and good by nature ": μειράκιον . . . καλόν τε κἀγαθὸν τὴν φύσιν. On the other hand, *Euthydemos* 271 b finds another youth " fair and good in appearance," καλὸς καὶ ἀγαθὸς τὴν ὄψιν. As in *Protagoras* 309 A, καλὸς μὲν ἐφαίνετο ἀνὴρ ἔτι, the general sense of *kalos* seems to be one made through the physical senses: " He was still a handsome man (in spite of his years)." In the same dialogue, 319 C, a certain one is lucky in being thrice blessed, " with striking good-looks, with wealth and with a lineage ": κἂν πάνυ καλὸς ᾖ καὶ πλούσιος καὶ τῶν γενναίων. The *Timaios* 88 C, ἅμα μὲν καλός, ἅμα δὲ ἀγαθός, shows that these two laudatory adjectives are never synonymous, and so, in *Euthydemos,* 299 B, " ᾧ καλὲ παῖ" is an address of love, stirred by personal beauty. Unless *kalos,* then, is qualified by some abstract virtue, its meaning and appeal to the Greek was physical. And of τοὺς καλοὺς παῖδάς τε καὶ νεανίσκους (*Sym.,* 211 D) Plato further says ἐπειδὰν δὲ ἀνδρωθῶσι, παιδεραστοῦσι (*id.,* 192 A).

Pindar, too, finds *kalos* an attribute appreciable to the senses, as in *Olympian,* VIII, 19, ἦν δ' ἐσορᾶν καλός. It is further synonymous with ὡραῖος (*Olym.,* IX, 94): ὡραῖος ἐὼν καὶ καλός. When it is ethical, he qualifies it (*Nem.,* III, 19): ἐὼν καλὸς ἔρδων τ' ἐοικότα μορφᾷ. In *Pyth.,* IV, 123 Jason is κάλλιστος ἀνδρῶν.

Sappho (fragment 101 Bergk) defines morally the component parts of the expression, καλὸς κἀγαθός:

ὁ μὲν γὰρ κάλος, ὅσσον ἴδην, πέλεται [ἄγαθος]:
ὁ δὲ κἄγαθος αὔτικα καὶ κάλος ἔσσεται.

This makes the good-looking only "good" as far as their looks go; that is to say, "Beauty is only skin-deep," but the noble and good man is fair and beautiful. According to an epigram of Solon (Hudson-Williams, *Early Greek Elegy,* p. 64, no. 13, ll. 39-40) both beauty and virtue can be at times only "seeming":

ἄλλος δειλὸς ἐὼν ἀγαθὸς δοκεῖ ἔμμεναι ἀνήρ,
καὶ καλός, μορφὴν οὐ χαρίεσσαν ἔχων.

One is reminded of Goldsmith's: "Handsome is as handsome does."

Perhaps it is not too much to say that of the *kalokagathia,* so stressed by writers of high moral sense, only the *kalos* element was directly felt by the majority of the ancient Greeks, as it is that element that most impressed itself on the poets (especially the lyric) and on the laymen (e. g. the vase-painters). Aristophanes [1] sees *kalokagathia* as something which anyone can acquire; in this passage the uncultured sausage dealer, Agorakritos, aspires to win his way to this social discrimination, not his by birth or desert. Xeno-

---

[1] *Knights,* 185.

phon [2] finds the *kalokagathia* only in deeds ἐφ' οἷς εὐδοκιμεῖ καλὸς κἀγαθὸς ἀνήρ. Gerlach [3] concludes that *agathos* up to the end of the fifth century represents no inner moral quality of the individual, but that it is exclusively a judgment of the outer world.

That the *kalos* element lent itself to the erotic emotions of the Greeks there is proof abundant. Suidas ends his definition with this: καὶ καλὸς ὁ ἐρώμενος. καὶ ἦν τῷ μὲν ἐρωστῇ Μελητος ὄνομα, τῷ καλῷ δὲ Τιμαγόρας (see Meletos in Chapter IV). We have *kalos* equal to *eromenos*, and *erastes* complementing it. He further says:[4] οὐχὶ δὲ μόνον οἱ ἐρώμενοι καλοῦνται τούτῳ τῷ ὀνόματι, ἀλλὰ καὶ πάντες οἱ σπουδαζόμενοι πάνυ κατὰ μεταφορὰν τὴν ἀπ' ἐκείνων.

Further confirmation comes from Plato,[5] who says: ὅτι ταύτης μετέχων τῆς μανίας ὁ ἐρῶν τῶν καλῶν ἐραστὴς καλεῖται. And, when in the *Symposion*, 178 E, he speaks of his στρατόπεδον ἐραστῶν τε καὶ παιδικῶν, we are to take *paidika* as synonymous with *kalos*; so in *Politeia*, III, 403 B, οὐδὲ κοινωνητέον αὐτῆς (τῆς ἡδονῆς) ἐραστῇ τε καὶ παιδικοῖς ὀρθῶς ἐρῶσί τε καὶ ἐρωμένοις, ... ἅπτεσθαι ὥσπερ υἱέος παιδικῶν ἐραστήν.

Of *paidika*, "amor puerorum impurus," Suidas says: ἐπὶ θηλειῶν καὶ ἀρρένων ἐρωμένων τάττεται ἡ λέξις. καὶ Κρατῖνος "Πανόπταις": "μισεῖς γὰρ τὰς γυναῖκας, πρὸς παιδικὰ δὲ τρέπει νῦν." Again, Xenophon [6] contrasts: ἢ γυναῖκας ... ἢ παιδικὰ ... φιλεῖν. The same author [7] says: τοῦ διαλέγεσθαι τοὺς ἐραστὰς εἴργουσιν ἀπὸ τῶν παίδων, and μηδὲν ἧττον ἐραστὰς παιδικῶν ἀπέχεσθαι. In sum, then, Xenophon's τὰ ἑαυτοῦ παιδικά, νεανίσκον ὄντα καλόν,[8] can be taken as the meaning and interpretation of the phenomenon of *kalos ho pais* on so many Attic vases.

Apropos of the reason for which such an emotional outburst should have appeared at all in so public a way, Suidas again is enlightening (*s. v. kaloi*—Aristophanes): Ἐν τοῖσι τοίχοις

---

[2] *Sym.*, VIII, 3.
[3] Ἀνὴρ Ἀγαθός, Dissertation, Munich, 1932, p. 50.
[4] Cf. Suidas, *s. v.* παιδικός.
[5] *Phaidros*, 249 E.   [7] *Reip. Laced.*, II, 12-13.
[6] *Kyroupaideia*, VII, 5, 60.   [8] *Hellenika*, VI, 4, 37.

ἔγραφον: "'Αθηναῖοι καλοί." Ἴδιον ἐραστῶν ἦν τὸ τὰ τῶν ἐρωμένων ὀνόματα γράφειν ἐν τοῖς τοίχοις ἢ δένδροις ἢ φύλλοις δένδρων, οὕτως · ὁ δεῖνα καλός... (He might have added " and on vases "!)

Eustathius on *Il.* VI, 169 (633) says practically the same: Χρήσιμον δὲ εἰς τὸν παρόντα τόπον καὶ τὸ παλαιὸν ἔθος, καθ' ὃ δένδροις ὅσα καὶ πίναξιν ἐνεκόλαπτον οἱ παλαιοὶ τὰ τῶν φιλουμένων ὀνόματα, ὡς εἴπερ ἔρωτες ἢ νύμφαι ὀρειναὶ τοῦτο ἐποίουν ...

Having seen how in the very heart of Hellenic paederasty stands the word *kalos,* we can follow its path through mythology [9] and the heroic age, its development through Crete, Thera, and the lyric poets, right down to an Attic vase. Noticing the varying conditions of boyhood in Athens, we shall see the changes in character and tone, the late fifth century decadence, and the falling away of the vase inscriptions (*ho pais kalos*) for that very good reason, the distress of the Peloponnesian War, the advent of a heterosexual norm, etc.

Wherever the idea of paederasty came from before it reached Athens, certain it is that the Homeric Greeks knew it traditionally and entertained it, in spite of Becker's theories to the contrary.[10] After Patroklos' death Antilochos took his

---

[9] For boy-love in Greek mythology cf. the dissertation by Rudolph Beyer, *Fabulae Graecae quatenus quave aetate puerorum amore commutatae sint,* Leipzig, 1910. Hyginos, Athenaios and others collected catalogues of pretty boys from the earliest stages of Greek myth and saga. The Pseudo-St. Clemens I (*Homilies,* V, 15; cf. also Clement of Alexandria, *Protr.* C. II) says: " Zeus loved Ganymede; Poseidon loved Pelops; Apollo loved Kinyras, Zakynthos, Hyakinthos, Phorbas, Hylas, Admetos, Kyparissos, Amyklas, Troilos, Branchos, Atymnios, Paros, Potnieus and Orpheus; Dionysos loved Adonis, Ampelos, Hymenaios, Hermaphroditos, Achilles; Asklepios loved Hippolytos; Hephaistos loved Peleus; Pan loved Daphnis; Hermes loved Perseus, Chryses, Therses, and Odryses; Herakles loved Abderos, Dryops, Iokastos, Philoktetes, Hylas, Polyphemos, Haimon, Diomos, and Peirithoos." Even from this catalogue, which contains only a few of the names of the god-lovers, the astonishing crowd of paidophilic motives in Greek myth can easily be conjectured. Apollo and Herakles, the hero, both Dorian favourites, have the longest list of beloveds, a fact that indicates the prevalence of paiderastic sentiments among the Dorians.

[10] *Charikles,* II, " Die Knabenliebe," pp. 199-230 (Leipzig, 1854).

place by Achilles' side, because Homer could not represent his hero without a beloved; we learn this from the *Odyssey*, XXIV, 78 ff., and further that the three were buried in a common grave. Whether Homer founded the relation between Achilles and Patroklos on sensuality for personal reasons only, there are other reasons for believing that paederasty was not unknown to Homer's people;[11] e. g., Agamemnon offers Achilles, after their quarrel has been settled, several noble youths. As Telemachos travels about for news of his father, it is mentioned quite casually that his host one night, Nestor, gave the son of Odysseus his only unmarried son, Peisistratos, for a bed-fellow and companion; this was part of the hospitality due to a guest.[12]

The historical Greeks were sometimes concerned as to the provenance of paederasty. Did this inclination develop independently in the Greek people, or is the phenomenon to be shared with their neighbors? Herodotos[13] says of the Persians: καὶ δὴ καὶ ἀπ' Ἑλλήνων μαθόντες παισὶ μίσγονται; that would lead us to seek the origin among the Greeks themselves, rather than among any of their neighbors who might have influenced them. Plutarch[14] states the contrary, and tries to show that the eunuchs of the Persians were acquainted with the perversion indigenously, but Plato[15] makes Pausanias say that both paederasty and gymnasia were in disfavour with the Oriental monarchs because of such resultants as the Harmodios and Aristogeiton conspiracy. Becker believes that there is not a trace of sensuality in the relations between the heroes of Homer, and that the emotional state of the later Greeks led their authors after Aischylos (see his *Myridons*), as we know from Athenaeus, XIII, 75, to falsify the material at hand in the interests of their own desires. He even believes that the myth of Ganymede has not the slightest suggestion of sensuality in Homer,[16] but that this interpretation was

---

[11] Cf. *Odyssey*, III, 109 ff.; XI, 467 ff.; XXIV, 15 ff.
[12] *Odyssey*, III, 400; IV, 303; XV, 4 ff.
[13] I, 135.
[14] *De Her. Malig.* 13.
[15] *Sym.*, 182.
[16] *Iliad*, XX, 235.

entertained after Pindar's tenth Olympian ode, line 105. Plato [17] does say that the Cretans admit that they follow the conduct of Zeus' example in cultivating boy-love, and this might argue that they turned the myth to suit their own proclivities. It is certainly true that in spite of what Becker thinks to be the innocent silence of the Homeric poems on this subject, the earliest appearance of the emotion among the Greeks goes as far back into their mythology, e. g., the Laios legend (Suidas *s. v. Thamyris*); though for this myth again our modern extant sources do not antedate Euripides' *Chrysippos*. According to Timaios [18] the Cretans handed down the custom to the Greeks. Plutarch [19] surely knew that the Cretan *harpagmos* was no chaste custom; "und er zieht, gewiss mit Rücksicht auf Sokrates und Plato, selbst die attische vor, wo doch in der That im Allgemeinen solche Liebe nicht als ein Tugendbund erscheint." [20] The general opinion now is that in the older and better days of the Cretan state the tendency of this practice was pure and chaste, but that by the time it was mentioned in the Platonic restatement of the laws governing it, it had already sunk to physical excess.[21]

As for the erotics of Crete, what Hesychios' gloss (κλεινοί: οἱ εἰς τὰ παιδικὰ ἐπὶ κάλλει ἁρπαζόμενοι παῖδες) tells us does not come from Ephoros, the authority, who interprets *kalos* (i. e., paederasty): ἐράσμιον δὲ νομίζουσιν οὐ τὸν κάλλει διαφέροντα ἀλλὰ τὸν ἀνδρείᾳ [22] καὶ κοσμιότητι. Athenaeus (XI, 782 C) says: σπουδὴ δὲ αὐτοῖς παῖδας ἁρπάζειν. καὶ τοῖς καλοῖς παρ' αὐτοῖς ἄδοξόν ἐστιν ἐραστοῦ μὴ τυχεῖν.

Ephoros [23] tells us about the Cretan *harpagmos*, or " rape " of boys by their lovers. That it was semi-official is clear. " If the man is the equal of the boy or superior to him, people follow and resist the rape only enough to satisfy the law, but are really glad to let him be carried off by one so noble."

---

[17] *Laws*, I, 636.
[18] Athenaeus, XIII, 602 f.
[19] *Educ. Puer.* 15.
[20] Becker, *op. cit.*, pp. 204-205.
[21] Hoeck, *Kreta*, III, pp. 106 ff.
[22] Cf. " Mikion kalos," Chapter IV, no. 176, p. 152.
[23] Mueller, F. H. G. I, p. 251.

The law here, in addition to preventing mis-alliances, specified what gifts were to be given the boy by his abductor; among others, a military habit, an ox, and a drinking cup, and things so numerous and costly that the friends of the erastes made contributions thereto. Athenaeus (502 B) also tells us that among the people of Gortyna it was customary for a lover to give to the boy whom he had carried off a cup similar to a Thericlean one but called a " chonnos." Abducted boys were called παρασταθέντες, those chosen as " stand-bys " by lovers. In dances and races they had places of highest honour. The boy was called κλεινός, his abductor φιλήτωρ. This was in the earlier state of Crete, as in the later laws of Gortyna, which Carpenter [24] says need not antedate the fifth century, the *harpagmos* was punishable by fines, determined according to whether the attacker or the assaulted was free or a slave.[25]

Among the Etruscans too Athenaeus (XII, 517 F) says that they enjoy ὁτὲ δὲ παῖδας πάνυ καλούς. Later (XII, 518 A) he says that, in preference to consorting with women, πολὺ μέντοι γε μᾶλλον χαίρουσι συνόντες τοῖς παισὶ καὶ τοῖς μειρακίοις. καὶ γὰρ γίνονται παρ' αὐτοῖς πάνυ καλοὶ τὰς ὄψεις, ἅτε τρυφερῶς διαιτώμενοι καὶ λεαινόμενοι τὰ σώματα.

The erotic of Crete was substantially the same as that of Sparta. For the Spartan the most appropriate place for study is the island of Thera, a Dorian colony, on which the rock-cut inscriptions bear a close resemblance to the *ho pais kalos* of Attic vases. These rock inscriptions were formerly dated as early as the geometric era,[26] but Professor Rhys Carpenter's recently published conclusions [27] would place them as late as the middle of the sixth century B. C. This is in astonishing agreement with the chronology of the *kalos* name in Athens, a synonymous and therefore logically contemporary

---

[24] *A. J. A.*, *XXXVII*, 1933, p. 26.

[25] Köhler-Ziebarth, *Stadtrecht von Gortyn*, II, 5, and pp. 77-78.

[26] Hiller von Gaertringen, *Thera*, III, p. 67.

[27] *A. J. A.*, XXXVII, 1933, p. 26; Ullman in *Classical Studies Presented to Edward Capps*, p. 341, however, thinks that the early writing of Thera might well go back to the ninth or even the tenth century B. C.

phenomenon. The *kalos* name, a product of the sixth century emotional ecstasy in Athens, has the same significance as in these Theran inscriptions, cut in the rock not seventy meters from the temple of Apollo Karneios and in the vicinity of the later gymnasium of the island. For the most part the inscriptions consist of a proper name and the Doric adjective *agathos*[28] but in one of them (*I. G.*, XII, 3, 549) we have -ς ἠμὶ πᾶσ[ι] καλός, an occurrence of the usual Attic lover's cliché, which suggests that it has the same force as the more usual Doric *agathos* on the island. The Dorians stressed ἀρετή, the Ionians κάλλος. But here, as in Attika, there is obvious proof that both imply eroticism. Here five times the word οἴφειν appears; e. g., *I. G.*, XII, 3, 537, where Delphinios is called to witness that "here Krimon lay with the son of Bathykles." Not only is praise of the best dancer among the boys found (*I. G.*, XII, 3, 546)—for this compare the Spartan *gymnopaidia* to Apollo[29]—" sondern auch direkte Zeugnisse für die Knabenliebe in der grobsinnlichsten Form ... sie zeigen uns die Roheit der dorischen Einwanderer."[30] On some of the later inscriptions there is no mistaking their significance; e. g. *I. G.*, XII, 3, 536, calls Enpylos a πόρνος, and another, dating from the third century A. D., says Δημήτριος κίναιδος.[31] About the character of the inscriptions Licht[32] says: "In unmittelbarer Nähe des Apollotempels auf dem heiligen Berge unter feierlichem Zeremoniell nach vorausgegangenem festlichen Reigentanze der Knaben fand der Vermählungsakt statt und wurde dem Gedächtnis der Späteren

---

[28] *I. G.*, XII, 3, 540, 544, 545, etc.

[29] Strabo, X, 483-484; Athen. XI, 782 c; Diels, *Hermes*, XXXI, 1896, pp. 353 ff.

[30] Thera, III, p. 68.

[31] Cf. *Epigraphische Nachtraege* zu Graef-Langlotz, *Die Vasen von der Akropolis*, Band II, Heft 3, p. 130, for another "Enpylos" from Attika. On the significance of the word *kinaidos* the epigram (*Anth.*, XI, 272) is explicit: ἀνέρες εἰσὶ γυναιξί, καὶ ἀνδράσιν εἰσὶ γυναῖκες. Cf. Suetonius (I, 52) on Caesar, whom Curio called, "omnium mulierum virum et omnium virorum mulierem."

[32] *Sittengeschichte Griechenlands, Ergaenzungsband*, p. 206.

durch die unverwüstliche Stimme der Steine aufbewahrt just dort, wo man das Gymnasium der Epheben erbaute und wo die Knaben und Jünglinge, die sich im Gymnasium durch ungezählte niedliche Schmierereien verewigten, tagtäglich es lasen und lesen mussten." The god was witness to all the notices of boy-love on that spot, and so it was sanctioned by the Dorian religious notions. Man and youth joined themselves together in a serious, sacred, and not dishonourable bond under the god's observation, so that the man's ἀρετή might be transferred to his young charge, his κλεινός.

A noteworthy similarity appears in the beginnings of epigraphy in Thera and in Athens as we compare one of the island inscriptions,[33]

Βάρβακς ὀρκheῖταί τε ἀγαθῶ[s]
ἐ[δ]ίδο[υ] [τε π]ο[τ]α[ν]ῆ,

a verse on an Attic Dipylon vase,[34] which some read:

ὃς νῦν ὀρχηστῶν πάντων
ἀταλώτατα παίζει, τούτον ἐκαύμην

("for him I burned with love"), and Theognis 1329:

Σοί τε διδοῦν ἔτι καλόν, ἐμοί τ' οὐκ αἰσχρόν ἐρῶντι
αἰτεῖν. ἀλλὰ γονέων λίσσομαι ἡμετέρων.
αἰδέο μ', ὦ παῖ καλέ, διδοὺς χάριν.

The contemporaneity of the Thera inscriptions with the first appearance of the kalos name on Attic vases might also be suggested by the fact that the very character of the scenes on Attic pottery of the time is in perfect accord with what we have seen to be the essentially physical significance of the island inscriptions: as, before the tone of the vase-scenes had been

---

[33] *I. G.*, XII, 3, 543.

[34] *Ath. Mitt.*, VI, 1881, pp. 106 ff.; XVIII, 1893, pp. 225-230. Carpenter, *loc. cit.*, p. 25, dates it c. 675 B. C. Cf. *Klio*, XVII, 1921, pp. 262 f., 267; *Arch. Anz.*, XXXVI, 1921, p. 343; *Musée Belge*, XXVII, 1923, p. 308; I. G. I², 919; Kirchner, *Imagines Inscriptionum Atticarum*, p. 9, no. 1, pl. 1 (eighth cent. B. C.).

subdued down into the polite, non-committal "conversational" groups of men and boys, prevalent in the fifth century, that same sentiment had first been expressed in the actual paederastic symplegmata so common on vases in the first decades after the middle of the sixth century and so hinted at on Thera's rocks at the same time.[35]

In Athens itself paederasty had become so deeply absorbed into society by Solon's time and was so ubiquitously recognized and felt as an honourable institution that he, almost the prototype of old Athens' moral code, depicted it clearly as an obvious pleasure of youth in the following distych (frg. 25):

> ἔσθ' ἥβης ἐρατοῖσιν ἐπ' ἄνθεσι παιδοφιλήσῃ
> μηρῶν ἱμείρων καὶ γλυκεροῦ στόματος.

"Er behielt sie durch seine Gesetzgebung ebenso wie die Gymnastik dem freien Manne vor, verbot sie dem Sklaven. Und so blieb es in Athen bis in die zweite Hälfte des fünften Jahrhunderts. Die Vasen jener Zeiten mit den Lieblingsaufschriften illustriren am besten."[36] The legal regulations of the institution made by Solon prove that boy-love was by that time something very customary for an Athenian. In fact, he himself fell in love with his cousin, the young Peisistratos (Plutarch, *Solon*, 1). According to them a slave could not traffic with a free-born; a young man could not sell his charms for money. But a way out of any difficulties was let in the πρόφασις φιλίας, by which anything mutually agreeable was excusable. The laws, fallen into desuetude by the time of Aischines, are found in that orator's speech, *Against Timarchos* (10-12). That the laws also contained regulations for the gymnasia and their hours of closing, is a confirmation of the belief that it was due to them that boy-love was such a common thing among the ancients. Undoubtedly the cause was the taking over of the gymnastic institution from the

---

[35] Graef-Langlotz, *Die Antiken Vasen von der Akropolis*, frag. 2242, text.

[36] "Die Dorische Knabenliebe," *Rheinisches Museum*, LXII, 1907, p. 441.

Cretans [37] and the frequency of the sight of nude men.[38] That the gymnasia fed the flame of boy-love is mentioned even by ancient writers; e. g. Cicero:[39] " quis est enim iste amor amicitiae? Cur neque deformem adulescentem quisquam amat neque formosum senem? Mihi quidem haec in Graecorum gymnasiis nata consuetudo videtur, in quibus isti liberi et concessi sunt amores. Bene ergo Ennius: ' Flagiti principium est nudare inter civis corpora.' " The stern Romans, who valued such exercises merely for their military and diaetetic advantages, judged unfavourably of Greek gymnastics. Plutarch [40] says: " For the Romans have a great prejudice against dry unction; and they are of the opinion that nothing hath been so great a cause to the Grecians of slavery and effeminacy ($\mu\alpha\lambda\alpha\kappa\iota\alpha\varsigma$) as their fencing and wrestling schools, insinuating so much debauchery and idleness into the citizens, vicious sloth and paederasty; they destroyed the very bodies of youths with sleeping, perambulations, dancing, and delicious feeding, whereby they insensibly fell from the use of arms, and instead of being good soldiers and horsemen, loved to be called agile, good wrestlers, and pretty men ($\kappa\alpha\lambda o\iota$)."

Bryant [41] says, " There was one experience that came to the Athenian boy which is happily quite unlike anything that comes in the way of the ordinary boy of today. The love of men for boys was never quite sanctioned by society, and the laws and the parents united in efforts to check and control it: but, sooner or later almost every attractive young fellow had to reckon with it; and to many a lad it was a determining influence for good or evil." The older man was the *erastes,* the younger was called *ta paidika* (a plural with singular

---

[37] Plato, *Rep.*, V, 452.

[38] Which Plato (*loc. cit.*) says only a short time ago was as shameful and ridiculous to the Greeks as it still was to the barbarians in his day; he says that the Dorian Spartans were the second after the Cretans to develop this institution.

[39] *Tusc.*, IV, 33.

[40] *Quaest. Rom.*, 40.

[41] " Boyhood in Athens," *Harvard Studies in Classical Philology,* XVIII, 1907, pp. 101 f.

force) or *ho kalos*.[42] Sometimes it was a boy of the same age, a school-fellow, that inspired the lad's affection,[43] sometimes, and more usually, an older man (cf. the cases of Sokrates and Alkibiades;[44] of Harmodios and Aristogeiton;[45] and the striking example of the young Menon[46]). This last curious double relationship is paralleled, however, in the case of Harmodios and Aristogeiton and elsewhere.[47]

In Aischines[48] we learn that the Solonian law provided for the closing of the schools except during the hours of daylight—an obvious precaution against the corruption of boys, directed against the abuses of the relation. Plato makes an offense against a boy a capital crime in his *Laws*, IX, 874 c: καὶ ἐὰν ἐλευθέραν γυναῖκα βιάζηταί τις ἢ παῖδα περὶ τὰ ἀφροδίσια,

---

[42] Plato, *Rep.*, V, 474 d; *Lysis*, 204 b: πρῶτον ἡδέως ἀκούσαιμ' ἄν, ἐπὶ τῷ καὶ εἴσειμι καὶ τίς ὁ καλός.

[43] E. g., Xen., *Sym.*, IV, 23, where it is said about Kritoboulos and Kleinias: οὐχ ὁρᾷς ὅτι τούτῳ μὲν παρὰ τὰ ὦτα ἄρτι ἴουλος καθέρπει, Κλεινίᾳ δὲ πρὸς τὸ ὄπισθεν ἤδη ἀναβαίνει; οὕτως οὖν συμφοιτῶν εἰς ταὐτὰ διδασκαλεῖα ἐκείνῳ τότε ἰσχυρῶς προσεκάθητο. ἃ δὴ αἰσθόμενος ὁ πατὴρ παρέδωκέ μοι αὐτόν, εἴ τι δυναίμην ὠφελῆσαι.

[44] Plato, *Gorgias*, 481 D: ἐγώ τε καὶ σὺ νῦν τυγχάνομεν ταὐτόν τι πεπονθότες, ἐρῶντε δύο ὄντε δυοῖν ἑκάτερος, ἐγὼ μὲν Ἀλκιβιάδου τε τοῦ Κλεινίου.

[45] Thuk., VI, 54, 2.

[46] Xen., *Anab.*, II, 6, 28. Cf. Chapter III, no. 61 below for the story of Menon, whose beauty won from Aristippos permission to command part of the forces, while, still an adolescent, he was living with Ariaios intimately and keeping the bearded Tharypas for his own beloved.

[47] Ps. Plato, *Hipparch*, 229 C: ἀλλὰ τὸν μὲν Ἁρμόδιον γεγονέναι παιδικὰ τοῦ Ἀριστογείτονος καὶ πεπαιδεῦσθαι ὑπ' ἐκείνου . . . ἐν ἐκείνῳ δὲ τῷ χρόνῳ αὐτὸν τὸν Ἁρμόδιον τυγχάνειν ἐρῶντά τινος τῶν νέων τε καὶ καλῶν καὶ γενναίων τῶν τότε· καὶ λέγουσι τοὔνομα αὐτοῦ, ἐγὼ δὲ οὐ μέμνημαι. Τὸν οὖν νεανίσκον τοῦτον τέως μὲν θαυμάζειν τόν τε Ἁρμόδιον καὶ τὸν Ἀριστογείτονα ὡς σοφούς, ἔπειτα συγγενόμενον τῷ Ἱππάρχῳ καταφρονῆσαι ἐκείνων· καὶ τοὺς περιαλγήσαντας ταύτῃ τῇ ἀτιμίᾳ οὕτως ἀποκτεῖναι τὸν Ἵππαρχον. Cf. Plutarch, *Alkib.* 3: παῖς ὢν Ἀλκιβιάδης ἐκ τῆς οἰκίας ἀπέδρα πρὸς Δημοκράτη τινὰ τῶν ἐραστῶν. Cf. Xen., *Hell.* IV 1, 40 for story of son of Pharnabazos who loved both Agesilaos and Eualkes.

[48] *Or. ag. Tim.*, 10-12.

νηποινὶ τεθνάτω ὑπό τε τοῦ ὑβρισθέντος βίᾳ καὶ ὑπὸ πατρὸς ἢ ἀδελφῶν ἢ υἱέων. We hear of men like Agesilaos who frowned on loose talking.[49] The very institution of the *Paidagogos* is proof enough of the attitude of the parents toward paederastia.[50] In the *Phaidros* Plato draws this picture of a young beloved: though in former days he may have mistrusted his passion because of the censure of his companions, when he is of a more mature age he will receive his lover as one who is "his mirror in whom he is beholding himself, but he is not aware of this. When he is with the lover, both cease from their pain, but when he is away then he longs as he is longed for."[51] With self-conscious blushes and embarrassed reticence the lovers reacted to inquiries about their beloveds;[52] praises were sung in prose and poetry by the lovers for their boys;[53] one followed the other about;[54] one was blind to the defects of his beloved, whose face was "charming" in spite of a snub-nose, or whose look was "royal" because of a hooknose, and who was always praised poetically for the colour of his complexion, whatever that might be;[55] one found his best

---

[49] Xen., *Ages*. VIII 2: μετεῖχε μὲν ἥδιστα παιδικῶν λόγων.

[50] Cf. Plato, *Sym*. 183 C, D: ἐπειδὰν δὲ παιδαγωγοὺς ἐπιστήσαντες οἱ πατέρες τοῖς ἐρωμένοις μὴ ἐῶσι διαλέγεσθαι τοὺς ἐραστὰς, καὶ τῷ παιδαγωγῷ ταῦτα προστεταγμένα ᾖ, ἡλικιῶται δὲ καὶ ἑταῖροι ὀνειδίζωσιν, ἐάν τι ὁρῶσι τοιοῦτο γιγνόμενον, καὶ τοὺς ὀνειδίζοντας αὖ οἱ πρεσβύτεροι μὴ διακωλύωσι μηδὲ λοιδορῶσιν ὡς οὐκ ὀρθῶς λέγοντας, εἰς δὲ ταῦτά τις αὖ βλέψας ἡγήσαιτ' ἂν πάλιν αἴσχιστον τὸ τοιοῦτον ἐνθάδε νομίζεσθαι. . . . πονηρὸς δ' ἔστιν ἐκεῖνος ὁ ἐραστὴς ὁ πάνδημος, ὁ τοῦ σώματος μᾶλλον ἢ τῆς ψυχῆς ἐρῶν.

[51] *Phaidros*, 255 D.

[52] Plato, *Lysis*, 204 C: ὃς ἀκούσας πολὺ ἔτι μᾶλλον ἠρυθρίασεν.

[53] *Ib.*, 204 C: ὁ οὖν Κτήσιππος, Ἀστεῖόν γε, ἦ δ' ὅς, ὅτι ἐρυθριᾷς, ὦ Ἱππόθαλες, καὶ ὀκνεῖς εἰπεῖν Σωκράτει τοὔνομα . . . ἡμῶν γοῦν, ὦ Σώκρατες, ἐκκεκώφηκε τὰ ὦτα καὶ ἐμπέπληκε Λύσιδος . . . ἀλλ' ἐπειδὰν τὰ ποιήματα ἡμῶν ἐπιχειρήσῃ καταντλεῖν καὶ συγγράμματα.

[54] Plato, *Euthydemos*, 273 A: οὔπω τούτω δύ' ἢ τρεῖς δρόμους περιεληλυθότε ἤστην, καὶ εἰσέρχεται Κλεινίας, ὃν σὺ φῂς πολὺ ἐπιδεδωκέναι, ἀληθῆ λέγων. ὄπισθεν δὲ αὐτοῦ ἐρασταὶ πάνυ πολλοί τε καὶ ἄλλοι καὶ Κτήσιππος, νεανίσκος τις Παιανιεύς, μάλα καλός τε κἀγαθὸς τὴν φύσιν, ὅσον μὴ ὑβριστὴς διὰ τὸ νέος εἶναι. Cf. *Phaidros*, 232 A, *Charmides*, 154 A.

[55] Plato, *Rep.*, V, 474 D: ἀνδρὶ δ' ἐρωτικῷ οὐ πρέπει ἀμνημονεῖν, ὅτι

incentive to virtue in an honourable lover;[56] one cherished a keepsake or looked at a possession of his beloved as the means of conjuring up the image of the "fair one," much as lovers of today guard a dance-program or a pressed flower from a corsage.[57] He lavished gifts, like the lover of today, too often, it seems, in the nature of a bribe,[58] sometimes in actual money—though this must have been very rare among the eleutheroi.[59] More usual was the doing of service, for the beloved, as in the case of Agesilaos' trying to get his favourite into the Olympic junior race, when that one, Eualkes, was over age.[60]

Of these lovers' jealousies Lysias [61] speaks, and he mentions

πάντες οἱ ἐν ὥρᾳ τὸν φιλόπαιδα καὶ ἐρωτικὸν ἀμῇ γέ πῇ δάκνουσί τε καὶ κινοῦσι, δοκοῦντες ἄξιοι εἶναι ἐπιμελείας τε καὶ τοῦ ἀσπάζεσθαι. ἦ οὐχ οὕτω ποιεῖτε πρὸς τοὺς καλούς; . . . μέλανας δὲ ἀνδρικοὺς ἰδεῖν, λευκοὺς δὲ θεῶν παῖδας εἶναι. μελιχλώρους δὲ καὶ τοὔνομα οἴει τινὸς ἄλλου ποίημα εἶναι. . . .

[56] Plato, *Sym.*, 178 C-E: οὐ γὰρ ἔγωγ' ἔχω εἰπεῖν ὅ τι μεῖζόν ἐστιν ἀγαθὸν εὐθὺς νέῳ ὄντι ἢ ἐραστὴς χρηστὸς καὶ ἐραστῇ παιδικά . . . φημὶ τοίνυν ἐγὼ ἄνδρα ὅστις ἐρᾷ εἴ τι αἰσχρὸν ποιῶν κατάδηλος γίγνοιτο ἢ πάσχων ὑπό του δι' ἀνανδρίαν μὴ ἀμυνόμενος, οὔτ' ἂν ὑπὸ πατρὸς ὀφθέντα οὕτως ἀλγῆσαι οὔτε ὑπὸ ἑταίρων οὔτε ὑπ' ἄλλου οὐδενὸς ὡς ὑπὸ παιδικῶν. ταὐτὸν δὲ τοῦτο καὶ τὸν ἐρώμενον ὁρῶμεν, ὅτι διαφερόντως τοὺς ἐραστὰς αἰσχύνεται, ὅταν ὀφθῇ ἐν αἰσχρῷ τινι ὤν. . . .

[57] Plato, *Phaidon*, 73 D: οὐκοῦν οἶσθα, ὅτι οἱ ἐρασταί, ὅταν ἴδωσι λύραν ἢ ἱμάτιον ἢ ἄλλο τι οἷς τὰ παιδικὰ αὐτῶν εἴωθε χρῆσθαι, πάσχουσι τοῦτο. ἔγνωσάν τε τὴν λύραν καὶ ἐν τῇ διανοίᾳ ἔλαβον τὸ εἶδος τοῦ παιδός, οὗ ἦν ἡ λύρα; . . .

[58] Aristoph., *Birds*, 704 ff.:
πολλοὺς δὲ καλοὺς ἀπομωμοκότας παῖδας πρὸς τέρμασιν ὥρας
διὰ τὴν ἰσχὺν τὴν ἡμετέραν διεμήρισαν ἄνδρες ἐρασταί,
ὁ μὲν ὄρτυγα δούς, ὁ δὲ πορφυρίων', ὁ δὲ χῆν', ὁ δὲ Περσικὸν ὄρνιν.

And so the birds call themselves "children of Eros," because they are an effective present to the beloved when the lover finds his own virtues insufficient.

[59] Lysias, *Simon*, 22. Cf. Aristoph., *Frogs*, 148: "or robbed his boylove (παῖδα) of the promised pay."

[60] Xen., *Hell.*, IV, 1, 40: ἐρασθέντος αὐτοῦ τοῦ Εὐάλκους υἱέος Ἀθηναίου πάντ' ἐποίησεν ὅπως ἂν δι' ἐκεῖνον ἐγκριθείη τὸ στάδιον ἐν Ὀλυμπίᾳ, μέγιστος ὢν τῶν παίδων.

[61] *Simon*, especially sec. 5: ἡμεῖς γὰρ ἐπεθυμήσαμεν, ὦ βουλή, Θεοδότου, Πλαταϊκοῦ μειρακίου.

the wrangling resulting from such attachments. In another case there is the comic scene of the men jostling each other to get a better view of the beautiful favourite, cf. Plato's *Charmides,* 155 C (see Chapter IV, p. 140 below). It is to such cases that the author of the *Hipparchos* attributes the overthrow of the Peisistratidc.[62] On the other side, a beautiful boy could be as arrogant as the most spoiled of modern coquettes.[63]

Plato in his *Symposion,* in which the speeches of Pausanias and Aristophanes describe this manly love, distinguishes two kinds of love—the love of the senses, whose patron goddess is Aphrodite Pandemos, and the love of the soul, which Uranian Aphrodite watches over. And he claims paederasty for the kingdom of the latter.[64] But the relations of ordinary lovers were not on this plane. The Athenian was particularly susceptible to the influence of the senses. Even the temperate and high-minded Sokrates requires all his iron will to banish at times unholy desires, as he confesses with humility himself.[65] To too many lovers the paramount interest was the

---

[62] Ps. Plato, *Hipparchos,* 229 C; for extract cf. footnote 47 above Cf. also Thuk. VI, 54, 3; Arist., *Pol.* V, 11, 15. In the speech of Pausanias in Plato's *Symposion* we read (182) why tyrants have reason to fear such attachments (Jowett): "In Ionia and other places . . . subject to the barbarians, the custom is held to be dishonourable; loves of youths share the evil repute in which philosophy and gymnastics are held, because they are inimical to tyranny; for the interests of rulers require that their subjects should be poor in spirit; and that there should be no strong bond of friendship or society among them, which love, above all motives is likely to inspire, as our Athenian tyrants learned by experience; for the love of Aristogeiton and the constancy of Harmodios had a strength which undid their power."

[63] As young Alkibiades in Plato, *Alk.,* I, 103 B: σχεδὸν οὖν κατανενόηκα ἐν τούτῳ τῷ χρόνῳ σκοπούμενος ὡς πρὸς τοὺς ἐραστὰς ἔσχες. πολλῶν γὰρ γενομένων καὶ μεγαλοφρόνων οὐδεὶς ὅς οὐκ ὑπερβληθεὶς τῷ φρονήματι ὑπὸ σοῦ πέφευγε.

[64] *Sym.,* 181 C, ὁ δὲ τῆς οὐρανίας πρῶτον μὲν οὐ μετεχούσης θήλεος ἀλλ' ἄρρενος μόνον. καὶ ἔστιν οὗτος ὁ τῶν παίδων ἔρως.

[65] Plato, *Charmides* 155 D, when he caught fire, as he beheld the inside of Charmides' garment.

body and not the soul of the boys for whose favour they sued.[66] For such a relation even Plato has nothing to say, though he admits its prevalence, at least outside of Athens.[67] It is easy, of course, to exaggerate the part which abuse of the relation played in community life; just as it is impossible to deny that its influence was on the whole bad.[68]

The *paides kaloi* of the earlier vases influenced the poets deeply, and whatever the formula had developed into by the time of Aristophanes, certain it is that with the earlier poets the sentiments were largely of a noble character. In elegiac and lyric poetry, in Theognis, Plato, Archilochos and Alkaios, Ibykos, Anakreon, Pindar and Stesichoros [69] the poet sings of this love for fair boys.

It is known that a famous skolion quoted by Plato, *Gorgias*, 451 E, attributed by some to Simonides, by others to Epicharmus (Bergk., *Poetae Lyrici Graeci*,[4] III, p. 645, no. 8) rated beauty as the second of "the four best things": δεύτερον

---

[66] In the following passages it is a sensual relation that is referred to: Aristoph., *Frogs*, 148; *Wasps*, 1025, 1068; *Clouds*, 1073; *Peace*, 11, 762; *Ploutos*, 153; *Birds*, 705; *Knights*, 1382 seq.; Plato, *Phaidros*, 227 C, 237 B, 255 A, B; *Sym.*, 217 A; *Rep.*, IX, 574 C; *Laws*, I, 636 B, VIII, 836 C, 840 A; Ps. Plato, *Hipparch.*, 229 C; Thuk., I, 132, 5; VI, 54, 2; Xen., *Anab.*, II, 6, 28; *Ages.*, 8, 2; *Mem.*, 1, 3, 8; *Hell.*, IV, 1, 40; IV, 8, 39; V, 3, 20; V, 4, 25; VI, 4, 37; *Hiero*, 1, 29, 31, 35, 36; Eurip., *Kyklops*, 502 seq.; Eupolis, frags., 100, 233, 337 (Kock); Kratin., frag., 152 (Kock); Krates, frag., 1 (Kock); Telekleid., frag., 49 (Kock); Aischin., *in Timarch.*, 13 (40); Antiphon, frag., 66 (Blass); Lysias, *Simon*, 5, 6, 10, 22; in *Alk.*, I, 27; Tisis, frag. 75.

[67] *Laws*, VIII, 836 C.

[68] Plato, *loc. cit.*: εἰ γάρ τις ἀκολουθῶν τῇ φύσει θήσει τὸν πρὸ τοῦ Λαΐου νόμον, λέγων ὡς ὀρθῶς εἶχεν τὸ τῶν ἀρρένων καὶ νέων μὴ κοινωνεῖν καθάπερ θηλειῶν πρὸς μεῖξιν ἀφροδισίων, μάρτυρα παραγόμενος τὴν τῶν θηρίων φύσιν καὶ δεικνὺς πρὸς τὰ τοιαῦτα οὐχ ἁπτόμενον ἄρρενα ἄρρενος διὰ τὸ μὴ φύσει τοῦτο εἶναι, τάχ᾽ ἂν χρῷτο πιθανῷ λόγῳ, καὶ ταῖς ὑμετέραις πόλεσιν οὐδαμῶς συμφωνοῖ . . . τοῦ δ᾽ εἰς μίμησιν τοῦ θήλεος ἰόντος τὴν τῆς εἰκόνος ὁμοιότητα ἆρ᾽ οὐ μέμψεται; . . . τὴν τῆς φιλίας τε καὶ ἐπιθυμίας ἅμα καὶ τῶν λεγομένων ἐρώτων φύσιν ἰδεῖν ἀναγκαῖον, εἰ μέλλει τις ταῦτα ὀρθῶς διανοηθήσεσθαι.

[69] Athenaeus, XIII, 601a, says of him: καὶ Στησίχορος δ᾽ οὐ μετρίως ἐρωτικὸς γενόμενος συνέστησε καὶ τοῦτον τὸν τρόπον τῶν ᾀσμάτων . . . ἐκαλεῖτο παιδεῖα καὶ παιδικά.

δὲ φυὰν καλὸν γενέσθαι. And even if Theognis had not written such lines as:

1280—ὦ καλὲ παῖ
1282—τῶν δὲ καλῶν παίδων
1336—σὺν καλῷ παιδί
1350—καλοῦ παιδός
1365—ὦ παίδων κάλλιστε
1369—παιδὸς ἔρως καλὸς μὲν ἔχειν
1377-9—καλὸς ἐών . . . ὦ παῖ

(in which the formula is accepted with many case-inflections, proving that it was a formula in the strictest sense), we should have the red-figured cup by the Brygos Painter [70] to remind us of his influence on the *kalos* inscription. The cup (see plate I, 2) has a scene of a reclining man, singing the first words of a distich by the poet: ὦ παίδων κάλλιστε. For κάλλιστος cf. the list in *C. V. A., Oxford*, fasc. 1, p. 2, also below C. III, nos. 4, 25, 53, 65, 78; C. IV, nos. 22, 29, 118. Theognis writes:

ὦ παίδων κάλλιστε καὶ ἱμεροέστατε πάντων,
στῆθ' αὐτοῦ καὶ μοῦ παῦρ' ἐπάκουσον ἔπη.

The words on the vase occur nowhere else in Greek poetry of suitable date save in this distich, 1365-66, by Theognis, and, while they are such as any erotic poet might have written, this fact is a strong one. This vase fixes the date of Theognis 1365 as probably not later than the beginning of the fifth century, just at the time when Theognis was alive and at work; he continued so at least as late as 490 B. C.[71] With this vase compare the red-figured cup by Epiktetos in the British Museum,[72] with a scene of a reclining man, singing "Hipparchos is fair"; and a black-figured Little Master, or "Little Mistress," cup with καλλίστη παρθένων, in the collection of Mr. Gallatin in New York.[73] Cf. pp. 87-88.

---

[70] *C. V. A., Athènes, Musée National*, fasc. 1, III I c, pl. 3, 1; Koehler, *Ath. Mitt.*, IX, 1884, p. 1, pl. 1.
[71] Harrison, *Studies in Theognis*, p. 286.
[72] Br. Mus., E 37; Hoppin, *Handb. R. F.*, I, p. 310.
[73] Beazley, *A. J. A.*, XXXI, 1927, p. 346, 3. Cf. also the Rhodian

The whole elegy from which the quotation on the Athens vase comes, is filled with variations on the formula and explanations as to its meaning, so that Koehler [74] could say: "Die epische Poesie den griechischen Vasenmalern eine Fülle von Stoffen zugeführt, so dass man die Frage aufwerfen kann, ob dieser Kunstzweig ohne jene Anregung zu haben sich so reich entfaltet haben würde." [75]

In line 1259 of Theognis we read:

ὦ παῖ, τὴν μορφὴν μὲν ἔφυς καλός,

and there is advice in 1255:

ὅστις μὴ παῖδάς τε φιλεῖ καὶ μώνυχας ἵππους
καὶ κύνας, οὔποτε οἱ θυμὸς ἐν εὐφροσύνῃ.

That the formula is here tantamount to paederasty is apparent in 1335-36:

Ὄλβιος ὅστις ἐρῶν γυμνάζεται, οἴκαδε δ' ἐλθὼν
εὕδει σὺν καλῷ παιδὶ πανημέριος.

"Theognis kalos" also occurs on a vase (v. sub. nom.), and it is more than likely that, as Koehler thinks, the Second Book was written by Theognis, and not by a later poet, as some scholars think. As for its morality, Herwerden [76] refers to passages of Pindar, Mimnermos, Solon, and Ibykos to show that its author sinned in very good company, as at one time it was thought that the paederastic motives in this second Book should refer it to a later author. The application of the epithets κάλλιστος καὶ ἱμεροέστατος to a beautiful boy, for that matter, did not originate with Theognis, but far antedates him and his favourite, Kyrnos, son of Polypais; it is borrowed from the Cyclic story of Oidipous, where we read (scholia to Eur., *Phoenissae,* 1760):

ἀλλ' ἔτι κάλλιστόν τε καὶ ἱμεροέστατον ἄλλων,
παῖδα φίλον Κρείοντος ἀμύμονος, Αἵμονα δῖον.

---

vase in the Metropolitan Museum, *A. J. P.*, XXIX, 1908, pp. 461-466, the inscription on which should be read with Tarbell, *Cl. Phil.*, XII, 1917, p. 191: καλλίστα γᾶς Ἀβρασία ὡς ἐμὶν δοκεῖ. Cf. p. 114 below.

[74] *Ath. Mitt.*, IX, 1884, p. 1.

[75] *Loc. cit.*   [76] *Animad. Phil. ad Theog.*

Of the other poets a brief mention must suffice. Anakreon [77] says:

> Ἀναπέτομαι δὴ πρὸς Ὄλυμπον πτερύγεσσι κούφαις
> διὰ τὸν Ἔρωτ'. οὐ γὰρ ἐμοὶ παῖς ἐθέλει συνηβᾶν.[78]

The Lyra Graeca (*Loeb Classical Library*) gives this, number 3, under Anakreon:

> Κλευβούλου μὲν ἔγωγ' ἐρέω,
> Κλευβούλῳ δ' ἐπιμαίνομαι,
> Κλεύβουλον δὲ διοσκέω.

Orsi,[79] in speaking of a vase with an inscription to Anakreon,[80] finds that the *ho pais kalos* on the same vase is appropriate and " alludente alle tendenze del poeta," as well as " alla modo della pittura vascolare."

For another instance of the influence of poetry on vase-painting, there is to be cited the vase attributed to Euphronios,[81] with a scene of a youthful symposiast playing a lyre; the inscriptions read: Λέαγρος καλός· μαμε και ποτεο. These words, sung to the reclining Leagros of the vase, Studniczka[82] believes to be an inaccurate rendering of Sappho's καὶ ποθήω καὶ μάομαι.[83] On the vase they stand μαμε και ποτεο, and the analogy is certainly striking.

Of Alkaios Cicero (*de Nat. Deorum,* i, 28) says, " The mole on the limb of a boy delights him." He had a passionate attachment with a youth named Lykos (Horace, i, 32, 11); for his feelings for " Menon kalos," see, no. 61 in Chapter III. The line, οἶνος, ὦ φίλε παῖ, καὶ ἀλάθεα, also instances his enthusiasm and sincerity for wine and this anomalous love.

---

[77] Bergk, *Poetae Lyrici Graeci*, 24. Cf. also Kritias, Chapter IV.
[78] Cf. Himerius, *Or.*, XIV, 1: ἐκεῖνος γάρ [Anakreon] ποτε ἐρασθεὶς ἐφήβου καλοῦ, ἐπειδήπερ ἑώρα τὸν ἔφηβον ὀλίγον αὑτοῦ φροντίζοντα.
[79] *Mon. Ant.*, XIX, 1909, pp. 96, 102-115.
[80] Br. Mus. E 18; Klein, pp. 59-60, no. 29.
[81] *C. V. A., Louvre*, fasc. 5, III I c, pl. 27, 8.
[82] *Jahrb.*, II, 1887, p. 162.
[83] Cf. Miller-Robinson, *Songs of Sappho*, Lexington, Kt., 1925, p. 102, no. 9; Bergk, *Poetae Lyrici Graeci*, III, p. 97, frag. 93.

Theokritos, too (*Idylls* XXIX and XXX) writes of the complicated sentiments of paederasty.

Simonides can be found in part under *Bryson, Milon,* and *Theognetos* in Chapter III below, *Eualkides* in Chapter IV; Plato, in part, under *Alexis* in Chapter III and *Agathon* in Chapter IV. To Plato also is attributed a quatrain to the favourite Dion and a lyrical thought for Aster:[84]

"Star gazing Aster, would I were the skies,
To gaze upon thee with a thousand eyes."

The name Aster calls to mind the namesake, who, during the siege of Olynthos, shot an arrow at Philip of Macedon (in 348 B. C.) that cost the latter an eye (cf. Gude, *History of Olynthus,* p. 41, no. 26, and pp. 85, 93). May this have been the same Aster, who moved to Amphipolis and then to Olynthos (Lucian, *On Way to Write History,* 38)? In any case, of these two favourites of Plato, Diogenes Laertius (III, 29) says: μειρακίου τινὸς ἀστρολογεῖν συνασκουμένου ἐρασθῆναι, ἀλλὰ καὶ Δίωνος τοῦ προειρημένου . . . ἔνιοι καὶ Φαίδρου φασί· δηλοῦν δὲ τὸν ἔρωτα αὐτοῦ τάδε τὰ ἐπιγράμματα, ἃ καὶ πρὸς αὐτοῦ γενέσθαι εἰς αὐτούς.

Peek[85] describes a vase with a skolion, "Huldigung an einen παῖς καλός." The inscription is of no use in explaining the ritualistic scene on the vase, as it was simply scratched on carelessly by the owner; if the inscription had any relation to the scene, it would have been painted on, Peek thinks, and so we may assume that only painted inscriptions and carefully incised ones like the signature of Hieron were put on in the vase-shops; carelessly inscribed ones were doubtless added by the buyer and owner. The inscription in this case reads:

Σοφροσσύνεν ἐνὶ κλά[δοις σ]μίλα[κος ἡειμένος]
[Στρόμβιχε, ἐλε]υθερίας καλὸν ἔχει στέφανον.

Peek translates, "Sophrosyne ist um dich in den Zweigen

---

[84] Bergk, *op. cit.,* II, pp. 620-622, nos. 7 (Dion) and 14 (Aster).

[85] "Epigraphische Nachträge," Graef-Langlotz, *Die Antiken Vasen von der Akropolis,* II, 3, no. 563, p. 130.

des Smilax, wie du den der Freiheit schönen Kranz auf dem Haupte trägst." The vase dates c. 480 B. C.

In literature and on vases gods and heroes are often called "fair." From the Prosopographia in Chapter IV almost all such have been eliminated, but, as an example, the third century dedication by Gorgos to *Phoibos kalos*[86] is cited here:

παῖς 'Ασκληπιάδεω καλῷ καλὸν εἵσατο Φοίβῳ
Γόργος ἀφ' ἱμερτᾶς τοῦτο γέρας κεφαλᾶς.

Phanokles composed an elegy called " Erotes " or " kaloi," rich illustrations out of mythology and heroic saga forming a history of boy-love. The longest fragment of this is preserved[87] and illustrates the love of Orpheus for the boy, Kallias. (In the earliest period of Greek religion Orpheus turns himself to the cultivation of paederasty because, after he failed to bring his dear wife, Eurydike, back to earth, he felt this the only way to remain true to his marriage-bond with her. Boy-love was not felt to be adulterous for a married man, cf. Apollod., I, 14; Ovid, *Heroides,* XI, 50 ff.)

To return, however, to the period in which the cultivation of paederasty was contemporary with the inscriptions on Attic vases, we must now, in an endeavor to understand the disappearance of the inscriptions from vases, look into the general public conditions. We must consider the opinions held in the time of the Peloponnesian War and of the critical activities of the comic poet, Aristophanes.

During the distress of the Peloponnesian War the earlier moral conditions went completely off the track.[88] Pauly[89] says: " Wenn bis dahin in der Knabenliebe eine sittliche Haltung das Übergewicht behauptet hatte, so ging diese jetzt sicherlich verloren. Auch gehören ja überhaupt die schlimmsten Berichte über päderastische Ausgelassenheit welche wir bei den Alten vorfinden, der Zeit nach dem peloponnesischen

---

[86] Ct. Rhianus, *Anth. Pal.*, VI, 278.
[87] In Stob., *Flor.*, LXIV, 14.
[88] Thuk., II, 53 ff.
[89] *Real-Encykl.* (1848), sub Paederastia.

Kriege an. Dahin gehören auch die Anklagen der attischen Redner, bei welchen das päderastische Treiben in den Jugendjahren noch zu ebenso schmachvollem als verderblichem Vorwurfe im Mannesalter gebraucht wird."

The comedies of Aristophanes are the most fertile field for the study of social conditions at the time. How different is his society from the graceful young men in a Platonic dialogue! How little time, however, separated the elegant Socratic circle from the "dramatis personae," either ill-mannered or affected, of Aristophanes! The first jibe comes when a character in the *Knights* (736 ff.) is told that he is like the "beloved boys" in his loose ways, in having turned from the serious, noble aspects of his position to a great commonness and indiscrimination:

> σὺ γὰρ
> ὅμοιος εἶ τοῖς παισὶ τοῖς ἐρωμένοις.
> τοὺς μὲν καλούς τε κἀγαθοὺς οὐ προσδέχει,
> σαυτὸν δὲ λυχνοπώλαισι καὶ νευρορράφοις
> καὶ σκυτοτόμοις καὶ βυρσοπώλαισιν δίδως.

In lines 1162-1163 of the same comedy Demos takes a fling at the manners of the "boys":

> ἀλλ' ἢ μεγάλως εὐδαιμονήσω τήμερον
> ὑπὸ τῶν ἐραστῶν νὴ Δί' ἢ 'γὼ θρύψομαι;

("Shall I play the coquette with them?")

The scene between the Dikaios Logos and the Adikos Logos in the *Clouds,* 889-1112, over the raising of young men is very important. The speeches of the Dikaios Logos deplore the impertinences of the boys, and ridicule the effeminacies and sensualities of the day. The Dikaios Logos says [90] on the training of boys in his day, an earlier one (the Socratic one):

> And every one's thigh was forward and high as they sat to be drilled in a row,
> So that nothing the while indecent or vile the eye of a stranger might meet,

---

[90] Rogers' translation, II, p. 125, ll. 972 ff. For "the Image in the Sand" cf. Hewitt in *Cl. Phil.,* XXX, 1935, pp. 10-22.

And then with their hand they would smooth down the sand whenever they rose from their seat,
To leave not a trace of themselves in the place for a vigilant lover to view.

The last gesture is further explained in 1084 ff., where the Adikos Logos sets out to show that εὐρυπρώκτος εἶναι at Athens is no great matter. Councillors, poets, orators, all Athenians are so called in this section, but the εὐρυπρωκτία which he declares to be so common is that of the boy-lover and not of the detected adulterer, as is shown by line 1103. Antimachos is designated as the same sort of person but in different terms in 1022: τῆς 'Αντιμάχου καταπυγοσύνης σ' ἀναπλήσει. The scholiast has this to add: 'Αντιμάχου: οὗτος εἰς θηλύτητα κωμῳδεῖται. *Euryproktia* is a constant insinuation against those in public life.[91]

The common way of cultivating one's favourite with gifts was by the time in disfavour with the "boys," who were now eager only for money. So in the *Ploutos*[92] we read:

> And those Corinthian huzzies so they say,
> If he who sues them for their love is poor,
> Turn up their noses at the man; but grant
> A wealthy suitor more than he desires.
> So too the boy-loves (τούς γε παῖδας);
>   just to get some money
> And not at all because they love their lovers.—
> Those are the baser (πόρνους), not the
>   nobler sort;
> They never ask for money. — No? what then?—
> O, one a hunter, one a pack of hounds."—
> Ah, they-re ashamed, I warrant, of their vice
> And seek to crust it over with a name.

Because of the lisping voices, mincing gaits, and soft wraps these boys affected (*Clouds,* 977-989), their suitors were in some disrepute with Aristophanes. In the *Wasps*[93] he says:

He (Aristophanes) never was found in the exercise-ground, corrupting the boys; he never complied

---

[91] *Acharn.*, 716; *Knights*, 877 ff.; *Eccl.*, 112 seq.
[92] Rogers' transl., 149 ff.   [93] Rogers' transl., 1025 ff.

With the suit of some dissolute knave, who loathed that the
  vigilant lash of the bard should chide
His vile, effeminate boy-love (παιδίχ' ἑαυτοῦ).

That the gymnasia were a haunt of such persons is clear in another passage, the speech of Peisthetairos in the *Birds,* 137 ff.:

> ὅπου ξυναντῶν μοι ταδί τις μέμψεται
> ὥσπερ ἀδικηθεὶς παιδὸς ὡραίου πατήρ·
> ' καλῶς γέ μου τὸν υἱόν, ὦ Στιλβωνίδη,
> εὑρὼν ἀπιόντ' ἀπὸ γυμνασίου λελουμένον
> οὐκ ἔκυσας, οὐ προσεῖπας, οὐ προσηγάγου,
> οὐκ ὠρχιπέδισας, ὢν ἐμοὶ πατρικὸς φίλος.'

Where is such a city? τὸν Ἠλεῖον Λέπρεον is the answer. The Felton edition of the comedy, note to ll. 137-142, says: "It is sufficient to say of the passage that it is one of many in Aristophanes founded upon the unnatural vices which marked the social morals of the historical ancients, and the increase of which, in progress of time, accelerated the downfall of both Greece and Rome."

Another proof of the popularity of boys at this time comes in *Clouds,* 1073-74, where one is told of what he should deny himself in order to be temperate:

> σκέψαι γάρ, ὦ μειράκιον, ἐν τῷ σωφρονεῖν ἅπαντα
> ἄνεστιν, ἡδονῶν θ' ὅσων μέλλεις ἀποστερεῖσθαι,
> παίδων, γυναικῶν, κοττάβων, ὄψων, πότων, κιχλισμῶν.

This proves: (I) that an ἀνὴρ σώφρων had nothing to do with boy-love in the time of the Dikaios Logos, the speaker; (II) that it was, all the same, one of the customary delights. In this connection, it is interesting to compare with this condition of things in Athens what we know of Sparta's attitude, as in Xenophon:[94] ὁ Λυκοῦργος ἐναντία καὶ τούτοις πᾶσι γνούς, εἰ μέν τις αὐτὸς ὤν, οἷον δεῖ, ἀγασθεὶς ψυχὴν παιδὸς πειρῷτο ἄμεμπτον φίλον ἀποτελέσασθαι καὶ συνεῖναι, ἐπήνει καὶ καλλίστην παιδείαν ταύτην ἐνόμιζεν. Here we see: (1) that there was a perfectly moral relationship possible, and, moreover, existent in Sparta

---

[94] *De Reip. Lac.,* II, 13.

in Lykourgos' day; (2) that the opposite (εἰ δέ τις παιδὸς σώματος ὀρεγόμενος φανείη) was shameful (αἴσχιστον).

But in Athens the purity of the early stages scarcely lasted past the Persian wars before it had sunk down into ἀρρενομιξία, a thing that formerly was punishable by death.[95] By a law of Solon[96] grown-up men were forbidden entrance to the palaistrai. This was true of an earlier time, but before the end of the fifth century, the law had fallen into desuetude, and persons of all ages were found there, conversing with the ephebes.[97] In Athens at the time of Aischines (*Speech against Timarchos*, 19), whoever had sold his body while a boy, or prostituted it, either unwillingly by force or wantonly,[98] lost his citizenship rights; he could not be one of the nine archons, nor a priest, a herald, an ambassador; he could not be an orator, nor wear a crown. Aischines goes on to say: "To which of these two classes will you reckon Timarchos? to those who have had a lover or those who have been prostitutes? . . . I do not take away the character of handsome lads. I do not deny that I have often loved . . . But . . . while the love of beautiful and temperate youths does honour to humanity . . . the buying of the person of a free boy for debauchery is a mark of insolence and ill-breeding." That such business was a fairly common one we know also from the speech of Lysias against Simon, in which a legal contest was waged over an actual contract drawn up for it.

The ephebes in Athens loitered around in the barber-shops,[99] in the perfumery shops,[100] in the ἰατρεῖα,[101] and around the

---

[95] Xen., *Reip. Lac.*, II, 13; *Symp.*, VIII, 34, 35; Aelian, *Var. Hist.*, III, 12.

[96] Aisch., I, 9.

[97] Even before this time the vases show pictures of boys being followed to school by their admirers; P. Girard, *Educ. Athen.*, p. 41; Aristophanes, *Peace*, 762 ff.

[98] Phaido was bought out of a brothel by Sokrates; Diog. Laert., II, 105.

[99] κουρεῖα: Demosth., *In Aristog.*, 786-7; Aristoph., *Ploutos*, 338.

[100] μυροπωλεῖα: Aristoph., *Knights*, 1375.

[101] Aelian, *Var. Hist.*, III, 7.

deserted and dark Pnyx,[102] where the male prostitution went on. The Kerameikos was also a good place for meeting people and for the animated conversation the Athenians liked so well. Athenaeus (242 E) quotes a passage from the *Odysseus* of Anaxandrides (Kock, II, p. 148) which refers to the profligate Theagenes who was known to Aristophanes (*Birds*, 823) and was called " Smoke ": " If one leers at the beauties, he is Smoke of the family of Theagenes " (Gulick in Loeb Classical Library, *Athenaeus,* III, p. 93).

We reflect that just a generation before this Plato [103] had been pouring all the ardent eloquence of his genius into describing the ideal love (that of boys) in passages like this:

Men who are sections of the male pursue the masculine, and as long as their boyhood lasts they show themselves to be slices of the male by making friends with men and delighting to lie with them and to be clasped in men's embraces; these are the finest boys and striplings, for they have the most manly nature. Some say they are shameless creatures, but falsely; for their behaviour is due not to shamelessness but to daring, manliness and virility, since they are quick to recognize their like. Sure evidence of this is the fact that on reaching maturity these alone prove in a public career to be men. So when they come to man's estate they are boy-lovers, and have no natural interest in wiving and getting children, but only do those things under stress of custom; they are quite contented to live together unwedded all their days. A man of this sort is born to be a lover of boys or the willing mate of a man, eagerly greeting his own kind.

He had seen (*Rep.,* III, 403 B) that for ideal ends there should be " a law to the effect that a friend should use no other familiarity to his love than a father would use to his son." He had distinguished its character in Athens: [104] " Now here and in Lacedaemon the rules about love are perplexing ($\pi o\iota\kappa\iota\lambda o\varsigma$), but in most cities they are simple and easily intelligible; in Elis and Boeotia, and in

---

[102] Aischines, I, 34, 81.
[103] *Sym.,* 191-192; Fowler's translation in Loeb Classical Library.
[104] *Sym.,* 182 A.

countries having no gifts of eloquence, they are very straightforward; the law is simply in favour of these connexions, and no one, whether young or old, has anything to say to their discredit; the reason being, as I suppose, that they are men of few words in those parts, and therefore the lovers do not like the trouble of pleading their suit" (Jowett). This would imply, I suppose, that one of the reasons for the complexity of the rules in Athens was due to the fact that, being forensically inclined, Athenian men liked to exert verbal persuasion on their youths and to quibble about which hung heavier in the scale, the spiritual or the sensual, in their relationships. Plato had, however, also said, in a whimsical passage and mood (*Sym.*, 181 E), that there should be a law against paederasty because of the waste of zeal and effort on an object so uncertain as a youth. This "uncertain" quality he had then explained as due to the impossibility of predicting whether a youth would end in vice or virtue of mind and body.

On the passage in the *Phaidros* (249 A), οὐ γὰρ πτεροῦται ... πλὴν ἡ τοῦ φιλοσοφήσαντος ἀδόλως ἢ παιδεραστήσαντος μετὰ φιλοσοφίας, purity had been wasted, so far as a later age was concerned; for, while Juvenal (II, 10) founds the imputation against Sokrates on this passage (Inter Socraticos notissima fossa cinaedos), we have seen that even as early as Aristophanes misunderstanding, obscenity and defamation were thrust upon this anomalous love. Aristotle had analyzed the poetic rapture of Plato into considering whether such habits were unnatural congenitally or habitually,[105] and saw the ugliness in the maiming of the anus of an effeminate man.[106] Lysias (Plato, *Phaidros,* 227 C) had put into writing a formula for the seducing of a *pais kalos,* and not by a lover; for with great ingenuity he had maintained that one ought to give his favours not to the lover, but to one not in love with him! How erotic a *cliché* the poet's song of yesterday had become is further to be seen in a fourth-century cure-inscription from

---

[105] *Eth. Nic.*, VII, 5 ff.
[106] *Probl.*, IV, 26.

Epidauros,[107] in which an ailing man dreamt that he was associating with a beautiful boy: παιδὶ καλῷ συγγίνεσθαι.

To sum up, then, the path of development which paederasty had taken, I quote John Addington Symonds:[108] "We find two separate forms of masculine passion clearly marked in early Hellas—a noble and a base, a spiritual and a sensual." As Maximus Tyrius [109] says: " The one is Greek, the other barbarous; the one is virile, the other effeminate." The mixed form (ποικίλος) on which the Greeks prided themselves and on which Plato was decisive,[110] was a passionate and enthusiastic attachment between man and youth, recognized by society and protected by opinion. Though it was not free from sensuality, it did not degenerate into mere licentiousness. The expanding emotions of boys living a communal life from early prepubertic years, athletic contests with close attention to comparative anatomical beauties, less veiled and illusive ideas of marriage, were all conducive to this fervid emotional enthusiasm, as well as the intellectual inferiority of Athenian women. Though it is not true that the company of an uncultured woman is any less stimulating to the mind than that of a callow boy, the deduction nonetheless, follows from the picture Plato draws in the *Phaidros* of a sublimated paederasty. This picture, however, does not profess to be founded on reality of experience, and it is certainly true that this commerce, like that with hetairai, was normally founded on physical attraction. The Greek love of beauty cast a glamour upon it, and the characteristic passion of Athens for culture was as sympathetic to the growth of paederasty as Dorian militarism.

It is an interesting and not ungrounded speculation that *kalos*-inscriptions may have ceased because of the advent of

---

[107] *I. G.*, IV, 951, l. 104.

[108] *A Problem in Greek Ethics, Being an Inquiry into the Phenomenon of Sexual Inversion* (for private circulation), London, 1901, p. 6.

[109] *Dissert.*, IX.

[110] In the *Phaidros, Symposion*, and *Laws*.

heterosexuality and its concomitant interest in the female,[111] which must be observed in art, both painting and sculpture, of the late days of the fifth century and the whole of the fourth, when the male-ideal of beauty had been lost. It is apparent in literature that the epic nobility of what *kalos* had meant to the pre-Periklean Greeks had been pretty well disintegrated by this time, and as Athenian law now recognized contracts between man and boy for the mutual exchange of the person of the one and the money of the other, the high character of the relationship had been lost.

Since *kalos* used in this sense was no longer a compliment for all people, it was not spoken of for what it had come to mean to the few. Its developing shades of meaning can be followed from the purely athletic scenes of the earlier vases on which the interest in bodies is still healthy, to the ensuing predilection for the " mantled " figures, already a step down from the more natural earlier interest. At this time the youth of Athens had been badly decimated by the Peloponnesian Wars, and this, too, was probably back of the new drift, for families had to be built up and sons had to give up the older philosophic loves for the wooing of the necessary female,[112] who now acquired more importance in Greek life

---

[111] " The female body begins to attract more attention than the male, while society turns at the same time from a homosexual to a normal basis. A decay in amateur athletics contributed to the change, lessening the interest in boys, which had naturally been felt when men of the upper classes exercised regularly in the gymnasia . . . . Statues of young athletes, scarce even in the 4th century . . .": says Lawrence, *Classical Sculpture*, p. 283, referring to a sculptural analogy at a later date. This seems to occur even earlier; transparent drapery on female statues c. 425 B. C. certainly gives them a more sensuous character, and at this time Aristophanes begins to ridicule what Plato, Sophokles, and serious advocates of the preceding generations deemed noble in character, paederasty.

[112] The legislator of Crete is said by Aristotle (*Pol.*, II, 10, p. 1272 Bekk.) to have favored paederasty so that there might not occur an over-population of the island, which could not support too many people: πρὸς τὴν διάζευξιν τῶν γυναικῶν, ἵνα μὴ πολυτεκνῶσι, τὴν πρὸς τοὺς ἄρρενας ποιήσας ὁμιλίαν

than she had ever had, as can be seen in the art of the period. Certainly some new flair must be the cause of the disappearance of the old scenes of the palaestra and the popular "conversational" groups and "couples in procession" of the vases to which *kalos* names had formerly lent themselves.

Not too much has been made of the literary and the ethical elements, interweaving with and conditioning the artistic as they do. Homoerotic sentiments opened the heart of the Greek people and enchanted the body of its lyric expression.[113] Indeed, they stood so solidly in the very centre of Greek culture that it has been asserted [114] that, without them, the civilization of this people would have struck out on utterly different paths. Even a modern psychopathic clinic would scarcely attempt to force the idiosyncrasy of a nation into pedantic rules, and, though it be a faint unintelligibility to see just how essentially related, as cause and effect, were Greek moral-ideals and Greek art, still no progress in interpretive appreciation can ever be made if the layman behaves like an ostrich in the face of something distasteful and ignores its reality. To see only the dazzling shimmer of its reflection in Hellenic art without admitting the strange shadows that, to our sense, so enshroud the sensitive soul of the Greek, is as purblind an occupation as that of separating the known homosexuality of this people from the fine jewel of art it produced in the Athenian Akropolis.

So *kalos* in art must be considered in relation to all the information to be gleaned from expressions of it in literature; with that it becomes less of an enigma. Still, where it appears as a character-trait of an entire folk, where it could be confessed with impunity and reckoned among the enriching experiences of life, where even the coryphées of the nation could scarce lift themselves above it, where the laws at most controlled it without judging against it, where the youth of

---

[113] Bethe, *Rheinisches Museum*, LXII, 1907, p. 438.

[114] Licht, *Sittengeschichte Griechenlands, Ergaenzungsband*, p. 220, sec. 167.

the land found in it a source of material gain and spiritual ennoblement, it is certainly a norm of conduct hopelessly at variance with ours.[115] Perhaps to look at the specific instances in the following chapter with a psycho-analytic curiosity can only give clearer, sharper outlines to the mysterious figure of Eros like " a rose without thorns." [116]

---

[115] Becker, *Charikles*, vol. II, *Die Knabenliebe*, pp. 199 ff.
[116] Carpenter, E. A., *Love's Coming of Age*, p. 127 (Vanguard Press, New York).

CHAPTER III

PROSOPOGRAPHIA OF LOVE-NAMES IN LITERATURE AND ART OTHER THAN VASES

Here we have listed alphabetically the names of eighty-one persons who are called "fair" in Greek literature and on art-monuments other than vases. Many are of the period of *ho pais kalos* on Attic vases, though we have included others of later times, as well as the names of a few philosophers, such as Plato and Sokrates, and of other famous Hellenes who are known to have cultivated the emotions. Where, in the last case, the name of the lover is more famous than that of his *pais kalos,* his name as well as that of his beloved is given in the alphabetic heading (e. g. Agorakritos kalos and Pheidias, no. 2). The *Mousa Paidike,* a late collection of erotic verses, compiled by Straton of Sardis from the writings of poets of different ages, some of them from the period of *ho pais kalos* on vases, has yielded many personal names. I have, however, limited myself to the mention of those only to which the adjective *kalos* is actually appended. Reference to this work we give as to the Twelfth Book of the Palatine Anthology, including, where known, the name of the poet within the reference (e. g. 3. Agrippa kalos; Anth. Pal., XII, 194; by Straton). When several ephebes are praised for beauty in the same poem, the names of those not given in the particular alphabetic heading are enclosed parenthetically within the reference to the work that mentions them; their own heading simply refers back to the one in which the work is cited (e. g. no. 6, Alexis kalos [and Phaidros; *Gk. Anth.,* VII, 100, Loeb]; no. 68, Phaidros [see Alexis]). That the number of those who in this chapter are definitely declared to have been the favourites of particular individuals is preponderant to those whose liaisons are unknown or unstated, is further evidence for the amorous consequences which a Greek youth met for being a *kalos*.

The following table shows the distribution of such of the names in this chapter as are or were known (on objects no longer extant) on monuments; the object on which the name was recorded is in each case mentioned:

Roof-tile from Olynthos	Menon
Rock-inscription	Alphinoos
Pheidias' Olympian Zeus (on the finger of the statue)	Pantarkes
Red marble fragment from Akropolis	Archias
Sling stone from Olynthos	Archias
Cave inscription	Achilles
Tile from building	Hippeos
Stones and buildings	Philokles
Mosaics from Olynthos	Aphrodite
	Eutychia
Bronze castanet	Lichas

The occupations and the ways in which the youths won their fame are listed in these tables:

Poets' favourites: Alexis and Phaidros (Plato)
Batrachos (Hesiod)
Bryson (Simonides)
Dositheos (anonymous)
Lysanias (Kallimachos)
Megistes and others (Anacreon)
Menon and others (Alcaeus)
Milon (Simonides)
Philokles (Aratos)
Theognetos (Simonides)
and
37 more from the *Mousa Paidike* of Straton

Adventurers: Alkibiades
Episthenes
Leon
Menon

Favourites of generals and rulers:
Aristokles (Antigonos)
Argilios (Pausanias of Sparta)
Asopichos (Epameinondas)
Bathyllos (Polykrates of Samos)
Dailochos (Hieron)
Demokles (Demetrios)

| | Euthydemos (Kritias)
| | Kephisodoros (Epameinondas)
| | Megabates (Agesilaos)
| | Menon (Ariaios)
| | Panteus (Kleomenes)
| | Pausanias (Philip of Macedon)
| | Smerdis (Polykrates of Samos)
| | Stesileos (Themistokles and Aristeides)

Athletes: Autolykos
                          Milon
                          Theognetos

Sculptor: Agorakritos
Favourites of   Agorakritos (Pheidias)
   Famous Men: Alkibiades (Sokrates)
                          Epikrates (Demosthenes)
                          Isokrates
                          Pantarkes (Pheidias)
                          Zeno (Parmenides)

1. Achilles kalos.

"Inscriptio amatoria" cited by Plutarch, *Bruta Animalia Ratione Uti*, II, 990 E: ἐν δὲ τῇ θόλῳ τοῦ Πτῴου Ἀπόλλωνος λαθών τις ὑμῶν ἐνέγραψεν: Ἀχιλλεὺς καλός, ἤδη τοῦ Ἀχιλλέως υἱὸν ἔχοντος, καὶ τὰ γράμματα πυνθάνομαι διαμένειν. Xenophon in the *Symposion*, VIII, 31, says: Ἀχιλλεὺς . . . οὐχ ὡς παιδικοῖς Πατρόκλῳ ἀλλ' ὡς ἑταίρῳ ἀποθανόντι ἐκπρεπέστατα τιμωρῆσαι.

2. Agorakritos kalos and Pheidias.

On Agorakritos, the sculptor and pupil of Pheidias, Pliny (*N. H.*, XXXVI, 17) says: "Agorakritos of Paros was also a pupil of Pheidias, who was attracted by his youthful beauty, and so is said to have allowed his name to appear on several of his own works." On Pheidias' love for Agorakritos and for Pantarkes, cf. Pausanias, V, 11, 3; VI, 10, 6; IX, 34, 1. That other artists as well were given to boy-love we know from what Aristophanes says of the poets Agathon and Euripides in the *Thesmophoriazusae*, 35, 54, 74, 210, 264.

3. Agrippa (*Anth. Pal.*, XII, 194; by Straton):

Ἀγρίππαν τὸν καλόν . . .

4. Aktaion kallistos.

Plutarch (*Amat. Narr.*, II, 7) tells a story about Aktaion, the fair son of Melissos of Corinth, and the object of the passion of Archias: τούτου δὴ τοῦ Μελίσσου υἱὸς 'Ακταίων γίνεται, κάλλιστος καὶ σωφρονέστατος τῶν ὁμηλίκων, οὗ πλεῖστοι μὲν ἐγένοντο ἐρασταί, διαφερόντως δ' 'Αρχίας, γένους μὲν ὢν τοῦ τῶν 'Ηρακλειδῶν, πλούτῳ δὲ καὶ τῇ ἄλλῃ δυνάμει λαμπρότατος Κορινθίων. 'Επεὶ δὲ πείθειν οὐκ ἠδύνατο τὴν παῖδα, ἔγνω βιάσασθαι καὶ συναρπάσαι τὸ μειράκιον. He came to the house of Melissos with a large company of friends and servants, but, during the struggle between his party and that of the father defending his son, the boy was killed, Archias ran away. Then the father carried his son to the Agora and demanded vengeance, but all the Corinthians did was to sympathize. Later a plague fell on Corinth, and, as the oracle declared that it would not abate until the boy's death was atoned for, Archias sailed to Sicily to found Syracuse, where ὑπὸ τοῦ Τηλέφου δολοφονεῖται, ὃς ἐγεγόνει μὲν αὐτοῦ παιδικά ... Diodorus Siculus, VIII, 10, tells the same story.

5. Alexander the Great.

Athenaeus (XIII, 603 a) says that he had a consuming passion for beautiful boys. Dikaiarchos (*F. H. G.*, II, 241) says that he fell so deeply in love with the eunuch Bogoas that he kissed him publicly in a theater, and repeated it for the benefit of the audience (cf. also Plutarch, *Alex.* 67). In the *Historic Memoirs* of Karystios (Müller, *F. H. G.*, IV, p. 357) we read: "Charon of Chalkis had relations with a beautiful boy. When Alexander saw this boy at a banquet in the house of Krateros and remarked that he was very fair, Krateros told the boy to give Alexander a kiss; Alexander replied, 'Don't, for it would give you more sorrow than me pleasure.' For Alexander was just as temperate as he was sensual, when it was a question of decency." In the light of his reputation for personal comeliness and of his relations with his friend, Hephaistion (cf. Alexander's words that 'Hephaistion was Alexander'), the great conqueror finds a place in this list.

6. Alexis kalos (and Phaidros; *Gk. Anth.*, VII, 100, Loeb):

" Now when I said nothing, except just that Alexis is fair, he is looked at everywhere and by everyone when he appears. Why, my heart, dost thou point out bones to dogs and have to sorrow for it afterwards? Was it not thus that I lost Phaidros?" This quatrain, attributed to Plato, bears the heading: εἰς Ἄλεξιν καὶ Φαῖδρον˙ οὗτοι εἰσὶν οἱ βεβηλοῦντες τὸν Πλάτωνος βίον.

Alexis (and Kleoboulos; *Anth. Pal.*, XII, 164, by Meleager):

Ἡδὺ δὲ παιδοφιλεῖν καὐτὸν ἐόντα καλόν,
οἷα τὸν ἁβροκόμην στέργει Κλεόβουλον Ἄλεξις.

7. Alphinoos kalos.

Coincidental with the use of καλός on vases and similar to the inscriptions of Thera is the rock-cut praise of Alphinoos on the northwest slope of Philopappos Hill in Athens. The inscription is mentioned by Judeich (*Topographie von Athen*, 2nd ed., p. 398), but attention is called here to the fact that the inscription lies seventy paces south-west of the "Siebensesselplatz," and not north-west, as Judeich says. At the date of its finding, it was published (in Ἀρχ. Ἐφ., 1899, pp. 239 ff.). The name is fragmentary, and was read " Olynthos " by the original publisher, but, following Judeich's preferable restoration, I read:

[Ἀλφίν]οος καλὸς μὲν ἰδὲν,
τερπνὸς δὲ προσειπεῖν.

Alphinoos may be identified with the cousin of the orator Hypereides (Kirchner 660); though, apart from the fact that he was " fair to behold and a joy to converse with," we know little else about him. Here, once for all, the reading into *kalos* of all sorts of epic, abstract virtues is taken out of the hands of moralists and given a strictly physical meaning and appeal: "Alphinoos is fair to behold " (cf. the inscribed statue base of the Sculptor Phaidimos in the National Museum, Athens, Papaspyridi, *Guide du Musée National*, p. 23, no. 81, with a "καλὸν ἰδεῖν"). The Alphinoos inscription is probably later than any of the vase inscriptions of this type.

8. Antileon (*Anth. Pal.,* XII, 138; by Mnasalcas):

Μεῖνον ἐπ' Ἀντιλέοντι πεσεῖν ὑπὸ τὴν γλυκὺν ὕπνον,
ὡς τότε τοῖς καλοῖς πάντα χαριζομένα.

9. Antiochos (*Anth. Pal.,* XII, 133; by Meleager):

Καὶ γὰρ ἐγὼ τὸν καλὸν ἐν ἠϊθέοισι φιλήσας
Ἀντίοχον, ψυχῆς ἡδὺ πέπωκα μέλι.

10. Aphrodite.

On a mosaic from Olynthos. Cf. Chapter I, p. 10, footnote 38 above.

11. Archestratos (*Anth. Pal.,* XII, 140; anonymous):

τὸν καλὸν ὡς ἰδόμαν Ἀρχέστρατον . . .

12. Archias kalos.

On an unpublished fourth century lead sling stone excavated by Professor D. M. Robinson at Olynthos is the inscription Ἀρχίας ὡραῖος. This reminds us of Pindar's ὡραῖος ἐὼν καὶ καλός (*Ol.,* IX, 94), from which we know that ὡραῖος is equivalent to καλός. The "Archias kalos" on Attic vases, however, and on a red marble fragment from the Akropolis is perhaps another person (Chapter IV, no. 35 below). The case is interesting in that it shows how the idea of celebrating a person for his physical beauty had travelled far from Athens, doubtless with the vases.

13. Argilios kalos and Pausanias, the Spartan general.

Thukydides (I, 132) tells us that Argilios (an ethnic?) was the beloved of Pausanias: ἀνὴρ Ἀργίλιος, παιδικά ποτε ὢν αὐτοῦ καὶ πιστότατος ἐκείνῳ. Cf. also Thukydides, IV, 103. That "paidika" is here, as generally, to be taken in the erotic sense, we know from Cornelius Nepos, *Paus.,* 4, 1;

"quem puerum Pausanias amore venerio dilexerat." All else we know of Argilios is that Nepos calls him "quidam adulescentulus."

14. Aribazos, a Persian (*Anth. Pal.*, XII, 62, anon.):

Ματέρες αἱ Περσῶν, καλὰ μὲν καλὰ τέκνα τέκεσθε.
ἀλλ' 'Αρίβαζος ἐμοὶ κάλλιον ἢ τὸ καλόν.

15. Aristagoras (*Anth. Pal.*, XII, 122, by Meleager):

τὸν καλὸν 'Αρισταγόρην . . .

16. Aristokles kalos and Antigonos.

This youth was a lyre-player and the most famous of the favourites of one of Alexander's generals, Antigonos, who was so in love with him that once, after a drinking-bout, he led the philosopher, Zeno, away with him to the boy's house. (Diog. Laert., VII, 1, 14; Athen., XIII, 603e). Cf. Zeno, no. 81, below.

17. Aristotle.

Aristotle (384-322 B. C.) was influenced by the beauty of one of his pupils, whose name is not known to us, only that he came from Phaselis, one of the coast cities of Lykia in Asia Minor (Athen., XIII, 566e).

18. Asopichos and Epameinondas.

Most famous of the favourites of Epameinondas, the victor at Leuktra (371) and Mantineia (362), Asopichos shared the fame of Leuktra with his lover (Plut., *Amat.*, XVII, 15; Athen., XIII, 605a).

19. Autolykos (cf. chapter IV, *s. v.* Kallias).

This youth was the beloved of Kallias (Xen., *Sym.*, VIII, 7, 37 and 42), who was himself called *kalos* on Attic vases (see Chapter IV *sub nom.*). Autolykos, son of Lykon, was the victor in the pankration in 421 or 420 B. C. The date for this victory is set by the *Autolykos* of Eupolis (cf. Athen., V, 216). When Aristophanes (*Wasps,* 1026) says, "nor if any lover paid court to the poet to lampoon the favourite with whom he is piqued," he is sneering at Eupolis, who had attacked Autolykos in his *Poleis* (424 B. C.) and again in the *Autolykos* (420 B. C.). Cf. *Poleis,* frag. 215, ὥσπερ ἐπὶ τὴν Λύκωνος ἔρρει πᾶς ἀνήρ (Zelle, *De Comoediarum Graecarum saeculo quinto ante Christum natum actarum temporibus definiendis,* p. 33). The beauty of Autolykos is most poetically described in Xenophon (*Symp.* I, 2 and 9): Καλλίας δὲ ὁ Ἱππονίκου ἐρῶν ἐτύγχανεν Αὐτολύκου παιδὸς ὄντος· καὶ νενικηκότα αὐτὸν παγκράτιον ἧκεν ἄγων ἐπὶ τὴν θέαν . . . πρῶτον μὲν γάρ, ὥσπερ ὅταν φέγγος τι ἐν νυκτὶ φανῇ, πάντων προσάγεται τὰ ὄμματα, οὕτω καὶ τότε τοῦ Αὐτολύκου τὸ κάλλος πάντων εἷλκε τὰς ὄψεις πρὸς αὐτόν.

20. Bathyllos and Polykrates of Samos.

Polykrates had a statue of Bathyllos, one of his favourites (Hor. *Ep.* XIV, 9; Max. Tyr., XXXVII), erected in the temple of Hera, an unusual honour for a pleasure-boy to attain. It was still standing in as late a day as that of Apuleius, who saw and described it (*Florida,* 15). For more material on Polykrates' preoccupation with boys, cf. below sub Smerdis.

21. Batrachos kalos and Hesiod.

Hesiod loved a youth named Batrachos, on whose early death he composed a dirge, a fragment of which remains (cf. Suidas *sub nom.*). For this name on Attic vases, cf. Chapter IV, sub Leagros.

22. Bryson.

An epigram of Simonides (*Diehl, Anthologia Lyrica,* II, p. 117, no. 159) celebrates the beauty of Bryson: "Opis, giving glory to his fatherland, the holy city of Athena, child of the black earth, offered these pleasant flutes, that he wrought by the help of Hephaistos, to Aphrodite, having been vanquished by love for beautiful Bryson." (Edmonds).

A headless, seated statue of Bryson, father of Aiakes, was found on Samos (*Ath. Mitt.,* XXXI, 1906, p. 152, Abb. 3).

This Bryson, an earlier one, was probably the grandfather of Polykrates, whose father was named Aiakes (c. 570 B. C.).

23. Charidemos (*Anth. Pal.*, XII, 68; by Meleager):

οὐκ ἐθέλω Χαρίδαμον· ὁ γὰρ καλὸς εἰς Δία λεύσσει.

24. Cyrus (*Anth. Pal.*, XII, 28; by Numenius of Tarsus):

Κῦρος κύριός ἐστι. τί μοι μέλει, εἰ παρὰ γράμμα;
οὐκ ἀναγιγνώσκω τὸν καλόν, ἀλλὰ βλέπω.

25. Dailochos kallistos and Hieron.

In Xenophon's *Hieron*, I, 29 ff., the tyrant says that it is better to be a private citizen than a ruler; for, even in matters of love, there is no contest for gaining the affections of another person, as everybody is ready to give a ruler what he wants. In section 31 Hieron is addressed: τυράννῳ οὐ φῇς παιδικῶν ἔρωτας ἐμφύεσθαι; πῶς μὴν σύ, ἔφη, ἐρᾷς Δαϊλόχου τοῦ καλλίστου ἐπικαλουμένου.

26. Damon (*Anth. Pal.*, XII, 35; by Diokles):

'Αλλ' ὁ περισσὸς
κάλλεϊ νῦν Δάμων οὐδὲ τὸ χαῖρε λέγει.

27. Demokles kalos and Demetrios of Phaleron.

Plutarch (*Demetrios*, XXIV, 899 d) says: τὴν δὲ Δημοκλέους ἀρετὴν καὶ σωφροσύνην . . . 'Εκεῖνος γὰρ ἦν ἔτι παῖς ἄνηβος, οὐκ ἔλαθε δὲ τὸν Δημήτριον ἔχων τῆς εὐμορφίας τὴν ἐπωνυμίαν κατήγορον· ἐκαλεῖτο γὰρ Δημοκλῆς ὁ καλός, " who, to escape importunities, avoided every place of resort, and when at last followed into a private bathing-room by Demetrios, seeing none at hand to help or deliver, seized the lid from the cauldron, and plunging into the boiling water, sought a death untimely and unmerited, but worthy of the country and of the beauty that occasioned it " (Clough). Demetrios, for ten years the leader of the Athenian state (317-307 B. C.), had numerous erotic adventures with the young men of Athens, who swarmed around him. Karystios (Athen., XII, 542 d-f; Plut., *Demet.*, 24) says: "All the young men of Athens were envious of the preference of Demetrios for Diognis, and wanted so much to be loved by him, that when Demetrios went walking, they followed after, so that they might be noticed by him." Athenaeus (542 C and D) describes Demetrios of Phaleron as careful of his appearance, with dyed blonde hair, rouge on his cheeks, and says that νεανίσκων ἔρωτες νυκτερινοί were conducted by him.

28. Dexandros (*Anth. Pal.*, XII, 69; anon.):

   Δέξανδρον ... τὸν καλόν.

29. Diodoros (*Anth. Pal.*, XII, 9):

   Ἄρτι καλός, Διόδωρε, σύ, καὶ φιλέουσι πέπειρος.
   ἀλλὰ καὶ ἢν γήμῃς, οὐκ ἀπολειψόμεθα.

30. Diokles (*Anth. Pal.*, XII, 51; by Kallimachos):

   Καλὸς ὁ παῖς ... λίην καλός.

31. Dionysios (*Anth. Pal.*, XII, 67; anon.).

   τὸν καλὸν οὐχ ὁρόω Διονύσιον ...
         (*id.*, no. 107; anon.):
   τὸν καλόν, ὦ Χάριτες, Διονύσιον, εἰ μὲν ἕλοιτο
   τἀμά, καὶ εἰς ὥρας αὖθις ἄγοιτο καλόν.

32. Diphilos (*Anth. Pal.*, XII, 224; by Straton):

   Δίφιλε, ... ἔστι μὲν ἐν υἱὶ κάλλος.

33. Dositheos kalos (*Anth. Pal.*, XII, 130; Loeb trans.):

"I said and said it again, 'He is fair, he is fair,' but I will still say it, that Dositheos is fair and has lovely eyes. These words we engraved on no oak or pine, no, nor on a wall, but Love burnt them into my heart. But if any man deny it, believe him not. Yea, by thyself, O God, I swear he lies, and I who say it alone know the truth."

34. Drakon (*Anth. Pal.*, XI, 22; by Straton):

   Ἔστι Δράκων τις ἔφηβος, ἄγαν καλός.

35. Epikrates kalos.

This is the youth praised in the *Erotikos,* attributed probably falsely to Demosthenes. It is obviously influenced by Plato's *Phaidros,* and praises Epikrates ὃν ᾤετο πολλῶν καὶ καλῶν κἀγαθῶν ὄντων νέων ἐν τῇ πόλει χαριέστατον εἶναι (LXI, 1 = 1401).

36. Episthenes.

Xenophon (*Anab.,* VII, 4, 7) tells of a famous Olynthian, Episthenes, who was so smitten with love for a *pais kalos* doomed to die, that he offered his own life to save that of the boy. Both were freed together, and what happened later we are not told.

Ἐπισθένης δ' ἦν τις Ὀλύνθιος παιδεραστής, ὃς ἰδὼν παῖδα καλὸν ἡβάσκοντα ἄρτι πέλτην ἔχοντα, μέλλοντα ἀποθνῄσκειν, προσδραμὼν Ξενοφῶντα ἱκέτευε βοηθῆσαι παιδὶ καλῷ.

Later this Episthenes formed a band of young men, and was celebrated as a hero among them. Cf. Gude, *A History of Olynthus,* p. 42, no. 42.

37. Eubiotos and Kleander (*Anth. Pal.,* XII, 163; by Asklepiades):

Εὗρεν Ἔρως τί καλῷ μίξει καλόν . . . Κλέανδρον Εὐβιότῳ

38. Euphragoras (*Anth. Pal.,* XII, 171; by Dioskorides):

. . . τὸν καλὸν . . . Εὐφραγόρην.

39. Euthydemos kalos. (cf. Kritias, no. 54.)

40. Eutychia kale.

On a mosaic from Olynthos. Cf. Chapter I, p. 10, footnote 38 above.

41. Euxitheos (*Anth. Pal.,* XII, 71; by Kallimachos):

Ἔγνων· Εὐξίθεός σε συνήρπασε· καὶ σὺ γὰρ ἐλθὼν
τὸν καλὸν, ὦ μοχθήρ', ἔβλεπες ἀμφοτέροις.

42. Harmodios.

Thukydides, VI, 54, 2, says: γενομένου δὲ Ἁρμοδίου ὥρᾳ ἡλικίας λαμπροῦ Ἀριστογείτων . . . ἐραστὴς ὢν εἶχεν αὐτόν . . . Εἶχεν is here used, as otherwise, of the marital relationship (cf. II, 29). Thukydides tells the story of the famous pair: δι' ἐρωτικὴν ξυντυχίαν ἐπεχειρήθη . . . πειραθεὶς δὲ ὁ Ἁρμόδιος ὑπὸ Ἱππάρχου τοῦ Πεισιστράτου καὶ οὐ πεισθεὶς καταγορεύει τῷ Ἀριστογείτονι. Ὁ δὲ ἐρωτικῶς περιαλγήσας . . . καὶ ἐν τούτῳ ὁ Ἵππαρχος ὡς αὖθις πειράσας οὐδὲν μᾶλλον ἔπειθε τὸν Ἁρμόδιον. And as on a second attempt he had no more success with Harmodios, he avenged himself by refusing to allow Harmodios' sister to be a basket-bearer in the Panathenaia. Aristotle (*Ath. Pol.*, 18) says of Hipparchos: ἐρασθεὶς γὰρ τοῦ Ἁρμοδίου καὶ διαμαρτάνων τῆς πρὸς αὐτὸν φιλίας . . . λοιδορήσας τι τὸν Ἁρμόδιον ὡς μαλακὸν ὄντα.

43. Herakleitos (*Anth. Pal.*, XII, 152; anon.):

πνεῦμα δ' ἐμὸν κάλλει ἐφελκόμενος.

(*id.*, 33; by Meleager):

Ἦν καλὸς Ἡράκλειτος . . .

44. Hiketas (*Anth. Pal.*, XII, 92, by Meleager. Cf. Chapter IV *sub nom.*):

τί . . . πρὸς δ' Ἱκέτην αὐτομολεῖτε τάχος;
ὀπτᾶσθ' ἐν κάλλει ("roast yourselves in his beauty").

45. Hippeos kalos.

On a tile from a remnant of a building (*C.I.G.*, 541) we read "Hippeos seems fair to Aristomedes": Ἵππεος καλὸς δοκεῖ Ἀριστομήδει. Cf. the roof-tile with Menon kalos, no. 61 in this chapter, below.

46. Hippias.

Ἱππίας ὁ καλός τε καὶ σοφός (Plato, *Hipp. Mai.*, 281a).

47. Isokrates kalos.

Plato (*Phaidros*, 278 E) speaks of Ἰσοκράτη τὸν καλόν, and further, in 279 B, has Sokrates say: ταῦτα . . . ἐγὼ . . . ὡς ἐμοῖς παιδικοῖς Ἰσοκράτει ἐξαγγέλλω.

48. Kalos Kothokides.

Sundwall (*Nachträge zur Pros. Att.*), in a list of Athenians living on Delos in the second century B. C., lists a man named

"Kalos Kothokides," and also Apelles, his son. This son was one of the Athenians mentioned in Delian inscriptions (*B. C. H.*, XXXII, 1908, p. 311, no. 50). This would be a unique case of the use of Kalos as a proper name, and so it is possible to speculate at least on the retention of an adjective, once popularly given to an earlier member of the family, and which, in this generation, had been adopted into a name.

49. Kephisodoros and Epameinondas.

A boy favourite of Epameinondas, later in his heart than Asopichos, Kephisodoros fought by the general's side at Mantineia, fell with him and was buried in his grave (Plut., *Amat.*, XVII, 15). Cf. the Kephisodoros on vases, Chapter IV, no. 139.

50. Kleander (cf. sub Eubiotos).

51. Kleoboulos (cf. sub Alexis).

52. Kleomenes.

Kleomenes of Sparta (255-220 B. C.) was called a born ruler by Polybios (V, 39). From Plutarch (*Kleom.*, III, XXXVII) we know that in his youth he was the beloved of Xenares. Later he was himself the lover of Panteus, "the most beautiful and most virtuous youth in Sparta," who killed himself out of faithfulness to his lover after Kleomenes died. When Panteus saw his lover dead before him, he touched his foot and saw that he could still move; whereupon he kissed him, and, gathering the corpse into his arms, he lay down beside him and killed himself with his sword. Panteus is called κάλλιστος and ἐρώμενος of Kleomenes.

53. Kleonymos kallistos.

Xenophon (*Hell.*, V, 4, 25) tells us of this "fairest and most estimable" of youths, Kleonymos, son of Sphodrias and beloved of Archidamos, the son of Agesilaos: ἦν υἱὸς τῷ Σφοδρίᾳ Κλεώνυμος ἡλικίαν τε ἔχων τὴν ἄρτι ἐκ παίδων, καὶ ἅμα κάλλιστός τε καὶ εὐδοκιμώτατος τῶν ἡλίκων. Τούτου δὲ ἐρῶν ἐτύγχανεν Ἀρχίδαμος ὁ Ἀγησιλάου.

54. Kritias.

The Kritias, whom Sokrates scorned for his passion for Euthydemos, was later one of the truly most powerful of the Thirty in Athens. Xenophon (*Mem.*, I, 2, 29) says: Κριτίαν μὲν τοίνυν αἰσθανόμενος (Sokrates) ἐρῶντα Εὐθυδήμου καὶ πειρῶντα χρῆσθαι καθάπερ οἱ πρὸς τἀφροδίσια τῶν σωμάτων ἀπολαύοντες. "From this endeavour he tried to deter him, pointing out how illiberal a thing it was, how ill-befitting a man of honour to appear as a beggar before him whom he loved. . . . But when this reasoning fell on deaf ears and Kritias refused to be turned aside, Sokrates, as the story goes, took occasion of the presence of a whole company and of Euthydemos to remark that Kritias appeared to be suffering from a swinish affection, or else why this desire to rub himself against Euthydemos like a herd of piglings scraping against stones. . . . The hatred of Kritias to Sokrates dates from this incident" (Dakyns' translation). Xenophon (*Mem.*, IV, 2, 1) speaks of Εὐθύδημον τὸν καλόν. Theramenes, forced to drink hemlock by his political enemy, Kritias, pours out the last drops and says: Κριτίᾳ τοῦτ' ἔστω τῷ καλῷ (Xen. *Hell.*, II, 3, 56). Cicero (*Tusc. Disput.*, I, 40, 96) says of this: "Graeci enim in conviviis solent nominare, cui poculum tradituri sint." For an earlier Kritias, cf. Chapter IV, *sub nom.*

55. Lado (*Anth. Pal.*, XII, 12; by Flaccus):

Ἄρτι γενειάζων ὁ καλὸς καὶ στερρὸς ἐρασταῖς
παιδὸς ἐρᾷ Λάδων· σύντομος ἡ Νέμεσις.

56. Leon kalos.

Herodotos (VII, 180) tells how, when a Greek ship from Troizene was captured by the Persians, the handsomest man on board was sacrificed by the Barbarians: τὸν καλλιστεύοντα ἀγαγόντες ἐπὶ τὴν πρώρην τῆς νεὸς ἔσφαξαν, διαδέξιον ποιεύμενοι τὸν οἶλον τῶν Ἑλλήνων πρῶτον καὶ κάλλιστον· τῷ δὲ σφαγιασθέντι τούτῳ οὔνομα ἦν Λέων· τάχα δ' ἄν τι καὶ τοῦ οὐνόματος ἐπαύροιτο.

57. Leptines (Theodoros and Philokles).

(*Anth. Pal.,* XII, 93; by Rhianus of Crete):

Χαίρετε καλοὶ παῖδες . . .

58. Lichas kalos.

On a bronze castanet in Amsterdam, cf. Chapter IV, no. 72, p. 101, sub Diphilos.

59. Lysanias kalos.

This ephebe is celebrated in an epigram by Kallimachos (*Anth. Pal.,* XII, 43):

Λυσανίη, σύ δὲ ναίχι καλὸς καλός· ἀλλὰ πρὶν εἰπεῖν
τοῦτο σαφῶς, ἠχὼ φησί τις: " "Αλλος ἔχει."

60. Megabates.

Agesilaos of Sparta, victor at Koroneia (394 B. C.), was attached to this youth. His love for him Xenophon records (*Ages.,* V, 4): τὸ δὲ Μεγαβάτου τοῦ Σπιθριδάτου παιδὸς ἐρασθέντα ὥσπερ ἂν τοῦ καλλίστου ἡ σφοδροτάτη φύσις ἐρασθείη. See also Xen. *Ages.,* XI, and Chapter IV sub Eualkes.

60A. Megistes.

A boy-love of the poet Anakreon, who had other such boy-loves as Bathyllos, Kleoboulos, Smerdis. It is said that Polykrates loved some boy of Anakreon's and in jealousy had his hair cut off without any remonstration from Polykrates (Athenaeus, XII, 540e; Aelian, V. H. IX, 4). But, since Anakreon's love seldom amounted to passion, these names have not been included in our prosopographia. Cf. Bowra, *Greek Lyric Poetry,* pp. 292, 307 where he opposed Wilamowitz's emendation of Himerius (*Or.* V, 3) to τὸν ξανθὸν Μεγίστην.

61. Menon kalos.

Xenophon (*Anab.,* II, 6, 28) mentions a Thessalian adventurer of this name, who was one of the commanders of Cyrus' Greek force. Xenophon says: παρὰ Ἀριστίππου μὲν ἔτι ὡραῖος ὢν στρατηγεῖν διεπράξατο τῶν ξένων, Ἀριαίῳ δὲ βαρβάρῳ ὄντι, ὅτι μειρακίοις καλοῖς ἥδετο, οἰκειότατος ἔτι ὡραῖος ὢν ἐγένετο, αὐτὸς δε παιδικὰ εἶχε Θαρύπαν ἀγένειος ὢν γενειῶντα. Xenophon speaks further of the preference of Ariaios, friend and satrap of the younger Cyrus, for boys.

There was also a Menon, who was a favourite of Alkaios. A fragment of the poet (Hephaistion, 44; Edmonds, *Lyra Graeca*, I, p. 398, no. 123; Bowra, *Greek Lyric Poetry*, p. 170, who also mentions Bucchis, Lykos and Thales as favourites of Alcaeus) says:

> κέλομαί τινα τὸν χαρίεντα Μένωνα κάλεσσαι
> αἰ χρὴ συμποσίας ἐπόνασιν ἔμοιγε γένεσθαι.

In the 1934 excavations of Olynthos David M. Robinson discovered a 5th century roof-tile inscribed "Menon kalos" (cf. *Ill. London News*, Nov. 10, 1934, p. 768, fig. 11 for illustration; *A. J. A.*, XXXIX, 1935, p. 224, fig. 19); with this compare the Menon of Chapter IV, *sub nom.*

62. Milon kalos.

A lyric poem of Simonides (*Gk. Anth.*, XVI, 24) celebrates the handsome Milon; it was inscribed on a monument, and mentions his athletic victories. It reads: "This is a beautiful statue of beautiful Milo, who, by the banks of Pisa, conquered seven times and never once fell on his knees." Frazer's commentary to *Pausanias*, VI, 14, 5, mentions the statue of Milo, son of Diotimos. Milo gained six victories at Olympia (Diod., XII, 9; Euseb., *Chron.*, I, p. 201, ed. Schoene). Eusebius says that he won also six prizes at the Pythian games, ten at the Isthmian, and nine at the Nemean; according to this writer, one of his Olympic victories was won in Olympiad 62 (532 B. C.). Cf. Suidas *sub nom.*, and Frazer, *Pausanias's Description of Greece*, IV, p. 44.

63. Myiskos kalos (*Anth. Pal.*, XII, 65; by Meleager):

> κἠμοὶ τὸν καλὸν ἐστὶν ⟨ἐνὶ⟩ σπλάγχνοισι Μυΐσκον κρύπτειν.

(*id.*, no. 154; by Meleager):

> καλὸς γάρ, ναὶ Κύπριν, ὅλος καλός . .

The name Myiskos occurs also on a vase from Thasos (*C. I. G.,* IV, 8518, III, 11).

64. Pantarkes kalos and Pheidias.

A favourite of Pheidias was named Pantarkes; the great sculptor carved his name on the finger of his colossal Olympian Zeus. Suidas (sub Ῥαμνουσία Νέμεσις) says: ὃς καὶ Ὀλυμπίασι τῷ δακτύλῳ τοῦ Διὸς ἐπέγραψεν, Παντάρκης· καλὸς δὲ ἦν οὗτος Ἀργεῖος, ἐρώμενος αὐτοῦ. Clement of Alexandria (*Protreptikos* 53 [16S]) uses the story to show the folly of a pagandom for which the beauty of a love took precedence over the beauty of its gods; he says: ὁ μὲν Ἀθηναῖος Φειδίας ἐπὶ τῷ δακτύλῳ τοῦ Διὸς τοῦ Ὀλυμπίου ἐπιγράψας, Παντάρκης καλός. οὐ γὰρ καλὸς αὐτῷ ὁ Ζεύς, ἀλλ' ὁ ἐρώμενος ἦν. Arnobius (*Adversus Nationes,* VI, 13), interprets the relationship thus: "Nomen autem fuerat amati ab se pueri, atque obscena cupiditate dilecti." For the Pausanias passages relating to this Argive youth, cf. V, 11, 3; VI, 10, 6; 15, 2.

65. Panteus kallistos. (cf. Kleomenes, no. 52.)

66. Pausanias.

Pausanias, the beloved of the great Philip of Macedon, was in his youth corrupted by Attalos (Justinus, IX, 6). It is said that, during a drunken brawl, Attalos satisfied first his own lusts on this youth, then offered him to all his guests as well. Pausanias complained of this disgrace to Philip, who had befriended him. Because he was held off with empty promises, while Attalos still held military ascendancy, his anger rose to such a pitch that in 336 B. C. he murdered Philip. Aristotle (*Politics,* 1311 B) says: ἐπεβούλευσαν δὲ καὶ Περιάνδρῳ τῷ ἐν Ἀμβρακίᾳ τυράννῳ διὰ τὸ συμπίνοντα μετὰ τῶν παιδικῶν ἐρωτῆσαι αὐτὸν εἰ ἤδη ἐξ αὐτοῦ κύει. ἡ δὲ Φιλίππου ὑπὸ Παυσανίου διὰ τὸ ἐᾶσαι ὑβρισθῆναι αὐτὸν ὑπὸ τῶν περὶ Ἄτταλον. Cf. Athenaeus 260 E. Cf. also Diod. Sic., XVI, 93, 94.

67. Periander (*Anth. Pal.,* XII, 20; by Julius Leonidas):

Θαῦμα γὰρ εἰ Περίανδρον ἰδὼν οὐχ ἥρπασε γαίης
τὸν καλόν· ἢ φιλόπαις οὐκέτι νῦν ὁ θεός;

68. Phaidros (cf. Alexis).

69. Philebos.

Plato, *Philebos,* 11 C, says: Φίληβος γὰρ ἡμῖν ὁ καλὸς ἀπείρηκεν.

70. Philokles (*Anth. Pal.,* XII, 129; by Aratos):

> Ἀργεῖος Φιλοκλῆς Ἄργει καλός· αἱ δὲ Κορίνθου
> στῆλαι, καὶ Μεγαρέων ταὐτὸ βοῶσι τάφοι·
> γέγραπται καὶ μέχρι λοετρῶν Ἀμφιαράου,
> ὡς καλός· Ἀλλ᾿ ὀλίγον· γράμμασι λειπόμεθα.
> τῷδ᾿ οὐ γὰρ πέτραι ἐπιμάρτυρες, ἀλλὰ Ῥιηνὸς
> αὐτὸς ἰδών· ἑτέρου δ᾿ ἐστὶ περισσότερος.

Cf. Leptines, no. 57 above.

71. Plato.

Paederasty fills his dialogues. Among the ephebes celebrated in epigrams attributed sometimes to Plato are Agathon, Aster, Alexis, and Dion (his favourite pupil). Cf. R. Lagerborg, *Die Platonische Liebe,* Leipzig, 1926. For the lyrics cf. Bergk, *Poetae Lyrici Graeci,* II, pp. 299 ff., 1, 7, 8, 14, 15; cf. also 22, 23, 32. Among his dialogues, cf. the *Symposion,* the *Alkibiades,* the *Phaidros,* and the doubtful *Erastai.*

72. Protarchos (*Anth. Pal.,* XII, 29; by Alcaeus, c. 200 B. C.)

> Πρώταρχος καλός ἐστι, καὶ οὐ θέλει· ἀλλὰ θελήσει
> ὕστερον· ἡ δ᾿ ὥρη λαμπάδ᾿ ἔχουσα τρέχει.

73. Smerdis and Polykrates.

Polykrates of Samos vied with the poet Anakreon (frags. 48, 49) for the love of the boy, Smerdis. Maximus Tyrius says that " Smerdis received gold and silver and everything a beautiful youth would naturally get from a powerful ruler who was in love with him; from Anakreon, however, he got poems and praises and the natural things a loving poet would offer " (XXVI, 309). Once Polykrates was so jealous of the youth's favours to the poet that he had the celebrated dark curls of Smerdis cut off; Anakreon refused to let his sorrow be seen, but in his next poem pretended that the boy had wilfully shorn his hair and reproached him mildly for it (Aelian, *Var. Hist.*, IX, 4).

74. Sokrates.

Diogenes Laertius (*Lives of the Philosophers*, V, *Sokrates*, III), quoting Aristoxenus, says that he was the *paidika* of his teacher, Archelaos. Porphyrius (*Hist. Phil.* Frag. XII, 5, Nauck, 1886, p. 10) adds that at the age of seventeen years he had not been disinclined to the attentions of this Archelaos, for at that time he had had a great sensuality, which later he sublimated in the interests of his work. Plato (*Sym.*, 173 B) mentions an Aristodemos as one of the most ardent lovers Sokrates had. Xenophon (*Mem.*, II, 6, 28) has Sokrates say: "I can perhaps help you in your hunt for pretty boys, as I understand quite well this love. I concentrate, once I have seen a man I love or long for or desire, on being loved or longed for or desired in return." In the *Symposion*, 177 D (Plato) Sokrates says, "I admit, I understand myself in nothing else than love-matters." Cf. Licht, *Sittengeschichte Griechenlands*, II, pp. 162-165; Kiefer, "Sokrates und die Homosexualität," *Jahrbuch für Sexuelle Wissenschaft*, IX, 1908, pp. 203 ff.

75. Sosiades (*Anth. Pal.*, XII, 204; by Straton):

Σωσιάδας ὁ καλός . . .

76. Stesileos.

Plutarch (*Aristeides*, II) says that the enmity between Themistokles, the Athenian victor at Salamis, and Aristeides the Just was over this youth: Ἀρίστων δ' ὁ Κεῖος ἐξ ἐρωτικῆς ἀρχῆς γενέσθαι φησὶ καὶ προελθεῖν ἐπὶ τοσοῦτον τὴν ἔχθραν αὐτῶν. Στησιλέω γάρ, ὃς γένει Κεῖος, ἰδέᾳ τε καὶ μορφῇ σώματος πολὺ τῶν ἐν ὥρᾳ λαμπρότατος, ἀμφοτέρους ἐρασθέντας οὐ μετρίως ἐνεγκεῖν τὸ πάθος οὐδ' ἅμα λήγοντι τῷ κάλλει τοῦ παιδὸς ἀποθέσθαι τὴν φιλονεικίαν. (Not even after the boy's beauty had faded did they lay aside their rivalry). Cf. *C. I. G.*, IV, 7590.

77. Theodoros (cf. Leptines).

78. Theognetos kallistos.

This is another Olympian victor celebrated for his prowess and beauty both by Simonides (*Gk. Anth.*, XVI, 2; Loeb translation); the quatrain must date after 476 B. C., in the year in which Theognetos won the crown. It reads: "Know Theognetos, when thou lookest on him, the boy who conquered at Olympia, the dexterous charioteer of wrestling, most lovely to behold, but in combat in nowise inferior to his beauty. He won a crown for the city of his noble fathers [Aigina]."

79. Theokritos (*Anth. Pal.*, XII, 230; by Kallimachos):

τὸν τὸ καλὸν μελανεῦντα Θεόκριτον . . .

He was also celebrated in a poem of Bacchylides (*Bacchyl.*, Kenyon, frag. 54):

ἦ καλὸς Θεόκριτος· οὐ μόνος ἀνθρώπων ἐρᾶς.

80. Theron (*Anth. Pal.*, XII, 41; by Meleager):

οὐκέτι μοι Θήρων γράφεται καλός . . .
(*id.*, 141; by Meleager):
σοὶ καλὸς οὐκ ἐφάνη Θήρων . . .

81. Zeno, ta paidika.

Parmenides, the Eleatic, was in love with his pupil, Zeno, according to Plato (*Parmen.*, 127 B): λέγεσθαι αὐτὸν [τὸν Ζήνωνα] παιδικὰ τοῦ Παρμενίδου γεγονέναι. Cf. also Diogenes Laertius, IX, 25. Cf. Antigonos, no. 16 above. Athenaeus (XI, 505 F) brands as the most outrageous thing of all Plato's statement that Zeno was the favourite of Parmenides.

CHAPTER IV

PROSOPOGRAPHIA OF LOVE-NAMES ON ATTIC VASES

In the following list, alphabetically arranged, are catalogued the love-names published in Klein, *Die Griechischen Vasen mit Lieblingsinschriften,* in the *Inschriften-Register* at the end of Beazley's *Attische Vasenmaler* and of the same author's *Attic Red-Figured Vases in American Museums,* in Hoppin's *Handbook of Black-Figured Vases* and his *Handbook of Red-Figured Vases,* and in sporadic journal articles. Some of the inscriptions have been noticed in personal visits to the great museums, and a few of these are otherwise unpublished. Many of the possible identifications are our own suggestions, often effected with the help of Kirchner's *Prosopographia Attica* and of Pape-Benseler's *Griechische Eigennamen.* Some of these have no more cogent reason for being suggested than that they accord chronologically with the dates of the vases, but even these have seemed worth mentioning because they draw together all references to like-named persons of the period. They also give us a certain picture of Athenian society of the day, of its occupations, and of the class and quality of the young men who were such favourites.

In the following table is contained a survey of the professional activities of some of these *paides kaloi* of ceramic fame. From it will be noted the fact that many of these ephebes grew up into positions of political and social importance, and hence that, even as boy-favourites, they were drafted in most cases from the upper strata of Athenian society:

Six were poets: Agathon
   Akestor
   Epilykos
   Krates
   Myllos
   Polyphrassmon

Five were scribes:	Diogenes
	Etearchos
	Kephisophon
	Phainippos
	Philon
Seven were orators: (speakers of decrees)	Chairestratos
	Diokles
	Dion
	Hestiaios
	Kineas
	Phrinos
	Lysikles
Nine belonged to the Socratic circle:	Agathon
	Alkibiades
	Aristarchos
	Charmides
	Diodoros
	Hermogenes
	Kallias
	Laches
	Lysis
Fifteen became archons:	Akestorides
	Alkaios
	Apollodoros
	Archinos
	Diokles
	Hipparchos (?)
	Hippokles II
	Isarchos
	Kalliades
	Krates
	Mikion
	Nikodemos
	Pedieus
	Praxiteles
	Theodoros
Twenty-two were Strategoi:	Alkibiades
	Archinos
	Aristeides
	Diphilos
	Eukleides

68   A STUDY OF THE GREEK LOVE-NAMES

Strategoi: (continued)	Eukrates
	Glaukon
	Hippodamas
	Leagros
	Leokrates
	Menandros
	Menon
	Miltiades
	Nikostratos II
	Olympiodoros
	Panaitios
	Pythaios
	Sokrates
	Sophanes
	Stesileos
	Teisias
	Timarchos
Seven were involved in the mutilation of the Herms (Hermokopids):	Alkibiades
	Diogenes
	Euphiletos (grandson)
	Eurymachos
	Meletos
	Polyeuktos
	Telenikos
Three were demagogues:	Eukrates
	Kleophon
	Lysikles
Five were prytany-presidents:	Kephisios
	Nikostratos I
	Polymainetos
	Timonides
	Timoxenos
Two were treasurers:	Demostratos
	Thaliarchos
Three were among the Thirty Tyrants:	Hippolochos
	Phaidimos
	Pheidon
Two were professional musicians:	Chairis(?)
	Kydias (pp. 93-94)
Two were athletes:	Eualkes
	Phayllos

Seven were poets' favourites:	Agathon (Pindar; Plato)
	Dorotheos
	Eualkides (Simonides)
	Kritias (Anakreon)
	Leokrates
	Philliades
	Stesias
Nineteen made Akropolis dedications:	Aischines
	Alkimachos
	Archias
	Demostratos
	Diogenes
	Dorotheos
	Leagros (Agora)
	Menandros
	Nausistratos
	Neokleides
	Onetor
	Pheidiades
	Philon
	Polykles
	Simon
	Smikros (Mikros)
	Smikythos
	Theodoros
	Thrasykleides

Where it has seemed advisable, we have kept the names of ephebes, closely allied by family ties or mutual association, together under the heading of one name; all other names in one such group, however, are noted in their proper alphabetic position, where reference to the longer discussion is given (*e. g.,* no. 29: Antiphanes—see Diodoros kalos). Where identifications have not been forthcoming, the love-name alone has been classified along with the place of its publication; if, in these cases, names of other ephebes or hetairai occur on the same vases, they too have been mentioned, in order to fill out what little is known of the love-name in question (*e. g.,* number 131, Kallipe kale—Klein, p. 144. Rodon, contemporary.). The names, listed by Wernicke and Klein, which, on closer inspection, have proved themselves not to be strictly of this type, have been dropped from the list (see beginning of Chapter One). On the other hand, many new names have been added, even though in some cases the adjective *kalos* does not actually accompany the inscription (for the right to do this, see Hauser's argument under Phayllos kalos, below in this chapter).

1. Agasias kalos.

This name, which appears on red-figured ware (Klein, p. 93: Adria, Museo Bocchi, 362) must refer to a person who lived sometime between 500-450 B. C. The only other reference to an Agasias is Kirchner's 97, whose son, Chairigenes, was an Attic cleruch to the island of Imbros in the fourth century. The grave-stone of the son is noted in Conze's *Reise im Thrakischen Meere,* 85.

2. Agasikles kalos.

On a red-figured kylix fragment found in the Athenian Agora recently (*Arch. Anz.,* LI, 1936, p. 107) this name is inscribed. *I. G.,* I, 433, col. II, 49 is a sepulchral monument of the year 459/8 B. C. on which an Agasikles of Erechtheis is mentioned.

3. Agathon kalos.

On a plain black-glaze fragment published by Graef-Langlotz [1] and dated around the middle of the fifth century is an incised graffito which is read by them:

'Αγάθων καλὸς. καὶ τὸν κοινε..ον: μὲ φέρε.

Hiller von Gaertringen thinks that there is an erotic significance in what he reads in this graffito as ἔφερε. But Peek in the *Epigraphische Nachtraege* to the Graef-Langlotz publication (Band II, Heft 3, p. 131) reads καὶ τὸν κοινεῖ [φίλ]ον: μ' ἔφερε and suggests that the inscription is rather to be taken as though the vase itself were speaking and saying, "Agathon brought me (a memorial of . . .) and of common friends."

---

[1] *Die Antiken Vasen von der Akropolis zu Athen,* II, 3, p. 126, no. 1493, pl. 93.

The first Athenian to be remembered, one who comes to mind almost automatically and with great point, when we are considering *kalos* names and the emotional implications of the inscriptions (one to whom even Hiller von Gaertringen's suspicion of an erotic episode, as in this inscription, would be applicable) is the famous Agathon, son of Teisamenes. Kirchner 83 has a full list of all the references to this person. Suffice it to say here that as a youth he was the darling of Pausanias. Plato [2] says: "Near him on the beds hard by lay Pausanias from the Kerameikos and with Pausanias a lad who was still quite young, νέον τι ἔτι μειράκιον ... καλόν τε κἀγαθὸν τὴν φύσιν, τὴν δ' οὖν ἰδέαν πάνυ καλός. ... οὐκ ἂν θαυμάζοιμι εἰ παιδικὰ Παυσανίου τυγχάνει ὤν. Plato [3] also mentions the two as a love-pair, and in 194d of the *Symposion* Agathon is called καλῷ. Xenophon [4] also calls Pausanias the lover of Agathon: Παυσανίας γε, ὁ 'Αγάθωνος τοῦ ποιητοῦ ἐραστής. Agathon wrote six plays, and Aristophanes [5] says he was ἀγαθὸς ποιητὴς καὶ ποθεινὸς τοῖς φίλοις. In his note to the Aristophanes passage cited, Rogers says that he was famous because of "his delicate beauty, his affectations and effeminacy, his graceful language and dainty conceits, and the social amiability which endeared him to his friends." He was depicted principally in Aristophanes' *Thesmophoriazusae* (411 B. C.), and seems to have gone in for the outré and exotic even in his art, as Plutarch [6] says that he "first in his tragedy of the Mysians ventured to introduce the chromatic airs." That he acquired a reputation because of his erotic habits we know from the *Thesmophoriazusae* 200, where Mnesilochos says to Agathon:

καὶ μὴν σύ γ', ὦ κατάπυγον, εὐρύπρωκτος εἶ
οὐ τοῖς λόγοισιν, ἀλλὰ τοῖς παθήμασιν.

However improbable it may seem that so famous a person should be celebrated on so crude and inartistic a vase, it is

---

[2] *Protag.*, 315c.
[3] *Sym.*, 177e.
[4] *Sym.*, VIII, 32.
[5] *Frogs*, 84.
[6] *Quaest. Conv.*, III, 1, 645d.

striking that all we have seen of Agathon should be in such accord with what we have learned of the *kalos* background of the vase inscriptions. Curiously, too, Pindar (fragment 128, as quoted by Athenaeus X, 427d) praised a person with the very same name for his beauty, if the disputed text can be read with Boeckh (frag. 90):

> Χάριτάς τ' Ἀφροδισίων ἐρώτων,
> ὄφρα σὺν χειμάρρῳ μεθύω,
> Ἀγάθωνι δὲ καλῷ κότταβον.

Bowra (*Pindari Carmina,* Oxford, 1935, frag. 113), however, reads the last line as follows: Ἀγάθωνί τε βάλλω κότταβον. Gulick (Athenaeus, *loc. cit.*) follows Schroeder in reading: Ἀγάθωνί τ' ἰάλω κότταβον. For Agathon and Pausanias cf. also Athenaeus 216 E and F; 217 A, B and C.

I. G., I, 448, col. I, 19, a sepulchral monument from the end of the fifth century found not far from the Metroon in Athens, has the name Agathon. One of Plato's favourite pupils was named Agathon also, and Plato was at one time in love with him. A poem which he wrote for him testifies to his feelings toward this Agathon (Bergk, *Poetae Lyrici Graeci,* II, p. 299, 1):

> τὴν ψυχήν, Ἀγάθωνα φιλῶν, ἐπὶ χείλεσιν ἔσχον.
> ἦλθε γὰρ ἡ τλήμων ὡς διαβησομένη.

Shelley, changing the name and sex of the beloved, has translated this lovely epigram:

> " Kissing Helena, together
> With my kiss, my soul beside it
> Came to my lips, and there I kept it—
> For the poor thing had wandered thither,
> To follow where the kiss should guide it,
> Oh cruel I to intercept it!"

4. Ainios kalos.

Wernicke, p. 19, gives the name as Ainias, and to prove that Ainias was a genuine Attic name cites an inscription from

Brauron (*I. G.*, II, 3-4, 1317): Αἰνίας Ξανθίππος Ξανθίδης νικήσαντες ἀνέθεσαν. But cf. Klein, p. 71, no. 6. The name is on a black-figured lekythos, formerly in the collection of Lord Guilford, and illustrated in Stackelberg, *Gräber der Hellenen*, pl. XII; also in *Arch. Zeit.*, 1853, pl. 51. It is not given by Hoppin nor in Haspels, *Attic Black-Figured Lekythoi*, though she mentions (p. 49) the vase as lost and having the inscription, Leagros.

5. Aischines kalos.

Cf. the Boston alabastron, 01. 8122. Beazley[7] creates a painter with this love-name, and attributes to this Aischines Painter fifty-five inconsequential pieces, fifty of them lekythoi. The name Aischines occurs only on the Boston vase. This painter is a minor artist of the ripe archaic period.

Aischines is probably the man from Lamptrai, who was arrested by Aristeides[8] before the battle of Plataea in 479 for plotting to subvert the democracy: "While Hellas was thus in suspense and Athens especially in danger, certain men of that city who were of prominent families and large wealth, but had been impoverished by the war, saw that with their riches all their influence in the city and their reputation had departed, while other men now had the honors and offices. They therefore met together secretly at a certain house in Plataea, and conspired to overthrow the democracy; or, if their plans did not succeed, to injure the general cause and betray it to the Barbarians." Aristeides got wind of the conspiracy and arrested some eight of the machinators. "Two of these, against whom the charge was first formally brought, and who were really the most guilty ones, Aischines of Lamptrae and Agesias of Acharnae, fled the camp (Perrin)."

This exploit and the noble origin of its perpetrators indicate that Aischines was of the finer pedigree of "fair boys." He would have been roughly forty-six years of age at the time of the cabal, if we reckon that he was at least the prescribed fifteen in the year of the vase's appearance (c. 510).

---

[7] *A. V.*, p. 322; *V. A.*, p. 74.   [8] Plut., *Arist.*, 13.

On a bronze base for a dedication [9] we read the name, Aischines. The inscription dates from the end of the sixth century, and may very probably refer to our Aischines. On the painted abacus of a column found northeast of the Erechtheion, in the Persian debris, is also an inscription [10] which agrees chronologically with the activities of the same Aischines. The name also occurs in several other inscriptions of the fifth century.[11] The dedicatory inscriptions on the feet of two kylikes,[12] also according chronologically with the date of the identification proposed for the "fair Aischines," doubtless refer to the same Aischines as the other inscriptions cited here. All can be taken as pointing to some wealthy and influential individual, who, if his looks and popularity warranted, might easily have been the Aischines celebrated on vases.

The Aischines, mentioned as a potter on a fragment of a black-figured krater in Athens,[13] is probably earlier.

6. Aischis kalos.

On a black-figured lekythos in Athens, and on an alabastron in the Hermitage, Leningrad, neither published. Klein, p. 51.

7. Aisimedes kalos.

On a red-figured kotyle (Berlin, 2316; Neugebauer, *Führer durch das Antiquarium,* II, p. 105) is the inscription, somewhat differently worded from the run of love-inscriptions, and referring to an Aisimedes who lived between 500 and 450. The inscription reads: Αἰσιμέδες καλὸς δοκεῖ ξυννοοῦντι. Neugebauer translates it, "Aisimedes scheint dem Xynoon schön." If one, however, reads the extra letters as given above, it would mean "Aisimedes seems fair to the one thinking about it," or

---

[9] *I. G.*, I (Suppl.), p. 98, no. 373[180].

[10] *I. G.*, I (Suppl.), 373[202], p. 100; *Ant. Denkmäler*, I, pl. 29.

[11] *I. G.*, I, 31, 299, 324, 446, 450, 451; Suppl. 432, p. 107; 462, d 21, p. 111.

[12] Graef-Langlotz, *Akrop. Vas.*, II, 3, 1357-8.

[13] Nicole, *Rev. Arch.*, series 5, vol. IV, 1916, p. 377, no. 11; where a votive capital (cf. note 10) with this name is cited, *Class. Rev.*, II, 1888, p. 188.

" to the one supposing so," who he was not being stated. So Klein, p. 98 would interpret the inscription. Kirchner 310 is the only other chronologically possible occurrence of Aisimedes. He was of the tribe Hippothontis, and his grave-stone, from the end of the fifth century, is given in *I. G.*, I, 447, col. III, 66.

8. Akestor kalos.

Klein, p. 90; Beazley, *A. V.*, p. 51; London, Mitchell collection. The scholiast to Aristophanes, *Birds,* 31, mentions an Akestor who was a tragic poet: ἐκαλεῖτο δὲ καὶ Σάκας διὰ τὸ ξένος εἶναι. Later, in spite of his foreign origin, he was made a citizen. Cf. Aristophanes, *Wasps,* 1221.

9. Akestorides kalos.

Klein, p. 153; Beazley, *A. V.*, p. 137. Cf. now for the white-ground lekythos mentioned by Klein, *C. V. A., Bruxelles,* fasc. 1, III J b, pl. 2, 4. Possible is an identification with the Akestorides who was archon in 474/3 B. C.; cf. Diodoros, XI, 51. In the Metropolitan Museum is a kylix with the name spelt in cockney fashion Hakestorides, dating about 460 B. C. which seems a little late for the use of the name of the man who had been an archon (Richter, *Red-Figured Athenian Vases*, p. 137).

10. Aleximachos kalos.

On a black-figured cup in the Louvre (F 66; *C. V. A.,* fasc. 8, III H e, pl. 77, 8-12) with many inscriptions and the name Ἀλεξ[ί]μα[χ]ος καλός. Cf. Pottier, *Catalogue,* p. 743; *Vases Antiques du Louvre,* p. 97, pl. 68; Beazley, *J. H. S.*, LII, 1932, p. 178, note 21. Pottier reads the inscription καλὸν ἔνι τὸ ποτήριον καλ[όν], " voilà un beau vase à boire." Beazley, however, considers the inscription to read καλὸν εἰμὶ, τὸ ποτήριον καλ[όν], although the Corpus suggests καυκάλιον, a kind of vase. Beazley compares his reading with that on the Rhodian cup with καλύν : εἰμί ποτέριον (*loc. cit.*) and the Boeotian kantharos with the Gorginis inscription (see Appendix below).

All the writers agree, however, on Aleximachos kalos.

This was a not uncommon name, as will be seen by consulting Kirchner (*Pros. Att.*, I, 538-544), though most of these instances are too late in date, appearing around the end of the fifth century. *I. G.*, I, 433, l. 70 may possibly refer to the man mentioned in this vase inscription, as it is dated 459-458 B. C. The scene on the vase, a bearded man running and turning his head, may also be taken to be a representation of him.

11. Alexomenos kalos.

Klein, 152; *Catalogue of Vases in Br. Mus.*, III, p. 354, E 719, a red-figured alabastron.

12. Alkaios kalos.

Klein, 158. Beazley, *A. V.*, p. 372; *J. H. S.*, XXXIV, 1914, p. 185. On the underside of a partly glazed krater, discarded probably c. 460 B. C., and found in the Athenian Agora (*Hesperia*, V, 1936, p. 348, no. 3b, fig. 18) is inscribed this inscription in praise of Alkaios: 'Αλ⟨λ⟩καῖος καλὸς τὸ δοκεῖ Μέλιτι. For the wording of it cf. Ἵππεος, Chapter III, no. 45 above; and 'Αφροδισία καλή. (οὔ)τως δοκεῖ Εὐχείρῳ, no. 32 below. Miss Talcott (*Hesperia, loc. cit.*) thinks that Melis is a term of endearment, not a name. The name of Alkaios is again inscribed on the underside of another partly glazed krater from the Agora (*Hesperia*, V, 1936, p. 350, no. 5, fig. 20), but this time he is condemned as κατάπυγον. A third fragment from the Agora (*Hesperia*, V, 1936, p. 350, fig. 19) also mentions his name. The name Alkaios is found also at a slightly later time than these vases, namely, that of the early work of the Achilles Painter, c. 460 (Beazley, *loc. cit.*). Diodoros, XII, 73, mentions an archon with this name in 422/1 (*I. G.*, I², 311); other references to this same person are Thukydides, V, 19, 25; Athenaeus, V, 215d, 218b and d. Kirchner 573 (*I. G.*, I², 955) is a grave-stone from the end of the fifth century with this name.

13. Alkibiades kalos.

In speaking of a white-ground lekythos in the Jatta collection, no. 1539 (Klein, p. 117; Beazley, *A. V.*, p. 194), with this inscription, Studniczka (*Jahrb.*, II, 1887, p. 164) is certain that the famous Alkibiades is the one meant. But the vase is generally considered to be a work of the Briseis Painter, dating 480-470 B. C. For complete bibliography cf. Philippart, *L'Antiquité Classique,* V, 1936, p. 21. He (p. 22) suggests that perhaps 'Αλκί(μαχο)ς καλός should be read. Besides the argument on the basis of the comparative rareness of the name, Studniczka adds: "Zu der Zeit, als er ganz Athen erfüllte, war mit der reichsten Blüte der Vasenmalerei auch die heitere Sitte dieser persönlichen Huldigungen im Aussterben begriffen; auf Vasen des ausgebildeten schönen Stils, wie der Kodros- und Erichthoniosschale oder der noch jüngeren des Erginos und Aristophanes, fehlen sie vollständig oder treten nur in verblasster Allgemeinheit auf." Alkibiades was about 32 years old when the Athenians named him strategos to Syracuse in 423 (Clinton-Kruger, *Fasti Hellenici*, p. 72, anno 423), so that the period of his adolescence and early manhood must have fallen around 440, in his 15th year, too late for our vase. Plato (*Alkib.,* I, 113 B) calls him 'Αλκιβιάδης ὁ καλός. He was the fascinating son of Kleinias. Cornelius Nepos (*Alc.* 2, 3) says: "As a boy he was loved by many men, among them Sokrates; when he was grown up, he himself loved not many less." Aristophanes (*Acharn.,* 716) says:

τῷ γέροντι μὲν γέρων καὶ νωδὸς ὁ ξυνήγορος,
τοῖς νέοισι δ' εὐρύπρωκτος καὶ λάλος χὠ Κλεινίου.

Athenaeus (187 E) says that Alkibiades "did not begin to have converse with Sokrates until he had passed out of his early bloom, when all who had lusted for his body had deserted him." Athenaeus draws a long picture of the manners of Alkibiades (219 B F), and imagines the worst from Plato's statement (*Sym.* 219b) that Sokrates "lay down to sleep with Alkibiades under the same coverlet." In 534 C Athenaeus represents Alkibiades as κάλλιστος δὲ ὢν τὴν μορφήν, and later (534 E) adds καὶ στρατηγῶν δὲ ἔτι καλὸς εἶναι ἤθελεν. Anytos is one of his lovers (534 E).

14. Alkides kalos.

Klein, pp. 126-7; Hoppin, *Handb. R. F.*, II, p. 416. On a red-figured stamnos in Brussels, 119. He was a contemporary of Xenon, Lysis, Antias, and Pheidiades.

15. Alkimachos kalos, I and II.

At least nine vases with this name have been added to Klein's list of seven, so that Caskey (*Attic Vase Paintings in Boston,* p. 44) gives a revised list of sixteen. His no. 3a is now republished by Philippart, *L'Antiquité Classique,* V, 1936, pp. 22-23, pl. 9 (about 470 B. C.). Cf. also Beazley, *V. A.,* pp. 134-138; *A. V.,* pp. 296-299, 355. On the lekythos in Boston (Caskey, *op. cit.,* plates XXII and XXVI) showing the death of Orpheus, the name is inscribed: Ἀλκίμαχος καλὸς Ἐπιχάρος. On number 4 in Klein (*L. I.,* p. 165), a bell krater in Goluchow [14] is an inscription: Ἀξιοπείθης καλός· Ἀλκίμαχος καλός, while on number 6 in Klein, a white lekythos in Boston (Caskey, *op. cit.,* pl. XXIV) is the inscription: Ἀξιοπείθης καλὸς Ἀλκιμάχο. This last is number 13 in Caskey; together with numbers 14 and 15 in his list it forms a trio of works by the Achilles Painter, who seems always to have used the patronymic. A volute krater in the Oxford-Ashmolean (*C. V. A.,* fasc. 1, pl. 21, 1) in the style of Polygnotos has the name of Alkimachos.

The Alkimachos celebrated was the son of an Epichares, perhaps the Epichares represented, c. 500 B. C. on a cup by the Panaitios Painter in the Cabinet des Médailles.[15] The Alkimachos Painter who decorated the London amphora (Hoppin, *Handb. R. F.,* I, p. 18) was active around 470 B. C. Alkimachos was a contemporary of Glaukon, as Epichares was of Leagros. Was the Alkimachos mentioned as the father of Axiopeithes on the Achilles Painter's lekythoi identical with Alkimachos, the son of Epichares? Miss Swindler (*Ancient Painting,* pp. 192-3) assumes an Alkimachos I in the period 470-460 B. C. and an Alkimachos II from the decade 450-

---

[14] Beazley, *A. V.,* p. 399, no. 10; *Vases in Poland,* p. 54, pls. 24, 25.
[15] Hartwig, *Meisterschalen,* pls. 15, 2, and 16.

440 B. C. There was a younger Alkimachos with whom Axiopeithes was contemporary, as we know from the Goluchow krater by the Lykaon Painter. Beazley, *Gr. Vases in Poland*, p. 55, n. 3 suggests that Axiopeithes and the younger Alkimachos were cousins. We can draw their section of the family-tree as follows:

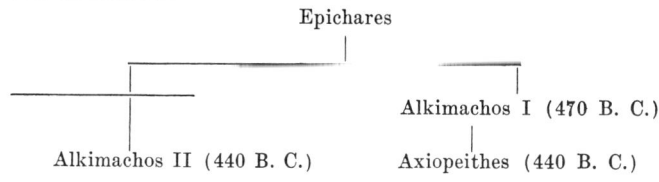

```
                        Epichares
                            |
          ┌─────────────────┴─────────────────┐
          |                                   |
          |                          Alkimachos I (470 B. C.)
          |                                   |
   Alkimachos II (440 B. C.)         Axiopeithes (440 B. C.)
```

On a drum of a fluted column with an Ionic capital is an inscription (*I. G.*, I, Suppl., 373[85], p. 87) with a dedication by an Alkimachos. The drum was found between the Propylaia and the Erechtheion in the north wall of the Akropolis, and its inscription dates after 508 B. C.

Also in a catalogue of names from after the middle of the fifth century (*I. G.*, I [Suppl.], 538 a, p. 54) occurs the name Alkimachos. This is probably Alkimachos the First.

On a sepulchral monument dating before 446 B. C. (*I. G.*, I, 435, 7) is found the name of Epichares, who is probably the father of Alkimachos I, though Kirchner, 4978-4980, has three men of this name on funeral monuments, any one of which would date suitably for our Epichares. It was a very common name.

16. Alkimedes kalos, son of Aischylides.

Klein, p. 162; Beazley, *A. V.*, p. 377. This name is found with its patronymic on vases of the mid-fifth century. *I. G.*, I (Suppl.), p. 100, 373[201] is a sixth century dedication from the Akropolis by the father, Aischylides. Cf. sub Diphilos.

17. Alkmeon kalos.

This name is inscribed on a red-figured vase in the Fatelli collection, Ruvo, mentioned by Klein, p. 129; on another in Beazley, *A. V.*, p. 182, London 99 (*J. H. S.*, XIX, 1899, p. 203). The American excavations in the Athenian Agora have yielded two red-figured fragments with this name; published by Miss Talcott (*Hesperia,* II, 1933, p. 230), and Thompson (*ibid.,* VI, 1937, p. 13, b. P 2231) and the style of the work suggests the Brygos Painter. It must date before 479 B. C. and the Persian sack of Athens. Of another vase, a lekythos, with this name (not listed in Klein) Miss Dickson, the publisher (*J. H. S.,* XIX, 1899, p. 202) says, " If we are to seek for the originals of the kalos or lovers' names among the Athenian aristocracy, it would not be easy to find a name better known. . . . But the only historically important Alkmaeon we know of lived long before the period of our vase." The Alkmeon to whom she refers was the father of the archon Megakles (Her. I, 59), and the whole line of the Alkmaeonidae was banished from Athens for a time for their murder of the Kylonian conspirators. (It is interesting to note that other names from this family are known on vases also: *v.* sub Megakles, Hippokrates, and Euryptolemos). There are, however, many other known Alkmeons; Pape-Benseler, *sub nom.,* says, " Bei den Attikern nicht selten," and it is not impossible to conjecture the identity of our Alkmeon kalos from them.

Kirchner, 649, cites an Alkmeon who was the father of Kallias, indicted for the mutilation of the herms which occurred on Munichion 30 in 415 B. C. (*A. J. A.,* XXXIV, 1930, p. 143), but freed of guilt and the charge by Andokides (Andok., I, 47, 68). Alkmeon kalos may well have been the father of Kallias kalos.

In 471/0 B. C. Themistokles was accused of betrayal. Plutarch [16] says that the accuser was Leobotes, the son of Alkmaion, but in the same author's *Aristeides,* 25, we read that Alkmaion himself was the accuser: ἀλλ' 'Αλκμαίωνος καὶ Κίμωνος καὶ πολλῶν ἄλλων ἐλαυνόντων καὶ κατηγορούντων. This person would well fit the chronological demands of our vase (Brygos Painter, 510-470 B. C.), and it is perfectly possible that the youth praised for his beauty and distinction at this

---

[16] *Them.,* 23. ὁ δὲ γραψάμενος αὐτὸν προδοσίας Λεωβώτης ἦν ὁ 'Αλκμαίωνος 'Αγρυλῆθεν.

time matured to a political importance and, as the accuser of Themistokles, left a further record of his name. If Leobotes was really the man who acted, however, the Alkmaion who was his father is probably the Alkmaion, the archon of 507/6 B. C. (Pollux, VIII, 110; Wilamowitz, *Aristoteles und Athen,* pp. 81, 417 not.). This Alkmaion is also probably the same as Kirchner's 652, Alkmaion of Agryle, father of Leobotes. If the accuser of Themistokles was Alkmaion himself, the demands of chronology would be better met and satisfied than by a man who was already old enough in 507/6 to be an archon. After all, the Alkmaion mentioned in Plutarch (*Arist.* 25) need not be the father of Leobotes at all nor the archon of 507, but simply one whose youth came in the first decade of the fifth century. The archon's youth, on the other hand, must have fallen sometime in the middle of the sixth century, and he can hardly be the Alkmaion mentioned on a vase which dates a half century later.

18. Alones kalos (*v.* sub Eualkos).

Miss Richter, *Red-Figured Athenian Vases in the Metropolitan Museum of Art,* p. 160, thinks that "Alones" is not a possible form and so must be a mistake. But cf. such names as Ἥλων, Ἠλώνη, Ἁλώνη, Ἁλόννησος, Ἁλόνησος, etc. in Pape-Benseler, *Gr. Eigennamen.* It is a new but possible name.

19. Amasis kalos.

Klein, 93; Beazley, *A. V.,* p. 75, no. 68; Hoppin, *Handb. R. F.,* II, p. 137.

20. Ambrosios kalos (*v.* sub Xanthes).

20A. Amphoe kale.

Klein, 46. Black-figured hydria in Museum of Fine Arts, Boston, 01.8058.

21. Andokides kalos.

Klein, 40; Hoppin, *Handb. B. F.,* p. 358; *C. V. A., Louvre,* fasc. 6, III H e, pl. 63, 1-4; Richter, *Red-Figured Athenian*

Vases in the Metropolitan Museum, p. 11. He was the eromenos of Timagoras; *v.* sub Meletos. This Andokides is probably not the well-known potter, though this vase (c. 540 B. C.) dates from his time but probably a young member of a distinguished family of this name, known from the middle of the sixth century on. Cf. Kirchner, *Pros. Att.*, 62 f.; Miss Richter, *Red-Figured Athenian Vases*, p. 11.

22. Andrias kallistos.

Klein, 51; Beazley, *J. H. S.*, LII, 1932, p. 184. All cases of this name in Kirchner are too late to refer to our man. On the black-figured vase in Munich, 7791, cited by Klein, he is *kallistos*.

23. Androxenos kalos.

This love-name does not appear in Klein's list. Kraiker gives it as a possibility in *Die Rot-figurigen Attischen Vasen (Universität Heidelberg)*, 1931, p. 44, no. 158. The vase is in the style of the followers of the Penthesileia Painter (480-450 B. C.), and has a picture of an ephebe with a lyre. The inscription is incompletely preserved, but Kraiker restores it to 'Ανδρόξ[ενος. This name, however, is not in Kirchner's or in Pape-Benseler's list of known people, and Fick-Bechtel does not have it in his list of roots and derived names. There was an Androxenos from Delphi (Curtius, *Anecdota Delphica*, 2).

24. Antheseos kalos.

Klein, 52. On one black-figured lekythos, unpublished, in Dorpat, Kunstmuseum.

25. Anthylla kale.

Klein, 44; Langlotz, *Gr. Vasen in Würzburg*, I, p. 55, no. 304. Black-figure; with Rodon, Mnesilla, Hegesila, Myrtale, Kallipe, Lysippides.

26. Antias kalos.

Klein, 97; Beazley, *A. V.*, p. 62; *Hesperia*, IV, 1935, p. 282, 144, either 'Αν]τίας or Φιν]τίας. *I. G.*, I, 447, col. III, 64, is a grave-stone to an Antias of Hippothontis from the end of the fifth century. Cf. *C. V. A., Brit. Mus.,* fasc. 3, III I c, pl. 19, 2.

27. Antimachos kalos.

Hoppin, *Handb. R. F.,* I, p. 29, no. 15 by Ambrosios Painter; II, p. 164, no. 6 by Lykaon Painter; I, p. 427, no. 58 by Panaitios Painter. Antimachos is also praised on black-figure vases; hence, Klein (*L. I.,* p. 35) calls this one distinguishingly Antimachos I, the red-figured one Antimachos II. This is incorrect, however, as it was the same person who straddled the two vase-styles. On Antimachos see Kirchner, 1102; *I. G.,* I, 432, col. I, 3, dating 465 B. C. For his effeminacy and perversity see Aristophanes, *Clouds,* 1022: τῆς Ἀντιμάχου καταπυγοσύνης ἀναπλήσει. An Antimachos was treasurer of the other gods in 421/0 (*I. G.,* I, 318).

28. Antimenes kalos.

Not in Klein. Cf. Beazley, *Attic Black Figure,* pp. 26, 41; *J. H. S.,* XLVII, 1927, p. 63. A black-figured hydria in Leyden (Beazley, *op. cit.,* pl. 12, 2) has a scene of a boy named Antimenes in a wash-house. Beazley thinks that " the name is a perfectly good one, and there is not the least reason for supposing that it is a miswriting for Automenes (as Klein does, *L. I.,* p. 48, no. 2) just because Automenes occurs on two other vases of the same period." Also on the Leyden hydria is a disputed inscription which Beazley reads Φίλων σε, " with an eloquent aposiopesis." [17] The date of the vase be-

---

[17] Klein gives two Philon vases, pp. 116-7; his no. 2 is of the same period as this vase; his no. 1 is later. Beazley adds a black-figured hydria of this period in the Peake collection with Philon kalos.

Philon was a common name in Athens at all times. A votive tablet of the 6th century (*I. G.,* I, Suppl., 373[79], p. 86), on a column dug up near the Parthenon, may be a dedication from the last quarter of the century by a Philon Aresiou. There are several sepulchral monuments which might refer to the demise of this Philon: *I. G.,* I, 439, l. 26, dates before 446; *id.,* 447, col. 3, after 446 B. C., records the death of Philon of Hippothontis. The Philon who was a scribe in 448 B. C. (*I. G.,* I, 293) may be the one on our vase, serving the

longs to early red-figured ware, to the time of Psiax and the earlier work of Oltos (530-510). Under his list of vases by the Antimenes Painter Beazley puts the hydria with Euphiletos kalos now in the Metropolitan Museum, and discussed under that name.

I. G., I, 433, col. I, 38, a sepulchral monument, dating c. 454, gives an Antimenes of Erechtheis who fell among those in action for Athens at Kypros, Egypt, Aigina, and Megara in that year.

In view of the fact that several other love-names are those of non-Attic persons (Xanthes, Eualkides, Pythaios, Alones) the Philon who twice prevailed in the Olympian boxing-matches and who was a Korkyraian by birth may be none-the-less the Philon who attracted the praise and comments of Athenian potters, perhaps during a sojourn in their city.

29. Antiphanes kallistos (see also *s. v.* Diodoros kalos).

In Miss Richter, *Red-Figured Athenian Vases in the Metropolitan Museum*, p. 73, no. 52 we have Ἀντιφάνης κ[άλλισ]τος, on a kylix by Makron, about 490-480 B. C. Cf. for Antiphanes also *ibid.*, p. 18, no. 3.

30. Antiphon kalos.

Klein, 119; Beazley, *A. V.*, p. 231; on vases of the Leagros circle. We recommend an identification with Kirchner's number 1275: Antiphon, father of Pyrilampes, the handsomest man in Greece (Plutarch, *de Gen. Sokr.*, 581d; Plato, *Charmides* 158 a; *Parmen.* 126 b and c). The last reference says that he was experienced in equestrian matters. Cf. below sub Kritias.

---

state in this way after advancing age precluded more vital activity: this has been restored Φ[ίλ]ωνος γ[ραμματεύοντος Πρ]ο[β]αλισίου ἐπιστάται. Pausanias (VI, 9, 9) mentions "a statue of Philon, a work of Glaukias the Aeginetan." On this Philon a very clever couplet may be readily be taken as referring to the Philon of vase fame; it was written by Simonides and quoted by Pausanias:

" My native land is Korkyra; Philon's my name; I am Glaukos'
Son, and am victor in boxing in two Olympiads."

31. Antoxenos kalos.

On a red-figured amphora with a scene of an Amazon with her war-axe are the names of Ἀντόξενος and Εὐφρόνιος (*C. V. A., Louvre*, fasc. 6, III I c, pl. 33, 5, 6, 7). The vase dates from the end of the 6th century or the beginning of the 5th. Pottier (*Vases Antiques du Louvre*, p. 158, G 106) and Hartwig (*Meisterschalen*, pp. 152-3) think that καλός was intended. There are no ready identifications for this ephebe.

32. Aphrodisia kale.

Klein, 150; Pfuhl, *Malerei und Zeichnung*, p. 278; *Catalogue of Vases in the British Museum*, III, p. 354, E 718. The inscription reads: Ἀφροδισία καλὴ. τὼς (= οὕτως) δοκεῖ Εὐχείρῳ. The name occurs also on a krater of the Chairippos Painter in Florence (Beazley, *A. V.*, p. 106, no. 8). Cf. Alkaios, no. 12 above.

33. Apollodoros kalos.

Klein, 105; Hartwig, *Meisterschalen*, p. 630, pl. 69, where the restoration of ἔγραφσεν instead of καλός is suggested. A fragment in the Louvre, unpublished in Pottier or the *C. V. A.* has the name of Euryptolemos as an associate of Apollodoros. Diodoros, XII 43, mentions an archon of 430/29 by this name. *I. G.*, I, 447, col. I, 57, is a sepulchral monument from the end of the fifth century. If our Apollodoros is slightly earlier, *I. G.*, I, 433, a grave-stone of the tribe Erechtheis, which has two mentions of men with this name (col. 1, 18; II, 21), may refer to him. *I. G.*, I, 118, 119 gives an Apollodoros who in the year 432/1 was the secretary of the treasury of the goddess.

34. Archedike kale.

Cf. Miss Richter, *Red-Figured Athenian Vases in the Metropolitan Museum*, p. 136, no. 104 (lekythos by the Sabouroff Painter). Perhaps this is the hetaira from Naukratis in Her. II, 135 and Athenaeus 596 D, though the name is common in Attica.

35. Archias kalos.

Klein, 38, a black-figured amphora in Cervetri, unpublished. On a fragment of marble painted red and from the Akropolis (*I. G.*, I, [Suppl.], 562, p. 191) we read the same love-name: καλὸς 'Αρχίας.

36. Archinos kalos.

Klein, 142; Beazley, *A. V.*, p. 127, 7 and 8; *C. V. A., Louvre*, fasc. 6, III I c, pl. 33, 8, by Painter of Dutuit Oinochoe. Mid-fifth century. Lolling, Κατάλογος τοῦ ἐν 'Αθήναις 'Επιγραφικοῦ Μουσείου, I, p. 73, no. 115, is a dedication of this time by an Archinos. Kirchner, 2526, refers to an Archinos from Koile, who was well-known and influential in the second half of the century. Dem. XXIV, 135 says of him: ὁ καταλαβὼν Φυλὴν (404 B. C.) καὶ αἰτιώτατος ὢν τῆς καθόδου τῷ δήμῳ καὶ ἄλλα πολλὰ καὶ καλὰ πεπολιτευμένος καὶ ἐστρατηγηκὼς πολλάκις. Aristophanes, *Frogs*, 367 with the scholia, also refers to him. It is said that he persuaded the Athenians to use the Ionic alphabet in the archonship of Eukleides (Phot. Lex. Suid. sub Σαμίων ὁ δῆμος).

37. Aristagoras kalos.

Klein, 100; Beazley, *A. V.*, pp. 205, 209, 218. *I. G.*, I, 439, 10, a sepulchral monument from the end of the fifth century, has the name. Cf. the epigram to Aristagoras kalos, Chapter III, no. 15.

38. Aristarchos kalos.

Klein, 97; Beazley, *A. V.*, p. 172, 5. Xenophon, *Mem.* II, 7, 1, mentions an Aristarchos who was the companion of Sokrates in 404 B. C. *I. G.*, II, 971 mentions an Aristarchos who was choregos in 422/1 B. C. Three persons with this name are cited on a grave-stone from the end of the century (*I. G.*, I, 447).

39. Aristeides kalos.

Klein, 97; Beazley, *A. V.*, p. 96. Ostraka with the name of Aristeides, banished in 483 B. C., were found in the Agora excavations (*Hesperia*, II, p. 460). Aristeides, son of Archippos, was strategos in 425/4 B. C., and was sent to Thrace and the Hellespont; in 424 he captured the city of Antandros (Thuk. IV, 50, 75; Diod. XII, 72, 3). Plato (*Theag.* 130 a) mentions an Aristeides, son of Lysimachos, and says that he was a pupil of Sokrates (*Theaet.* 151 a). *I. G.*, II, 1257 gives an Aristeides who was choregos at the end of the fifth century; he was of the tribe Antiochis. *I. G.*, I, 447, col. III, 30 is a grave-stone from the end of the fifth century with the name of Aristeides of Leontis. Cf. page 7, above, for vase by the Eucharides Painter with the inscription: Ἀριστείδες εἶ σὺ καλός.

40. Aristoleon kalos.

Klein, 148, a red-figured lekythos in the Russo collection, Terranuova. Kirchner 1943 says of this name: " De origine Attica dubitari licet."

41. Aristomenes kalos.

Klein, 37. On a black-figured amphora in the Louvre, *C. V. A.*, fasc. 4, III H e, pl. 40, nos. 4 and 5. No identifications are available.

42. Artemidos kalos (?).

This is taken to be a kalos name by the writer of *C. V. A., Madrid*, fasc. 1, III H e, pl. 17. It is on a black-figured amphora in Madrid with a scene of Herakles unloading the Erymanthian boar on Eurystheus who protests from the pithos; Athena is on the right, on the left is Artemis wearing a polos. Between Artemis and Herakles are a dog and the inscription. This name, however, occurs nowhere in compilations of proper names; Artemidoros, of which it is conceivably a shortened form, is late, the earliest case dating from the end of the third century. Artemis, the goddess, is probably represented as protectress either of Herakles or of the boar. She is often called ἡ καλή or καλλίστη or " KALLISTO " as goddess of the animal world (Aisch., *Agam.*, 140). Euripides, *Hippolytos*, 66, calls her καλλίστα πολὺ παρθένων, which reminds one of καλλίστη παρθένων on a black-figured cup in the Gallatin collection, *A. J. A.*, XXXI, 1927, p. 346. That Herakles was associated with her we know from Pausanias, IV, 31, 10, where it is said that in the group of Damophon in the "Hieron" at Messene the two were represented. Pauly-Wissowa, 2, 1415, records her presence in mythical scenes of archaic art at the contest for the tripod and the Erymanthian boar scene.

Though the *C. V. A.* takes it thus, this, then, is not a *kalos* name, but must be understood as, "This is the figure of Artemis," with an automatic, non-particularized *kalos* thrown in, to which interpretation the fact that the name of the goddess is in the genitive case lends itself. Compare the British Museum amphora with scene of the Delphic tripod and the goddess' name also in the genitive; Graef, *Die Antiken Vasen von der Akropolis zu Athen*, pl. 56, fragment 836 a, text 2, where the name is in that case too. The genitive is also used on the amphora signed by Menon as potter in Philadelphia (Hoppin, *Handb. R. F.*, II, p. 202). The fact that the goddess Artemis is present on all these vases makes it probable that the inscription refers to her, though it is faintly possible that a scene of her activities would call to mind an Athenian of a derived name. It is included here until more can be learned of the use of this as a proper name.

42A. Athena(i)a kale.

On an unpublished vase in the Walters Art Gallery in Baltimore, a black-figured krater from the Massarenti collection (48.30) representing Athena and Herakles in a quadriga. The inscription here probably, however, refers to the goddess.

43. Athenodotos kalos.

Klein, 91; Beazley, *A. V.*, pp. 50, 166-8, 201, 210, 228. Graef, *Die Antiken Vasen im der Akropolis*, I, p. 184, no. 1785; *A. J. A.*, XXXI, 1927, p. 348. Athenodotos occurs, sometimes with Leagros, on more than twelve vases dating about 500 B. C.. An Athenian of the deme Oinoe with this name is cited in Ross, *Dem. Att.*, no. 16; *I. G.*, II, 1226.

44. Automenes kalos.

Klein, 48, black-figured. This name is found also on a red-figured vase by Oltos, Beazley, *A. V.,* p. 16, 53. An Automenes was the father of Arignotos and Ariphrades. Arignotos (Kirchner, 1612) was a κιθαρῳδός (Aristoph., *Knights,* 1277-8; *Wasps,* 1278). Ariphrades is censured in the *Knights,* 1281; *Wasps,* 1280; *Peace,* 883; *Eccl.,* 129, as corrupted by the discipline of Anaxagoras.

45. Axiopeithes kalos.

Klein, 166. Cf. no. 15 above. The name is doubtfully Attic. He is son of Alkimachos, Beazley, *A. V.,* p. 378, no. 37.

46. Brachas kalos.

Klein, 118. On a red-figured vase in the Victoria and Albert Museum, South Kensington, London; *Burlington—Greek Art,* 1904, p. 117, pl. 96, I 67. In *L'Antiquité Classique,* IV, 1935, p. 219 Philippart says that the inscription is " probablement moderne." H. R. W. Smith, *New Aspects of the Menon Painter,* p. 59 is inclined to attribute the cup to the Menon Painter.

46A. Chachrylion kalos. Cf. Beazley, *A. V.,* p. 49, no. 2. The famous potter working for Peithinos.

47. Chairaia kale.

Klein, 38; Hoppin, *Handb. B. F.,* p. 194, an amphora by Nikosthenes in Castle Ashby. The inscription: Χαιραία καλή.

48. Chairephon kalos.

Klein, 127; Beazley, *A. V.,* p. 59, 4. On vases he is a contemporary of Philliades. There was a companion of Sokrates with this name (Plato, *Apol.* 21 a; Xen., *Mem.,* I, 2, 18; II, 3, 1), whose serious studies and sallow complexion made him the butt of comedy jests (Aristoph., *Clouds,* 156; *Birds,* 1296, 1564).

49. Chairestratos kalos.

Klein, 99; Beazley, *A. V.,* pp. 199-202, 208-9, 474. *I. G.,* I (Suppl.), 27 c, p. 165, mentions a person by this name, who was the speaker of a decree in the year 430 B. C.

50. Chairias kalos.

Klein, 88-89; Beazley, *A. V.*, pp. 49-50, 57, 159. Kirchner, 15212-15215 are all grave-stones with this name, and their dates, 459/8 and 438 B. C., allow any one of them to be a reference to the decease of our Chairias. This name should not be regarded as relating to the same person described under Chairis kalos. He is celebrated on vases by Phintias (510-500 B. C.) and the later Syriskos Painter, so that Beazley assumes a Chairias I and II. Cf. page 4, above.

51. Chairippos.

Klein, 150. On a red-figured alabastron, *Cat. of Vases in the British Museum*, III, p. 395, D 15; also on the krater of Chairippos Painter in Florence (Beazley, *A. V.*, p. 106, no. 1). For the kylix of Epiktetos in Adria cf. also Beazley, *A. V.*, p. 26, no. 34.

52. Chairis kalos.

Boston oinochoe, 13, 192 (cf. Caskey, *op. cit.*, p. 40, no. 43, and pl. XVIII; Beazley, *V. A.*, p. 157; *A. V.*, p. 355, no. 1). Attributed to the manner of Chicago Painter by Beazley. C. 450 B. C.

A youth moves off to the right, his body *en face*, his face looking back to a man at the left; a mantle is draped over his raised left arm, in his right he holds a skyphos temptingly to a bearded man, bent slightly forward with his right hand and arm in supplication, the left holding a stick. Below the skyphos is the inscription. Caskey says: "A break runs across the fourth letter of the name; but it is almost certainly a 'rho.' The other letters are clear, and there were but five. The only occurrence of this love-name."

Kirchner II, 15251, gives Χαῖρις on a sepulchral monument from the end of the fifth century. This reveals nothing in the life of Chairis, except that it protects him from being included in the list of eight vases tagged with the glory of Chairias (Klein, pp. 88, 89) and attributed to Phintias (520-500). Our vase is too late to be thinking of the Chairias on those vases, and anyhow there are far too many caprices indulged in by

the root of this name—Chairias, Chaireas, Charias. But there was a Chairis, a Theban scorned for his bad playing of the flute by Aristophanes (c. 428-420),[18] and spoken of as a bad penny who keeps turning up where there is little gratitude for his musical ministrations. The scholiast to *Birds* 857, calls him a κιθαρῳδός, but in the passages cited he is αὐλητής.

53. Chares kalos.

Klein, 70-1; *Arch. Zeit.*, 1853, pl. 51. Cf. Leagros. Diod., XI, 53 mentions Chares, archon in 472/1 B. C. Cf. for name *C. V. A., Louvre,* fasc. 5, III I c, pl. 28, 5, and 6; fasc. 6, pl. 51, 1.

54. Charmaios kalos.

This love-name is painted on a red-figured kylix in the collection of Capt. E. G. Spencer-Churchill. It is a cup with a scene of Eos and Tithonos, and dates c. 470 B. C., according to Beazley (*A. J. A.*, XXXI, 1927, p. 350, 11). The name Charmaios is not found elsewhere in lists of Attic names, and does not occur on any other vases (not in Klein). It stands, however, to χάρμη as Alkaios to ἀλκή. Fick-Bechtel (*Die Griechischen Personennamen,* p. 290) gives the development of the name from its root so: Χαρμᾶς → Χαρμάδας → Χαρμαῖος (when " a " is thought of as " ᾳ ")→ Χαρμαίδης. We must assume that we have here a new name or that the inscription, as it stands, is a mistake for something like Charminos, for example, the oligarch and admiral in the Peloponnesian War (Thuk., VIII, 30, 41, 42, 73; Aristoph., *Thesm.,* 804).

55. Charmides kalos. (Klein, 142-146; *C. V. A., Oxford,* fasc. 1, p. 16 (pl. 17, 6); *C. V. A., Louvre,* fasc. 6, III I c, pl. 50, 6.)

Charmides gives his name to the Charmides Painter (Beazley, *A. V.,* pp. 129-130). He is praised also by the Nikon Painter (Beazley, *op. cit.,* p. 131) and by the painter of the Munich cups (*ibid.,* p. 476). *Hesperia,* V, 1936, p. 350, no. 6

---

[18] *Achar.,* 16; *Peace,* 951; *Birds,* 858.

mentions a partly glazed krater found in the Agora, on the base of which the name of Charmides is inscribed along with Therikles and Timoxenos. The name is very common on vases, but not so elsewhere. On a sepulchral monument of the late 5th century (*I. G.*, I², 960) it is found, and also as the name of a Treasurer of the Other Gods in accounts of the statues of Athena and Hephaistos in 420-419 B. C. (*I. G.*, I², 370). Charmides is known on vases as a contemporary of Glaukon. In the Platonic dialogue by this name we have a good picture of what sort of youth he may have been (*v.* sub Lysis). Athenaeus (V, 187 F) says that Plato represents Sokrates "inconsistently as sometime in a state of vertigo and intoxication for love of the lad (Charmides) and beside himself, and as a fawn cowering before the strength of a lion (*Charm.* 155 D) and then again he declares that he takes no thought of the lad's beauty." Cf. also Graef-Langlotz, *op. cit.*, 1499-1500.

56. Charops kalos.

Klein, 66; *C. V. A., Copenhague,* fasc. 3, III, I, pl. 136, 1 a-c. Red-figured.

57. Chironeia kale.

Klein, 111; Hoppin, *Handb. R. F.,* I, p. 422, no. 39, by the Panaitios Painter. Hoppin wrongly gives Chireneia.

58. Choiros kalos.

Klein, 46; Gerhard, *Auserlesene Griechische Vasenbilder,* II, 95. The black-figured hydria mentioned by Klein is now in the Museum of Fine Arts, Boston, 01.8058 and has three other kalos names, Eupar(i)tos; Mnesila, and Amphoe.

59. Damas kalos.

Klein, 125; Hoppin, *Handb. R. F.,* I, pp. 444, 461; Beazley, *A. V.,* pp. 110, 184. Chairestratos is an associate.

60. Demos kalos.

See page 10, footnote 37, where it is impersonal, and p. 131, where it is personal on a vase fragment.

61. Demostratos kalos.

The Louvre amphora G 42 (*C. V. A.*, fasc. 5, III I c, pl. 28, nos. 5 and 6) with a scene from the palaistra has the following inscriptions: Σοτίνος, Σόστρατος, Χάρες . . . · χαῖρε, Δεμόστρατε, καλὸς Σο.ίθε.. The last name is taken in the *Index Analytique,* fasc. 7, as So(s)ithe(os), but Hoppin (*Handb. R. F.,* II, p. 368) wrongly reads it as Sosias.

Demostratos can be identified with the dedicator of an Akropolis inscription, which dates before the middle of the fifth century (Lolling, Κατάλογος, I, p. 76, no. 12). He may also have lived to be the secretary of the treasures of the goddess in 438 B. C. (*I. G.,* I, Suppl., 298, p. 146). His name is in the vocative here, as the χαῖρε clearly shows. Hence, not all the names ending in epsilon or eta on Attic vases should be understood as derisive feminizations (unless we have further testimony from literature, as in the case of Sostratos and others in this chapter), but rather they are to be taken with a χαῖρε that is understood. Hoppin, *Euthymides and His Fellows,* p. 124, and Beazley, *A. V.,* p. 57, give this amphora to Phintias.

62. Dexios (cf. Euthymos kalos).

63. Dikaios kalos.

This inscription is on a large red-figured amphora in the Louvre (*C. V. A.*, fasc. 5, III I c, pl. 29, 5; pl. 30, 2-5; pl. 31, 1; *Jahrb.,* XXXI, 1916, p. 140, fig. 16), which Beazley (*J. H. S.,* XXX, 1910, p. 41) attributed to the hand of Kleophrades. Hoppin discusses it in *Euthymides and His Fellows,* p. 67. The name is not given by Klein in his list, because he considered it to be an adverb, δικαίως, as also on the British Museum psykter E 767 (*C. V. A.,* fasc. 6, III I c, pl. 104, 2). On the one side of this psykter is the inscription κάρτα Δίκαιος . . . χαρχων, and on the other, scattered through a scene of two bearded men and a small boy dancing, is Κυδίας χαῖρε. The name Kydias is written over the shoulder of the first man, who is playing a kithara; Plato (*Charmides,* 155 D) mentions a celebrated kitharist, Kydias, known to be from Hermione, and Hoppin (*loc. cit.*) believes that we have here a complimentary reference to the musician. The name on the first side he restores to [Νι]χάρχων, but knows no other instances of this name. For Kydias, cf. Graef-Langlotz, *Akrop. Vas.*, II, 3, 1332.

The Louvre amphora has the inscription Δίκαιος καλὸς χαῖρε. On the one side it has "conversational" scenes between lovers and their beloveds, three groups, the middle one showing the beloved in his lover's arms preparatory to a kiss; the two other groups consist of a naked boy exercising and a draped ephebe watching him. On the second side of this vase is a scene of an Asiatic archer between two hoplites.

There is no reason for doubting that this Dikaios is the son of Theokydes, the Athenian who, according to Herodotos, VIII, 65, "was at this time an exile and had gained a good report among the Medes." As a companion of the Peisistratidae, Dikaios had been with Xerxes during his invasion of Greece. Herodotos reports that, while walking in the Thriasian plain with Demaretos, the Spartan king, after the Persians had wasted Attika in 480 B. C., this Dikaios saw a cloud of dust advancing from Eleusis, "such as a host of 30,000 men might raise," and in the accompanying din heard the mystic hymn to Iakchos. He explained to Demaretos: "Beyond a doubt some mighty calamity is about to befall the King's army. For it is manifest, inasmuch as Attica is deserted by its inhabitants, that the sound which we have heard is an unearthly one, and is now upon its way from Eleusis to aid the Athenians and their confederates. If it descends upon the Peloponnese, danger will threaten the King himself and his land army; if it moves towards the ships at Salamis, 'twill go hard, but the King's fleet there suffers destruction. Every year the Athenians celebrate this feast to the Mother and the Daughter; and all who wish, whether they be Athenians or any other Greeks, are initiated. The sound thou hearest is the Bacchic song, which is wont to be sung at that festival" (Rawlinson). Demaretos thereupon cautioned him to peace lest, if the King were to hear, he lose his head. But the dust and the voice moved toward Salamis, and the prophecy was fulfilled. Plutarch (*Them.* 15) tells the same story without mentioning the name of the narrator, and also changes its time to the day of the battle.

Trautwein (*Hermes*, XXV, 1890, p. 527) understands Herodotos' words " Ἔφη δὲ Δίκαιος " as meaning not a verbal informant, but that the literary evidence of the *Memoirs* of Dikaios was his source. But all that we know from Herodotos is that Dikaios was an exile from his native Athens, and that he was in the Persian headquarters, where he enjoyed a certain esteem, before the battle of Salamis. Duncker (*Gesch. des Altertums*, VII, p. 64) thinks that Dikaios was one of the "faithful," who followed the banished Hippias to Asia and who now on the Xerxes expedition was again in the retinue of the Peisistratids. But Trautwein believes that his relation to Demaretos, which is actually mentioned by Herodotos, should be stressed; that he was banished soon after the Kleisthenic reform, fled to Sparta where Demaretos was still in power, and grew intimate with him, and that later both, expatriate, were naturally in the Persian section to be re-established. Trautwein thinks that in his *Memoirs* Dikaios included the intricate relations of the Spartan King with the Persian court. The chief defect of the theory lies " in undertaking to realize too definitely the contents of the *Memoirs*." [19] Macan in his notes on Herodotos, VIII, 65, suggests that Thukydes or Theokydes may be the same person, as " Thukydes implies Thukydides," and so fances a possible connection between the father of Dikaios and the famous historian-son of Olorus.

The career of " Dikaios kalos " is surely to be identified with as much as we do know of this person, especially when we note the Asiatic archer in one scene on this same vase. What is more natural than that a vase-painter who was thinking of Dikaios should draw a picture of a Persian on

---

[19] Cf. Macan, *Herodotus*, VII, VIII, IX, Intr. sec. 10, p. LXXXV.

his vase, or vice versa? And certainly at the time of our vase, c. 500 B. C., the Persian power was already felt by the Greeks. Assuming that Dikaios was at least fifteen years of age when his name graced the vase, he would have been about thirty-five at the time of the Herodotean episode, and fifty-six when he died, if we identify him with the Dikaios of the tribe Erechtheis in the list of those who fell in 459-458 in the war activity of Athens in Egypt, Kypros, Aigina, Megara, etc.[20]

There is no reason to believe that the Dikaios on the British Museum psykter, E 767, does not refer to the same man. The inscription reads κάρτα Δίκαιος χαῖρε; for both vases date about the same time.

64. Diodoros.

This love-name, without the usual appended *kalos*, occurs on vases by, and of the period of the Ambrosios Painter (one of which is written up under the name Xanthes, *sub nom.* below). On another vase, the Louvre psykter G 58 (*C. V. A.*, fasc. 8, III I c, pl. 58, 3, 6, 9), the name occurs with those of Eukleides, Antiphanes, and Diomnestos; Beazley, *A. V.*, p. 62, no. 5, attributes it to Smikros.

A Diodoros was the companion of Sokrates (Xen. *Mem.*, II, 10, 1-6), but, unless he was older than Sokrates, it is more likely that the Diodoros on the Erechtheid grave monument of 459/8 (*I. G.*, I², 929, l. 148) is the one on our vase. Cf. the epigram to Diodoros kalos, Chapter III, no. 29.

With the Antiphanes of the vase Kirchner's numbers 1206-8, 1222-3 should be compared, grave-stones from the second half of the fifth century, to any of which our love-name might apply. There was also an ἀγαλματοποιός, Antiphanes, in the year 407, as known from *I. G.*, I, 323, 324 c (Loewy, *Inschriften Griechischer Bildhauer*, no. 526).

Eukleides is a very common name. Kirchner's numbers 5670-2, 5681-2 are suitably dated sepulchral stones from the fifth century. 5680 is the Eukleides, one of the Thirty (Xen., *Hell.*, II, 3, 2), of the phyle Aigeis, who is probably also the strategos of 410/9 at Eretria (*I. G.*, I, 188, l. 17).

---

[20] Tod, *Greek Historical Inscriptions*, no. 26, l. 78.

Diomnestos was the brother of the orator Isokrates, and came from the deme of Erchia (*Vitae X Orat.*, 836e). Both were sons of Theodoros. This boy occurs again as the dancing ephebe on a Louvre vase (*C. V. A.*, fasc. 8, III I c, pl. 59, 5, 7).

65. Diogenes kalos.

Klein 101; Beazley, *A. V.*, pp. 111, 187; *C. V. A., Oxford*, fasc. 1, pl. 2, 5, a red-figured vase in the Ashmolean Museum. A Diogenes is mentioned in *I. G.*, I, 315 as an ἀρχῆς γραμματεύς in 434/3 B. C. In 415 B. C. a Diogenes was charged with the profanation of the mysteries (Andok., I, 13). Lolling, Κατάλογος, I, p. 77, no. 128 (*I. G.*, I, 398) is a dedication on the Akropolis by Diogenes, son of Aischylos. Cf. also no. 270 below.

66. Diokles kalos.

Klein, 149; Beazley, *A. V.*, p. 129, 7; *C. V. A., Br. Mus.*, fasc. 5, III I c, pl. 50, 3, by the Boston Tithonos Painter. *I. G.*, I, 59 from the year 410/9 gives a Diokles as the speaker of a decree. An archon in 409/9 by this name is mentioned by Diodoros, XIII, 54. Cf. the epigram to Diokles by Kallimachos, Chapter III, no. 30.

67. Diomnestos (*v.* sub Diodoros).

68. Dion kalos.

Klein, 168; Beazley, *A. V.*, pp. 263-265; Hoppin, *Handb. R. F.*, I, p. 295, an amphora in Boston. Plato (*Menex.*, 234 b) mentions a Dion who was an orator at the end of the fifth century. Our "fair Dion" is not, then, the Dion of Syracuse to whom Plato wrote some of his poems (Bergk, *Poetae Lyrici Graeci*, II, p. 621, no. 7).

69. Dionokles kalos.

Klein, 147; Beazley, *A. V.*, p. 137; *C. V. A., Br. Mus.*, fasc. 5, III I c, pl. 50, 1a. On red-figured vases with Akestorides and Kallias. The name should be Oionokles according to Beazley and Miss Richter, *Red-Figured Athenian Vases*, p. 55, n. 1.

70. Diotimos kalos.

Cf. Miss Richter, *Red-Figured Athenian Vases in the Metropolitan Museum,* p. 150, no. 116, pl. 115 (white lekythos by the Achilles Painter c. 450-440 B. C.). Perhaps Diotimos, son of Strombichos, one of the generals at the Battle of Sybota in 433 B. C. (Thuk. 1, 45, 2).

71. Dioxippos.

Klein, 81; Beazley, *A. V.,* p. 14, 30, by Oltos.

72. Diphilos.

A distinct group of love-names occurs on Attic funeral lekythoi. The ephebes are: Diphilos, son of Melanopos (Klein, 159; Beazley, *A. V.,* p. 377, 8 by Achilles Painter; Hoppin, *Handb. R. F.,* I, p. 132, 62 by Brygos Painter); Alkimedes, son of Aischylides (see no. 16; Klein, p. 162); Axiopeithes (Klein, p. 166); Alkimachos (Klein, pp. 165-6; here, *sub nom.*); Dromippos (Klein, p. 159); Hygiainon (Klein, p. 167); Lichas (Klein, p. 160). Beazley sees the Achilles Painter in all of them in singularities of style.

An inscription found at Olympia (Dittenberger und Purgold, *Die Inschriften von Olympia,* 30) supplies fresh information that youths thus honoured were of good stock. It is a decree of Elis conferring proxenia on a Diphilos, son of Melanopos of Athens: Ἔδοξεν Ἀλειοῖς ... Δίφιλον τὸν Ἀθαναῖον, Μελανώπω υἱύν, πρόξενον καὶ εὐεργέταν τῶν Ἀλειῶν γράψαι ἐν Ὀλυνπίᾳ ἔδοξεν. Bosanquet inclines to identify him with the Diphilos on vases, and perhaps also with the one who commanded a fleet in 413 B. C. (Thuk., VII, 34, 3; Kirchner, *Pros. Att.,* 4464). Kourouniotis (Ἀρχ. Ἐφ. 1906, p. 21; on Diphilos-Dromippos) agrees with the Olympia identification, but doubts the latter.[21] In Melanopos Bosanquet (*J. H. S.,* XIX, 1899, p. 179, n. 1) seems to agree with Dittenberger and Purgold (*loc. cit.*) in seeing the father of the other son, Laches (also *kalos* on vases; here, sub Lysis; *v.* Klein, p. 95) who held a command in 427 B. C. (Thuk., III, 86, VI, 75;

---

[21] On the grounds that Diphilos would have been too old in 413.

Aristoph., *Lys.*, 304, *Wasps*, 240; Plato, *Symp.*, 221 a; Plato's *Laches* named after him).

All vases with Diphilos are by the same hand, Bosanquet says in the *J. H. S.*, XVI, 1896, pp. 164-177, pls. IV-VII. He counted twelve vases by the same master; four of them reflective of the beauty of Diphilos; three, of Glaukon; two, of Dromippos; one, of Lichas; one each, of Alkimedes and Axiopeithes. This group dates c. 465 B. C., on grounds of technique and also because of the possibility of linking " kalos Lichas " with a historical character, of which more will be said later. McMahon in the *A. J. A.*, XI, 1907, p. 18, says that he has seen eleven vases with the name of Diphilos and relates the whole group to the Achilles Painter on grounds of inscriptions, manner of writing and forming of letters, artistic technique and decorative patterns. All these names have an added patronymic (e. g., *C. V. A., Bruxelles,* fasc. 1, III J b, pl. 4, 3, a white lekythos with Δίφιλος καλὸς ὁ Μηλανόπ ..), a phenomenon that is practically peculiar to this group. That there is a group of names on these vases which do not occur on any other shapes is curious (for, with the single exception of Glaukon, these names are peculiar to lekythoi: Diphilos, Dromippos, Lichas, Axiopeithes, Alkimachos, Alkimedes, Hygiainon). If there is anything in Pottier's theory, that painters made a call for the patronage of great houses by celebrating the scions of those houses on their vases, the lekythos industry must have been supported by the ones in point, particularly the atelier of the Achilles Painter. But the exception in the case of Glaukon, as well as the general conduct of these inscriptions, suggests that the names and the use of them were merely a convention. In the case of the merged Diphilos, Dromippos-Hygiainon group, these three youths were probably all favourites of the Achilles Master at successive intervals.[22] Beazley [23] has counted more than forty-four white lekythoi as forming a group by this one master.

---

[22] The best place to study the Diphilos-Dromippos group is in Riezler's *Weissgrundige Attische Lekythen*, pls. II-IX.

[23] *J. H. S.*, XXXIV, 1914, p. 179.

All the names are inscribed *stoichedon* and have have an added patronymic. The Borelli lekythos (in Philadelphia) forms the transition of the Achilles Master from the Diphilos-Dromippos period (it has an inscription to Diphilos) to that of Hygiainon.[24] If we add this group, this painter is responsible for more than fifty lekythoi.

Hygiainon of vase-fame (*Cat. of Vases in Br. Mus.*, III, p. 402, D 48; *C. V. A., Copenhague,* fasc. 4, III J, pl. 170, 6) is probably the one of that name mentioned by Aristotle (*Rhet.,* III, 15) and to whom Euripides had to answer in an exchange-case for having written a verse encouraging perjury. The verse is *Hippolytos* 612: "My tongue has sworn; my mind remains unsworn."

Dromippos, son of Dromokleides, is celebrated on three vases, one of which is in Berlin, 2443 (Neugebauer, *Führer durch das Antiquarium,* II, *Vasen,* p. 58).

Lichas is not an Attic name (*J. H. S.,* XVI, 1896, p. 166, pl. VI). He is described as "the Samian" (*Cat. of Vases in the Br. Mus.,* III, D 50), but Bosanquet (*J. H. S.,* loc. *cit.*) prefers to read Σαμίου, " son of Samios " for several reasons:

1. The last letter may be completed as upsilon. Sigma on these vases generally is lunate, but rather a blurred zigzag than a plain curve.
2. In the other three line inscriptions of this group, the third word is the father's name.
3. That a Lichas should be the son of Samios is probable, since both are Spartan names (Lichas occurs in other Dorian states, Samios is peculiar to Sparta). The use of the patronymic may have been occasioned by increasing population, to distinguish like-named persons. Bosanquet gives this genealogy on the basis of Herodotos, III, 55. At the siege of Samos in 525 a Spartan so distinguished himself for valour that, though overpowered within the walls which he entered, and killed, the Samians gave him an honourable burial. In memory of his heroic conduct and of the chivalry of the

---

[24] Luce, *A. J. A.,* XXIII, 1919, p. 19.

Samians, a son of this hero, Archias, received the name of Samios. Our Lichas may be the son of the first Samios and the brother of the second Archias, from whom Herodotos gets the story. The genealogy is thus:

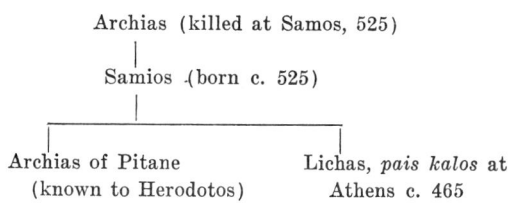

```
          Archias (killed at Samos, 525)
                    |
          Samios (born c. 525)
                    |
       _____
       |                         |
  Archias of Pitane        Lichas, pais kalos at
  (known to Herodotos)       Athens c. 465
```

These Lichas vases date c. 465 B. C. because the presence of a young Spartan in Athens at this time accords with the well-known *Lakonismos* of Kimon (*proxenos* of Sparta and father of Lakedaimonios) at his height between 470-464. Chronology of the vases certainly confirms this, for this Lichas vase [25] is later in style than the Glaukon vase of pl. IV (*J. H. S.* XVI). The earlier Lichas vases are doubtless contemporary with later Glaukon group. In Amsterdam there is a bronze castanet with the inscription ΚΑ...ΛΙΧΑΣ. Cf. Allard Pierson Museum, *Algemeene Gids,* 1937, p. 87, no. 759.

A less common name on lekythoi and one recently identified is Euaion, which appears on a dozen vases dated between 460-440. They are not all by one painter; this fortifies the theory that this is not an ordinary favourite of an individual painter, but a youth of prominence. Suidas says that the tragic poet, Aischylos, had a son of this name, and this is confirmed by the inscription on a small white lekythos in Heidelberg: [26] Εὐαίων καλὸς Αἰσχύλου.

The name Olympichos appears on only one lekythos, and that the oldest of this group (Klein, 149, Neugebauer, *Führer durch das Antiquarium,* p. 61, 2252). The name was common in Athens. Among the kleruchs from that city to Lemnos (*I. G.,* I, 443) on a sepulchral stone of c. 430 B. C. is

---

[25] *J. H. S.*, XVI, 1896, pl. VI.
[26] Beazley, *A. J. A.*, XXXIII, 1929, p. 365.

Ὀλύμπιχος Ἱπποθοντίδος. Eros flies over the one side of this vase: "The Eros of the vase-painter is the love, not untouched by passion, of man for man, and these sedate and austere Erotes help us to understand that to the Greek mind such loves were serious and beautiful, of the soul, as Plato says, rather than of the body, aloof from common things and from the emotional squalour of mere domestic felicity," as Miss Jane Harrison [27] says.

The appearance of something so vital as a *kalos* name on a funeral lekythos, which seems an "anomaly" to McMahon (*loc. cit.*), is an index more probably of the conventional usage to which the salute was put; for in more cases than those to the contrary we have noted the complete lack of connection between inscription and scene.

73. Dorotheos kalos.

Five examples are cited by Klein (p. 61), all belonging to the archaic period; a sixth occurs on the psykter by Oltos in the Metropolitan Museum (Beazley, *V. A.,* p. 8); a seventh is in Koenigsberg. The Panaitios Painter (Beazley, *A. V.,* p. 166, 8) and the Kerberos Painter (Hoppin, *Handb. R. F.,* I, p. 144, 2) also use this love-name. Other ephebes on vases of his group are Hipparchos, Memnon, Xenophon, Kephisophon. One of the most remarkable occurrences of the name is on a red-figured jug in Munich (334):

καλὸς Νικόλα, Δωρόθεος
καλὸς κἀμοὶ δοκεῖ. ναί·
χἄτερος παῖς καλός, Μέμνον
κἀμοὶ καλὸς φίλος.

Dorotheos is probably the father of Lampon, who was the co-founder of Thurii in 446 B. C. (Thuk., V, 19, 24), soothsayer and friend of Perikles. Cf. Lampon, *sub. nom.* below.

The following inscriptions memorialize the name of Dorotheos:

---

[27] *Prolegomena,* p. 637.

1. Kirchner, 4586, cites a small bronze dedication from the Akropolis,[28] reading [τάθην]αίαι Δωρόθεος ἀνέθηκε[ν] and dating after 508 B. C. The circle of Dorotheos and his vase-gracing confreres dates c. 520-510.

2. A dedication ('Αρχ. 'Εφ., 1898, p. 13, no. 6) on a square base of white stone, and dating after the beginning of the fifth century. The co-dedicator was Simylos.

3. *I. G.*, I, 447, col. III, 55, a sepulchral monument from the end of the fifth century, commemorating Dorotheos of Kekropis.

4. *I. G.*, I, 444, a grave-stone of the members of the phyle of Hippothontis from the last half of the fifth century.

It is likely that (1) and (2) are dedications by the same person, and that (3) *or* (4) marks the end of that person's activity.

74. Dromippos (*v.* sub Diphilos).

75. Echekles kalos.

The name Echekles is on a Panathenaic amphora dating from the period between Peisistratos and the Persian Wars (Graef-Langlotz, *Akrop. Vas.*, I, 2, no. 914, p. 109, pl. 60). Cf. Echekles, son of Aktor and commander of the Myrmidons (*Iliad,* XVI, 189). One other instance of the name is known, on a fourth century gravestone from Aigina with the inscription: Echekles of Rhamnous (Kirchner 6171). It is likely, then, that a handsome Athenian was called by this name at the time of our vase.

75A. Elita kale.

Graef-Langlotz, *Akrop. Vas.*, II, p. 51, no. 560.

76. Elpinikos kalos.

Klein, p. 86, gives three vases with this name, number 1 of which is now in the Manchester Art Gallery (Webster, *Memoirs Manch. Lit. and Phil. Society,* vol. 78, Feb. 1934, p. 2, pl. 1, 1; *L'Antiquité Classique,* IV, 1935, p. 223). A

---

[28] *J. H. S.*, XIII, 1892, p. 127, no. 45, pl. VI

kylix in Boston (Caskey, *op. cit.,* p. 6, no. 7, pl. III) is ascribed to the same hand as Klein's three vases by Beazley (*A. V.,* pp. 51-3, 468), who adds a fifth piece, Leipzig T 609, without an inscription. He says of the painter whom he names after the *pais kalos* on his vases, " The Elpinikos Painter, interesting for his daintiness, minute detail, and technical experiments, belongs to the same group as the Epidromos Painter and Apollodoros."

There are no instances of this name in Kirchner, but *C. I. G.,* II, 3523, an inscription from far-off Mysia, grants *proxenia* and exemption from taxation to an Elpinikos, son of Agasistratos of Tenedos.

77. Epainetos kalos.

Cf. Miss Richter, *Red-Figured Athenian Vases in the Metropolitan Museum,* p. 18, no. 3, pl. 4 (psykter by Oltos about 520-510 B. C.).

78. Epeleios kalos.

Klein, 65; Beazley, *A. V.,* p. 48. Contemporary with Isarchos kalos and Theodoros kalos. Cf. Miss Richter,*Red-Figured Athenian Vases in the Metropolitan Museum,* p. 23, no. 8, pl. 7 (kylix by the Epeleios Painter about 510 B. C.). ὁ παῖς καλὸς 'Επέλειος.

79. Epidromos kalos.

Klein, 83; Beazley, *A. V.,* pp. 50-2, 166; in Leagros' group. *I. G.,* I, 447, col. I, 41, is a grave-stone with this name from c. 425 B. C. Cf. *C. V. A., Robinson Collection,* fasc. 2, III I, pl. vi.

80. Epilykos kalos.

Beazley, *A. V.,* pp. 40-42.

Nicole (*Rev. Arch.,* IV, 1916, pp. 398-9) believes that Epilykos should be classed as a painter, in spite of Buschor (*Jahrb.,* XXX, 1915, pp. 36-40) who thinks that he is a " pretty boy " only, who in the last years of the Peisistratidean era excited attention in the palaistra along with Memnon, Miltiades, and Hipparchos. Nicole thinks he was a fellow-artist of Skythes and Epiktetos, and that Buschor's idea is weakened by the Louvre cup, G 10, which can't be read Ἐπίλυκος καλὸς. Σκύθες ἔγραψεν but rather Ἐπίλυκος ἔγραφσεν καλōς, as Rizzo does (*Mon. Piot.*, XX, pp. 101-154). Buschor, on the other hand, refuses to recognize a painter Epilykos, but straightens out the difficulties in the fragments to his own satisfaction, so that they always read that Epilykos was the pretty boy and Skythes his adoring painter.

Hoppin (*Handb. R. F.*, I, p. 342) says: " Only one undisputed signature of Epilykos exists. The Berlin Fragments are probably signed by Skythes, and Epilykos is used as a kalos name on them (4041). Most probably they were partners." The vase to which Hoppin refers is the Louvre kylix, G 10.

Robert (Pauly-Wissowa, VI, p. 159) identified Epilykos with the father of Teisandros, mentioned in Plutarch (*Per.,* 36) and given by Kirchner as number 62. Suidas mentions an Epilykos, κωμικὸς ποιητὴς, and brother of the Athenian comic poet, Krates (451 B. C.); this, too, might be our Epilykos.

81. Epimedes kalos.

Klein, 127; Beazley, *A. V.*, p. 478.

82. Erasippos kalos.

Klein, 50; Beazley, *Attic Black-Figure,* p. 41, reads it ℎερασπος.

83. Erinos. Cf. Phrinos below, no. 224, *sub. nom.*

Beazley, *A. J. A.,* XXXIX, 1935, p. 482 reads the name on the white cup found in the Athenian Agora, which Miss Talcott (*Hesperia,* II, 1933, p. 229) interpreted as Phrinos, as Erinos. Cf. also Philippart, *L'Antiquité Classique,* V, 1936, pp. 18-19. The scholiast to Aristophanes cited p. 173 makes Phrinos preferable.

83A. Eris kale.

Cf. Graef-Langlotz, *Akrop. Vas.,* I, p. 243, no. 2500.

84. Erosantheo.

Klein, 150; *Cat. of Vases in Br. Mus.*, III, p. 354. On red-figured ware with Aphrodisia kale.

85. Erothemis kale.

Klein, 113; Beazley, *A. V.*, p. 172. On red-figured ware with Lykos kalos.

86. Etearchos (*v.* sub Phayllos kalos).

87. Euagra kale.

Klein, 134, a red-figured hydria in Altenburg with the additional name, Kallipos.

88. Euainetos kalos.

Klein, 131; Beazley, *A. V.*, p. 399. *I. G.*, I (Suppl.), 321, p. 76, col. II, 21, mentions a Euainetos of Alopeke (409 B. C.).

89. Euaion kalos (see Diphilos, p. 101).

Son of the tragic poet Aischylos. Cf. *A. J. A.*, XXXIII, 1929, p. 365.

90. Eualkides kalos.

This name is on a red-figured stamnos in Brussels (Beazley, *A. V.*, p. 62; Hoppin, *Handb. R. F.*, II, p. 417). Incorrectly given as "Alkides" by Klein.[29] The vase is by Smikros (510-500 B. C.). Other love-names on this vase are Pheidiades and Antias.

This may be the Eretrian mentioned by Herodotos[30] as killed in the battle at Ephesos (498 B. C.). "The Ionians drew out against them in battle array; and a fight ensued, wherein the Greeks had very greatly the worse. Vast numbers were slain by the Persians; among other men of note they killed the captain of the Eretrians, a certain Eualkides, a man who had gained crowns at the games and received much praise from Simonides the Cean." The Athenian strategos had perhaps a superior authority over the Eretrian contingent, though

---

[29] *L. I.*, pp. 22 and 127, no. 1.
[30] Her., V, 102. Rawlinson, vol. 3, pp. 302-303.

Eualkides is also called *strategos*. It is said of him: στεφανη-
φόρους τε ἀγῶνας ἀναραιρηκότα καὶ ὑπὸ Σιμωνίδεω τοῦ Κηίου πολλὰ
αἰνεθέντα.

His crown and poetical lauds did not save him on this occasion: the verses in question were Epinikia.[31]

It seems probable that Eualkides, after gaining renown at the games and the celebration of Simonides, may have been in Athens between these conquests and the defeat quoted, especially since he was working as commander of the Eretrian forces in conjunction with those of Athens. Eualkides as a boy was a prize boxer at Olympia, and Simonides' ode was written between 516 and 508 B. C. Cf. Bowra, *Greek Lyric Poetry*, p. 331.

(Cf. Klein, p. 127, no. 3, where under this group appears the name, without *kalos*, of Teisis, ἐρώμενος of Pytheas; *v. sub nom.*, below).

91. Eualkos kalos (Alones kalos).

These two love-names are found on a kalyx krater by an associate of Polygnotos (about 440 B. C.) in the Metropolitan Museum, 07.286.66, now published by Miss Richter, *Red-Figured Athenian Vases in the Metropolitan Museum of Art*, p. 160, no. 127, pl. 126. It is mentioned by Beazley (*V. A.*, p. 175), but the love-names are not given. A vase of the early free style, it has on the one side a scene of Athena abetting Kadmos in slaying the dragon at the fountain of Ares; above Kadmos is the inscription to Eualkos. In the space between the dragon, Harmonia, and Ares is the inscription to Alones.

The name Eualkos, son of Eualkos, is found in Kirchner, 5262 = *I. G.*, II, 2036; this is a grave-stone dating after 403 B. C. with Eualkos of Aigeis. Eualkes was, incidentally, the name of a favourite of Agesilaos [32] of whom Plutarch [33] says: ἠράσθη ἀθλητοῦ παιδὸς ἐξ Ἀθηνῶν. This Eualkes was at this

---
[31] Bergk., *Poet. Lyr. Gr.*, III⁴, p. 391, no. 9.
[32] Xen., *Hell.*, IV, 1, 40.
[33] *Ages.*, 13.

time, c. 394, too old to be admitted to the contests of boys at Olympia, or in the Pindaric expression,[34] συλαθεὶς ἀγενείων, but set his heart on this desire to the point of engaging Agesilaos' efforts in this direction. Eualkos' youth must have been rather completely gone by the year 398 or 394, and, though it is conceivable that at the age of forty-six (assuming the very latest possible date for our vase, 430 B. C.) he still hankered after contests with boys, he was certainly no longer a *pais* nor capable of inspiring anything but the most decadent of enthusiasms as the eromenos of Agesilaos.

The Eualkes of Lamptrai mentioned in an altar-like dedication to Apollo (*I. G.*, II,[5] 1220 b) from Attika cannot possibly be the person on our vase, even if it is one of the latest to carry a *kalos* inscription. It might, however, be a reference to Agesilaos' favourite, if he is not identical with the Eualkes of our vase.

92. Eucharides kalos.

Klein, 128; *C. V. A., Copenhague,* fasc. 3, III I, pl. 134. The "Eucharides Painter" is named after this *pais kalos*; Beazley, *A. V.,* p. 95, 18; Hoppin, *Handb. R. F.,* I, p. 356; Robinson-Harcum-Iliffe, *Greek Vases at Toronto,* pp. 155-157; Smets, *L'Antiquité Classique,* V, 1936, p. 93; Miss Richter, *Red-Figured Athenian Vases,* pp. 44-45.

93. Eudemos kalos (*v.* sub Phayllos).

94. Eukleides (*v.* sub Diodoros kalos).

95. Eukrates (*v.* sub Phayllos).

96. Eumares kalos.

This inscription is on a fragmentary plate, found in the Agora, the knowledge kindly given us by Miss Lucy Talcott and Dr. Shear, still unpublished. The signature and *kalos* name are painted in glazed circles around the center. The top

---

[34] Pindar, *Ol.,* IX, 89.

of the plate is reserved, save for three concentric circles in black glaze, between which is the inscription also in glaze:

EVMARES: KAVS N K T
SAVA+S -ro.. SEN INAI:

We think immediately of the celebrated Athenian painter of this name. Kirchner 5812 gives all the references to his name, and, among others, we remember Pliny's statement (*N. H.,* XXXV, 56): " et qui primus in pictura marem a femina discreverit, Eumarum Atheniensem, figuras omnes imitari ausum, quique inventa eius excoluerit, Cimonem Cleonaeum." Eumares (-os) had his place between the monochromists and Kimon of Kleonai. Miss Swindler (*Ancient Painting,* p. 136) says that Kimon worked about the end of the sixth century and dates Eumares in the early part of this century. It is likely that Eumares was the father of the sculptor Antenor, who made a statue dedicated by Nearchos after the middle of the sixth century. Payne, *Archaic Marble Sculpture from the Acropolis,* p. 31, wrongly doubts the connection of the kore and the base. For the inscription, cf. Kirchner, *Imagines Inscriptionum Atticarum,* pl. 5, 10. Our Eumares, then may have been advertised on vases sometime around the end of the first half of the sixth century, before he had developed into the famous black-figured artist, who is known to have been the first to use white for the flesh of women in his paintings. The lively polychromy which Antenor used on his statues may well have been due to the influence of his father, Eumares (Reinach, *Recueil Milliet,* 1921, I, p. 76). To this same Eumares the inscriptions, *I. G.,* I (Supplement), p. 88, no. 373[91] and p. 181, no 373[93] probably refer; they are dedications of the art of the master.

Since it is difficult to date a piece like the Agora fragment, I add two other Athenians of this name, of the fifth century B. C.: (1) *I. G.,* II, 3713, p. 298, a sepulchral monument to a Eumaros or Eumares, and dating in the fifth, not fourth century; (2) Kirchner, 177, cites a Eumares, father of Agoratos, and a slave (Lys., XIII, 64): "Agoratum civem esse ex decreto anno 410/9 facto."

97. Eumele kale.

Klein, 136; Graef-Langlotz, *Akrop. Vasen,* I, p. 261, no. 2742, pl. 113. On a spinning whorl in Athens, Akropolis Museum.

98. Eupar(aite)tos or Eupar[itos] kalos.

Klein, 46. Cf. Amphoe, Choiros, Mnesilla, Rodon above. A careful examination of the inscription on this Boston hydria (01.8058) shows that only one letter is missing between EVΓAP and TOS. So Euparaitetos as given by Beazley, *C. V. A. Oxford,* fasc. II, p. 3, is impossible.

99. Euphamidas kalos.

On a black-figured alabastron in the Hermitage, Leningrad (inv. 2632), of the late style (beginning of the fifth century). The scene has a quadriga to the right and two warriors fighting and running; below a dog. Provenance unknown. The vase seems still to be unpublished.

100. Euphiletos kale or kalos.

Black-figured olpe in Metropolitan Museum, acc., .06.1021. 47. Klein,[35] p. 41, no. 2, gives it as a name without the adjective. Beazley (*J. H. S.,* XLVII, 1927, p. 87, footnote) also construes it alone. The Antimenes Painter (530-510) is the artist. For the British Museum Panathenaic amphora (530-515 B. C.) with Euphiletos kalos cf. *C. V. A.,* III H e, pl. 2, 2a-b and Smets, *L'Antiquité Classique,* V, 1936, p. 88, no. 10.

On the New York vase a man is playing a lyre before three ladies. There are inscriptions for the three women, but *kale* seems to belong to Euphiletos in the same derisive way as

---

[35] 'Αρχ. 'Εφ., 1888, plate 12, 2, whence Hoppin, *Handbook of Black-Figured Vases,* p. 89, a plaque from Eleusis on which he restores ἔγραφσεν. Middle of sixth century.

Pithon kale. Beazley mentions six vases which he groups under the Antimenes Painter (*loc. cit.*), and quotes the plaque in Eleusis with " Euphiletos ......n," which he says is a generation earlier than the vases, and that the name is usually supposed to have been followed by ἐποίεσεν or ἔγραφσεν. This can hardly be the Euphiletos of the sepulchral monument, *I. G.*, I, 447, 40 (which dates after 446 and before 403), and the father of Charoiades (Kirchner, 15529), a strategos in 427-26 along with Laches (Thuk., III, 86, 1) when Athens sent twenty ships to Sicily.

It was a popular name: one Euphiletos was among the Hermokopids put to death [36] for mutilation of the Herms and profanation of the Eleusinian Mysteries. The name is mentioned frequently as the originator of the plan by Andokides,[37] but this event of 415 suggests that he was the grandson of our Euphiletos and participated in the event. The treasurer of the sacred moneys of Athena in 420/9 B. C. by this name [38] is probably the Hermokopid of 415.

Klein assumed that the *kale* on the vase now in New York referred to one of the ladies present, but, since the same feminization occurs undisputed on two other vases of the same period (*v.* Hippodamas and Pithon later; cf. also, p. 11, note 39), we are justified in accepting this interpretation of the Metropolitan Museum vase. It is very striking that all three cases of a derisive use of this formula concerned contemporaries. Hippodamas and Pithon are mentioned together on the same grave monument (*I. G.,* I, 433) as having fallen in the same year, while Euphiletos, appearing late on the black-figured stage, c. 500, must have been a contemporary " precious " γύννις. The year of the monument mentioned is 459/8 B. C.

It has been suggested that the adjective may be understood as a vocative (cf. Chase, *Harvard Studies in Classical Philology,* XVII, 1906, p. 148. Cf. sub Pithon), though this is un-

---

[36] *I. G.*, I, 274-7.
[37] *De Mysteriis*, 35, 51, 61, 62, and 64.
[38] *I. G.*, I, 170-3.

precedented. Much more probably it is an aesthete notorious for his elegance (note the ornate ephebe on the New York vase) or of Dorian habit. Aristophanes [39] ridicules Kleisthenes as a γυνή; Nero called his spouse Sporus " Sabina;" [40] Aristophanes [41] gives Amynia instead of Amynias and Sostrate instead of Sostratos, as Tacitus [42] speaks of Gaia Caesar; Suetonius (I, 49) speaks of Julius Caesar as " Bythinicam reginam." Cf. the *nom-de-guerre* of the *kinaidos* Euantete on the cup by the Ambrosios Painter *C. V. A. Oxford-Ashmolean*, fasc. 1, III I, pl. I, no. 6, and pl. V, nos. 5 and 6.

101. Eurymachos kalos.

Klein, 127, 2; Hoppin, *Handb. R. F.*, II, p. 418 (*C. V. A., Brit. Mus.*, fasc. 3, III I c, pl. 19, 2, signed by Smikros). Τεῦκρος ἐπὶ τοῖς Ἑρμαῖς ἐμήνυσεν . . . Εὐρύμαχον in 415 B. C. (Andok., I, 35).

102. Euryptolemos kalos.

Klein, 105. On three vases by Apollodoros (Beazley, *J. H. S.*, LIII, 1933, p. 70). We recommend the identification of the fair Euryptolemos with Kirchner's number 5984, Euryptolemos, the son of Peisianax of Alopeke. Plutarch (*Perikles*, 7) relates that Pericles: ἐν οἷς ἐπολιτεύσατο χρόνοις μακροῖς γενομένοις πρὸς μηδένα τῶν φίλων ἐπὶ δεῖπνον ἐλθεῖν, πλὴν Εὐρυπτολέμου τοῦ ἀνεψιοῦ γαμοῦντος ἄχρι τῶν σπονδῶν παραγενόμενος εὐθὺς ἐξανέστη. As he was almost an equal of Perikles, our Euryptolemos is probably not the one sent in 409 B. C. as legate to the Persian king (Xen., *Hell.*, I, 3, 12.13). This Euryptolemos of ours is from the famous line of the Alkmeonidae; cf. Alkmeon.

103. Euthymos kalos.

A red-figured skyphos, dated c. 470 B. C. (Graef-Langlotz, *Die Antiken Vasen von der Akropolis*, II, 2, no. 557, p. 50, pl. 41) has the inscriptions:

Εὔθυμος Ῥόδω καλ[ός]· Δέξιος.

---

[39] *Thesm.*, 235, 571.
[40] Cassius Dio, LXII, 13.
[41] *Clouds*, 678, 690.
[42] *Ann.*, VI, 5.

The publication reads καλ[ή] but καλ[ός] seems preferable. The name Euthymos is not in Kirchner.

Dexios here is definitely a personal name, and this occurrence helps solve an argument occasioned by such an inscription as the words Δέξιος Πάλος on a vase in the British Museum (*C. V. A.*, fasc. 3, III I c, pl. 3, 1a and 1b). The inscription on that vase is read as meaning, "the cast is propitious," on the assumption, doubtless, that Hoppin's statement (*Euthymides and His Fellows*, p. 127) is true; "We must either adopt this reading or else assume that Δέξιος καλός was intended, and the Γ written in error for K, which is unsatisfactory as there are no instances of Dexios as a proper name." But there are not only instances of Dexios as a proper name; Palos also is one (*v. sub nom.*), as we know from other vases. So it is perfectly possible that the British Museum amphora has a salute to both Dexios and Palos, or we can assume that Δέξιος καλός is meant. That Dexios was a very good proper name we know from inscriptions. The only one of these which, in point of time, could refer to the Dexios of vase-fame is *I. G.*, I, 446, a military list dating 425/4 B. C., where among the τοξόται, "bowmen," we find Δέξιος. Two sepulchral inscriptions of the fourth century (*I. G.*, II, 3590 and 3591) have the name Dexios. Lysias defended with a speech a man named Dexios (Bekker, *Anecdota Graeca*, 129; Harpokration, sub Στρομβιχίδης). Of the authenticity of Dexios as a proper name and as a person intended by the inscription on vases we can no longer doubt.

The third name on our vase, Rodon, is one of the few female favourites of the vase-painters. The name is listed by Klein, p. 44 (Beazley, *B. F.*, p. 41), but there it is found on black-figured vases.

103A. Ganymedes kalos.

Cf. Miss Richter, *Red-Figured Athenian Vases in the Metropolitan Museum*, p. 199, no. 159, pl. 158 (oinochoe of Meidias Painter, about 420-410 B. C.). Ganymede was "the most beautiful of all mortals," Homer, *Il.* XX, 233; but it is a new kalos name on vases.

104. Glaukon kalos.

Klein, pp. 154 ff., *Jb. Arch. I.*, II, 1887, p. 162; VII, 1892, p. 187; IX, 1894, pp. 59, 75; Beazley, *A. V.*, pp. 131, 133-4, 144, 260-1. Add to this a lekythos in Baltimore, *C. V. A., Robinson Coll.*, fasc. 1, III I e, pl. 39, 1. Glaukon, son of Leagros, was, like his father, a strategos in his mature years. In 433/2 he commanded at Korkyra, and fell there in the latter year (Thuk., I, 51). Three times his name is inscribed on vases along with his patronymic, in memory of his handsome and popular father (cf. lekythos in the Ashmolean Museum, *C. V. A., Oxford*, fasc. 1, pl. 38, no. 10). Some fifteen vases from the end of the career of Euphronios praise this aristocratic youth. The vases date 480-460 B. C., as the Nolan amphora in Amsterdam, 1403 (1754), by the Providence Painter (475 B. C.). Cf. *C. V. A. Musée Scheurleer*, fasc. 1, III I c, pl. 4, no. 4; Allard Pierson Museum, *Algemeene Gids*, 1937, p. 150. We assume that Glaukon was born c. the year 495, in which event Leagros, his father, must have married somewhere in his thirties, the usual age for the Greeks. Glaukon was also strategos at Samos in 441/0 B. C.; a complete list of the literary references to the two activities we know from his life is given in Pauly-Wissowa *s. v.* A vase in the British Museum (E 298) with a scene of a Nike and a tripod, has the inscriptions Ἀκαμαντὶς ἐνίκα φυλέ and Γλαύκων καλός (Klein, *L. I.*, p. 155). Cf. *C. V. A., Brit. Mus.*, fasc. 5, III I c, pl. 51, 1.

105. Glaukytes (*v.* sub Megakles).

106. Habrasia kallista.

A. J. P., XXIX, 1908, pp. 461 ff.; *Cl. Phil.*, XII, 1917, pp. 190-1. The name is found on a Rhodian vase in the Metropolitan Museum. Tarbell (*Cl. Phil., loc. cit.*) reads the inscription: καλλίστα γᾶς Ἀβρασία ὡς ἐμὶν δοκεῖ, and thinks that this is a woman's name compounded of ἀβρ- and Ἀσία, the second element a place name as in Ἀριστόκυπρος. Cf. Chapter II, note 73.

107. Hediste kale.

Klein, p. 128; *Arch. Anz.*, XI, 1896, p. 97, no. 37. In Boston.

107A. Hegeleos kalos.

Cf. Miss Richter, *Red-Figured Athenian Vases in the Metropolitan Museum*, p. 152, no. 118, pl. 119 (bell-krater of the Meletos Painter, about 460-450 B. C.). καλως Εγελεως is for καλὸς Ἡγέλεως. This is the only case of this kalos name. For a later Athenian of this name, cf. Kirchner, no. 6277.

107B. Hegesilla kale.

Cf. Beazley, *A. J. A.*, XXXIII, 1929, p. 363 (black-figured hydria in the British Museum, B 330). In *C. V. A., Brit. Mus.*, fasc. 6, III H e, pl. 88 (1931) the inscription is still wrongly read, Ἐ(ρ)έσιλ(λ)α καλή.

108. Heras kale.

Klein, p. 158; Beazley, *A. V.*, pp. 131, 277.

109. Hermogenes kalos.

Klein, p. 105. Beazley, *A. V.*, p. 203, 42 by Duris. See p. 11 above for the inscription. Kirchner 5123 is Hermogenes, son of Hipponikos; he was familiar with Sokrates (Xen., *Apol.*, 2; *Sym.*, I, 3). He was present at Sokrates' death (Plato, *Phaedo*, 59 b). He was the brother of Kallias (Plato, *Kratyl.* 391 c), and named among τοὺς ἐπιχωρίους (Plato, *Phaedo*, 59 b).

110. Hestiaios kalos.

This name is on a plate in Boston, acc. 13.193, attributed to Euthymides by Beazley, *A. V.*, p. 64, no. 13. A photograph is given by Beazley, *V. A.*, p. 31. Hoppin rejects the attribution and Beazley, who in 1918 (*V. A.*) admitted less confidence in attributing the work, in 1924 (*A. V.*) apparently accepted it with good faith, since this disputed plate is, in the later book, still among the elect. Kirchner, I, 5194, relates to a stele-inscription [43] of c. 460-446, concerning the sanctuary of Athena Nike, which is to be provided with a new door and a stone altar, according to the plans of the architect

---

[43] Dittenberger, *Syll.*[8], 911; Ἀρχ. Ἐφ., 1897, p. 177, pl. 11, illustrates name and inscription.

Kallikrates, one of the builders of the Parthenon and the μακρὸν τεῖχος to the Peiraieus. Hestiaios makes the suggestion that three men be selected from the Boule to present the plans of Kallikrates before it.

The vase, a plate with a scene of an ithyphallic Seilen running with a horn and a flute-case in his hands, dates in the decade from 510 to 500 B. C. The love-name is written in a semi-circle around the Seilen, and, referring as it does to a youth of fifteen or more years in, let us say, 510, would offer a memory, tinged with the faint Greek melancholy before the advance of years, to a seventy-five year old man offering his suggestions for a new sanctuary to Athena Nike in 450 B. C.

A son of Hestiaios is mentioned in a sepuchral monument,[44] c. 430: . . . τος 'Εστιαίου, to the son of Hestiaios.

111. Hiketes kalos.

Klein, 94, lists four red-figured vases with this name. Beazley, *A. V.*, 208-9; *C. V. A., Oxford*, fasc. 2, pl. 62, 6. It is a Sicilian name. Pape-Benseler gives several instances of its use. We know of a later Hiketas who, in the middle of the fourth century, aimed at making himself lord of Syracuse (Diod. Sic., XVI, 67-77; Plut., *Tim.*, 1-33), a tyrant of Syracuse by this name (Diod. Sic., XXI, 22, 32, 153), and a similarly named Pythagorean from Syracuse. The Hiketes on the vases of Douris may not have been of high class, as the name seems servile. Meleager, however, had praised a boy named Hiketas (*v.* no. 44, Chap. III) for his beauty.

112. Hilaros kalos.

Philippart, *Coll. de Céramique Grecque en Italie*, p. 5, 8, tome II, p. 78. The inscription is read by Patroni (*Cat. dei Vasi del Museo Campano*, 1902) as Ἴλαρος καλός. Pape-Benseler suggests *C. I. G.*, 276, a late Attic inscription, which has:

'Ακαμαντίδος Ἴλαρος 'Επαγάθου.

---

[44] *I. G.*, I, 445.

113. Hipparchos kalos.

Beazley, *A. V.*, pp. 25-6, 29, 37: ten vases by, or related to Epiktetos; Klein, 61. This love-name is an important one in matters of vase chronology, though not so reliable as the Leagros one, because of differences of opinion as to identification. Studniczka (*Jahrb.*, II, 1887, pp. 165 ff.) supposed that the Hipparchos praised for his beauty on Epiktetan bowls must be the tyrant of that name, for after the expulsion those Peisistratid names were " damnatae memoriae " and excluded from use till the time of Aristophanes. Euthymides forgets himself once and almost uses it (Klein, p. 79, no. 38; Neugebauer, *Führer durch das Antiquarium,* II, *Vasen,* p. 94, F 2180 in Berlin), but checks it to HIΓΓ+ΟϞ. Now Hipparchos was very popular in the Kerameikos, the section of the city in which the fame of the ephebes was born, both for his beauty and wanton exploits and as a patron of the arts incubated there. It is incredible, Studniczka says, that a potter should have had the audacity to glorify this name any time after the freedom. Klein has argued that this name does not disappear from Attic history after 514, for in 496 there was an archon of that name (Kirchner 7600). Thus to identify the favourite of 520-510 with the son of Peisistratos he finds preposterous, since all the later cups of Epiktetos on which he is celebrated would be compressed into too narrow an interval, otherwise a fifty-year old would be praised for the bloom of youth. In the *Jahrbuch* for 1929 (p. 175, note 3) Kraiker prefers to follow Pottier in identifying this name with the archon of 496/5 B. C. But Langlotz (*Zeitbestimmung,* 1920, pp. 54 ff.) advances most cogent reasons that the Hipparchos mentioned is the tyrant. He finds that the vases on which this name occurs are generally earlier than the early Euphronios period; now, if this period dates c. 510, Hipparchos vases can have appeared before the death of the tyrant in 514 B. C. His main point, it seems to us, comes when he proves that *kalos* does relate to men as well as to boys. (*v.* Chapter I.) He feels that literary references particularly point to the tyrant as being meant on the vases. Aristotle (*Ath. Pol.,* 18, 1) calls him παιδιώδης καὶ ἐρωτικὸς καὶ φιλόμουσος, and even in his later years his murder was motivated by an erotic adventure (cf. Thuk., VI, 54, 3, for the Harmodios and Aristogeiton episode). He was the one who called the poets Anakreon and Simonides (whose relation to this type of inscription we have already noted) to his court. Idomeneus (Athen., XII, 532 F) characterizes him as well as the Peisistratid period as occupied in εὑρεῖν θαλίας καὶ κώμους. To Langlotz even the vase in Copenhagen with a scene of a hermoglyph at work and inscribed "Hipparchos is fair" (Beazley, *V. A.*, p. 17, fig. 9 bis) is reminiscent of the tyrant's setting-up of herms with inscribed epigrams (Plato, *Hipparch.* 228 d) on the streets. The reclining, singing reveller on the interior of an Epiktetan cup (Hoppin, *Handbook R. F.*, I, p. 310) may be a portrait of the tyrant himself in his later years, when the hair on his temples was turning gray. In spite of his assurance that the Hipparchos on the older vases ought to be the tyrant, Langlotz, however, admits the difficulty over the later vases to be a real one, and in a work subsequent to his *Zeitbestimmung* (*Griechische Vasen in Wuerzburg*, 1932, p. 58, no. 310), in speaking of a vase dated c. 510 B. C. says: "The Hipparchos celebrated on many vases at the end of the sixth century, can be identical only with the archon of 495 B. C., on the latest vases with this name, especially here where the inscription reads: Ἵππαρχος ὁ παῖς καλὸς Δοροθέος." In fine, though Langlotz has proved that Hipparchos need not have been still a youth on the vases on which he is called "handsome," it is necessary to date all the vases with his name before 514 if it is the tyrant who is meant, or else to take the archon for our identification. Studniczka (*loc. cit.*, p. 166) admits that there were others of this name: the son of Charmos, Hipparchos, against whom ostracism was directed in January, 487 B. C. (*Hesperia*, II, 1933, p. 460 for one of the actual sherds; for his relation with the tyrants, cf. Androtion in Harpokration, *s. v.*; Plut., *Nikias*, 11; Arist., *Ath. Pol.* 22, 4; Lykourgos, *Ag. Leokrates*, 117); and the archon of 496/5 (Dionys., *Antiq.*, 6, 1). But as the youth of both these men would have to reach back into the period of the famous Hipparchos, son of Peisistratos, he sees no reason for preferring an identification with either of them to one with the tyrant. It is certainly a more attractive identification and one completely in the spirit of things to see in the fair Hipparchos, of before 514 at least, the tyrant's son. Miss Richter, *Red-Figured Athenian Vases,* pp. 11-12 calls attention to an alabastron in the Metropolitan Museum (*Handbook,* 1930, p. 140) with Ἵππαρχος καλὸς ναί, but thinks it is the archon of 495.

114. Hippodamas kale.

Pyxis fragment in Athens, Akropolis F 40; Beazley, *V. A.,* p. 106, no. 108; *J. H. S.,* XIV, 1894, p. 195, pl. 3, 2. Richards (*J. H. S., loc. cit.*) restores it as *kalos,* but Beazley (*B. S. A.,* XXIX, 1927-1928, p. 192, footnote 6) reads *kale* (*v.* sub Euphiletos, Pithon, and p. 11, note 39). This boy was popular in the work-shops of Makron and Douris (Makron writes his name with two " p "s, Douris has thrice two and thrice one); he is toasted on six cups by Douris, nos. 41, 43, 44, 54, 66, and 74 in Beazley, *A. V.,* pp. 203-205; on five vases by Makron (one of these signed by the painter; two of them by the potter Hieron, Beazley, pp. 211 and 216, nos. 4 and 83; the other two are unsigned, nos. 69 and 132 in *A. V.*). There is a sixth vase also with this name to be added to Makron's five others, an aryballos (*B. S. A., loc. cit.,* pl. IV) in Oxford. The boy who attracted all this notice is none other than the one painted [45] on the cup by Makron in Berlin, for the boy in the picture has the name written beside him without the *kalos* and one naturally takes it as the name of the boy.

The name on the pyxis fragment is written on the tainia and is illustrated in Graef's *Die Antiken Vasen von der Akropolis* (II, 2, pl. 43, p. 51, no. 560; cf. also p. 27, nos. 311-312). Kirchner I, 7611, mentions a Hippodamas of Erechtheis, strategos,[46] who fell in battle in the Athenian

---

[45] Wiener Vorlegeblätter, series A, pl. V; Hoppin, *Handb. R. F.,* II, p. 42.

[46] *I. G.,* I, 433, 93.

activities in 459/8 B. C. As a *pais kalos* he appears on vases from 500-480; assuming that he was fifteen to twenty-five years at this time, in the year of his death he would have been about fifty-five or sixty years, which is perfectly agreeable with conditions (Leagros was sixty or seventy when he fell, strategos, in 465; Perikles was seventy; Phokion, eighty). Hoppin, *Handb. R. F.*, II, p. 64, no. 16, shows groups of erast and eromenos on a vase in Munich (804) with his name.

The pyxis fragment by Makron dates c. 500. Now this name occurs also on vases from the late period of Douris [47] which can hardly date before 480-470 B. C. Thus a period of twenty to twenty-five years is covered by *Hippodamas kalos*. Langlotz sees in this a refutation of Hartwig's outworn "decade" theory and believes it is the same person on all these vases.

115. Hippokles I kalos.

Hippokles is called fair on an amphora in the style of Amasis (Graef-Langlotz, *op. cit.*, I, 2, no. 923, pl. 59). The name was very common, but the only instance, contemporary with black-figure, of any person known at the time of the vase's fabrication is the *Hippoklos* who was the tyrant of Lampsakos in the Hellespont, and to whose son, Aiantides, Hippias gave his daughter, Archedike, in marriage (Her., IV, 138; Thuk., VI, 59). Whether because of this alliance of power Hippokles became well-known in Athens and was praised on this vase for a political reason, or whether we must look elsewhere for the person mentioned in the inscription, is indeterminable, especially in view of the ending, os for es.

116. Hippokles II kalos.

A Hippokles appears much later, on Attic vases of the red-figured style in the last quarter of the fifth century, and Beazley (*V. A.*, p. 182; *A. J. A.*, XXXIII, 1929, p. 366, no. 11) identifies him with the person of this name who was one of the Ten Archons in 404 B. C. (Lys., XII, 55), and who

---

[47] Klein, *L. I.*, p. 104, fig. 27.

may be the same as Hippokles, son of Menippos, in charge of the ships from Sicily (Thuk., VIII, 13; Beloch, *Att. Polit.,* 310; Kirchner, 7620) in 413 B. C.

117. Hippokrates kalos.

On two vases listed by Klein, p. 46; *C. V. A., Br. Mus.,* fasc. 6, III H e, pl. 88, 3. Hippokrates, a contemporary of Leagros, has been identified by Studniczka (*Jahrb.,* II, 1887, p. 161) with the person of that name who was the brother of Kleisthenes and the father of the ostracized Megakles. He was a descendant of Alkmeon (Kirchner 7633). This may have been the Hippokrates, banished in 485 B. C., concerning whom two ostraka were found in the Athenian Agora (*Hesperia,* II, 1933, p. 460). The love-name appears on a bilingual amphora by the Menon Painter (Beazley, *A. V.,* p. 9, no. 2).

118. Hippokritos kallistos.

Klein, 49; Hoppin, *Handb. B. F.,* p. 114, nos. 2, 4; Neugebauer, *Führer durch das Antiquarium, Vasen, Berlin,* p. 68 (F 1799); Hoppin, *Handb. R. F.,* I, p. 372, no. 20, a red-figured kylix, E 21 in the British Museum, with this name. Hippokritos may have straddled the two styles.

119. Hippolochos kalos.

Klein, 102, an alabastron in Tarentum with the additional name, Diogenes kalos. Hippolochos of the phyle Aigeis was one of the Thirty in 404 (Xen., *Hell.* II, 3, 2).

120. Hippon (I) kalos.

Klein, 35, a black-figured vase mentioned in the *Auction Catalogue of the Castellani Collection,* I, p. 10, no. 58. Stylistic differences separate this from Hippon II.

121. Hippon (II) kalos.

Klein, 140; Beazley, *A. V.,* p. 130, 7 by Charmides Painter; p. 131, 3; p. 133, 15, and p. 135, 42-6 by Providence Painter. *I. G.,* I, 447, col. I, 61, is a grave-stone from the end of the fifth century with this name but our name must belong to about 480. Cf. Miss Richter, *Red-Figured Vases in the Metropolitan Museum*, pp. 53, 54, no. 31, pl. 30 (lekythos of Providence Painter); *C. V. A. Oxford*, fasc. I, III I, pl. 38, 5 (a lekythos by the Pan Painter).

122. Hippoteles kalos.

Klein, 50, a black-figured vase in Munich (10).

123. Hippoxenos kalos.

Klein, 141; Beazley, *A. V.*, p. 134. On one vase by the Providence Painter in Leningrad (701).

124. Hygiainon kalos (*v.* sub Diphilos).

Cf. Klein, pp. 167-168; Beazley, *A. V.*, pp. 377-378.

125. Iphis kale.

Klein, 168, a red-figured amphora in Pisareff collection.

126. Isarchos kalos.

Klein, 65; Beazley, *A. V.*, p. 48. An archon of the year 424/3 B. C. had this name (Diodoros, XII, 65).

127. Kalliades kalos.

The inscription Καλιάδες καλός· Γετάλε φεσί· Ἐρυδόρῳ is on a black-figured skyphos (Graef-Langlotz, *op. cit.*, II, 1498, pl. 93). Kalliades is called fair also on a Louvre piece (*C. V. A.*, fasc. 2, III I c, pl. 12, 8). For Kalliades cf. Kirchner 7773, an archon of the year 480/79 (Her., VIII, 51); 7775, a strategos at Arginusae in 406/5 (Diodoros, XIII, 101); 7776, a taxiarch in 405/4 (Lysias, XXX, 14). The first of these is preferable for identification with our Kalliades.

128. Kallias kalos (cf. p. 52, *s. v.* Autolykos).

Klein, 146; Beazley, *A. V.*, pp. 131, 137. Plato (*Protag.* 362) says: Καλλίᾳ τῷ καλῷ χαριζόμενος. He was the lover of Autolykos (*v. sub nom.*, Chapter III, no. 19). Cf. also the Kallias, son of Kalliades, who proposed the treaties with Rhegium and Leontini in 433/2 (*I. G.*, I², 51, 52), and who may be the same as this contemporary of Timoxenos and

Charmides, who is praised as fair on vases by the Nikon Painter. The son of Telokles, another Kallias, was one of those prosecuted for mutilating the herms. However the Kallias on vases is probably the son of Hipponikos.

According to Herakleides of Pontus (quoted by Athenaeus, 536 F, 537), "It was at the time when the Persians made their first expedition into Euboea, they say, that a man of Eretria named Diomnestos came into possession of the commanding officer's money." This Diomnestos remained in possession of the gold when the officer had died, but, when the Persian king sent another punitive expedition against Eretria, the survivors of Diomnestos had to send the fortune to Athens for safe-keeping with Hipponikos, the son of Kallias. When all the Eretrians were removed by the king to Ecbatana, the money was retained by Hipponikos and Kallias. A later Hipponikos, the grandson of the recipient of the money, requested of the Athenians permission to build a storehouse on the Akropolis for the fortune. He changed his mind, however, and Kallias (the third of the name, born c. 455 B. C.) became posesssor of the sum and lived for pleasure with it.

These three names, Hipponikos, Kallias, and Diomnestos are known on vases. On the Oxford vase, given under *Xanthes* in Chapter IV, the names of Hipponikos and Diomnestos occur. Is it not possible that these names on vases refer to the characters mentioned by Athenaeus? The invasions of the Persians referred to happened in 490 and 480 B. C. (Her., VI, 100 and VIII, 4), and so the generations of the family of Hipponikos involved in this story lived in Athens in the fifth century. Diomnestos is a rare name, and might very well have become known in Athens as the original owner of the fortune on which the Athenian family later lived. Kallias, the son of Hipponikos, is mentioned by Athenaeus (V, 187 f.; 216 d) as the lover of Autolykos, who is listed in Chapter III.

129. Kallides kalos.

Klein, 148; *C. V. A., Br. Mus.*, fasc. 5, III I c, pl. 50, no. 2. Wernicke (*op. cit.*, p. 70) reads the name as "Kallitheos," incorrectly.

130. Kallikles kalos.

Klein, 141; Beazley, *A. V.*, pp. 134, 471. *I. G.*, I, 446, col. I, 28, is a sepulchral monument of the year 425 B. C. with the name, Kallikles of Hippothontis.

130A. Kallikrates kalos.

Broad-bodied lekythos by the Diosphos Painter from Koropi, in Athens market. Incised inscription behind the chariot which faces to right. Cf. Haspels, *Attic Black-Figured Lekythoi*, 1936, p. 233, no. 16.

131. Kallipe kale.

Klein, 44; *Cat. of Vases in Br. Mus.*, III, B 330; *C. V. A. Brit. Mus.*, fasc. 6, III H e, pl. 88. Cf. Rodon.

132. Kallippos kalos.

Klein, 134, a hydria in Altenburg. *I. G.*, I (Suppl.), 446a, p. 108; a grave-stone which mentions a person with this name from the year 438, of the tribe Oineis.

133. Kallistanthe kale.

Klein, 50, a black-figured cup in Munich (36).

134. Kallisthenes kalos.

No. 69 in Tarentum, of which Professor Zahn writes us that he discovered the inscription more than 28 years ago on a severe red-figured vase, with a picture of a man muffled in a mantle; alongside of the figure is an almost obliterated vertical inscription, the last two letters of which are confused.

Possible identifications for Kallisthenes, neither of which, however, is very probable, are:

(1) Kirchner, 8092: *I. G.*, I, 443, col. 18, dating c. 430 B. C.: Kallisthenes of Aigeis.

(2) Kirchner, 8093: *I. G.*, I (Suppl.), 446, p. 109. This Kallisthenes died fighting under Alkibiades at the Hellespont.

135. Kallisto.

Klein, 104; Hoppin, *Handb. R. F.*, I, p. 132, 62, by the Brygos Painter; II, p. 192, 47, by the Meidias Painter.

136. Karton kalos.

Klein, 130; Beazley, *A. V.,* p. 156; *Cat. of Vases in the Br. Mus.,* III, p. 234, E 350, where it is suggested that Karton may be a variation of Kraton, as *karteros* is for *krateros; C. V. A. Brit. Mus.,* fasc. 3, III I c, pl. 18, by the Copenhagen Painter.

137. Karystios kalos (Moryllos, Smikrion kaloi).

A British Museum alabastron, acquired in 1900, and published by Murray (*Mélanges Perrot,* p. 252) with an illustration. The figures are opaque white on a black ground, and are two grooms exercising horses (precursors of certain parts of the west frieze of the Parthenon). The inscription is in one straight horizontal line at the top of the picture: καλὸς Καρύστιος Μόρυλος. Lower and separated from each other are Σμίκριον καλός. While many names to be thought of as those of "pretty boys" do not always have the adjective, it is improbable that three persons are meant, since only two figures appear in the scene, and there is no reason to doubt the connection here. Murray thinks that Karystios has a local significance or is an ethnikon derived from Karystos, a town of Euboia (though this vase was found at Eretria). It is very easy and very natural to understand the top line as a single inscription, a parallel for which is found in Klein, p. 161: Λίχας καλὸς Σάμιος (cf. Diphilos above; the ethnikon there has been disputed).

There is a black-figured amphora (*C. V. A., Br. Mus.,* fasc. 3, III H c, pl. 37, 2a and 2b) with a scene of Herakles and Apollo contesting for the Delphic tripod, Athena and Artemis in attendance; all four of the figures in the scene are named by the inscription. Between the legs of Apollo and Herakles is an inscription καλός . . . Κάρ, which the Corpus restores as "kalos Karystios."

Klein (*op. cit.,* p. 49: now in Petit Palais, Paris, Dutuit collection, no. 312) cites a black-figured hydria with painting on a white ground. Hermes and Maia are pictured; the inscription is καλὸς Καρύστιος. This vase and the foregoing are related to the style of Skythes.

The letters *kalos Kar* on the British Museum amphora are also suggestive of the Hermokopid inscription,[48] where among the effects of Kephisodoros confiscated is a *Kar pais* and a *Karikon paidion,* both being Karian slave-lads. The Karystios who is mentioned on the alabastron and the hydria was celebrated on vases dating from 515 to 505 B. C. The name is not found in Kirchner; nearest to it is *Karystonikos* of the tribe Kekropis (*Pros. Att.,* I, 8260) from a sepulchral monument of c. 438 B. C.

Smikrion may be the one mentioned in Kirchner, 12747, of the tribe Pandionis, on a grave-stone from the year 438. If he had been born c. 525, he would have lived to an age of eighty-seven by this time.

Moryllos (Pauly-Wissowa, *Real-Encycl.,* XVI, 326-327): the inhabitants of a part of Chalkidike are called Morylli by Pliny (*N. H.,* IV, 10, 17).

If we read with Murray, " Moryllos from Karystos is fair," there is still the difficulty of knowing how to take *Karystios* on the Paris black-figured hydria and the British Museum amphora, where, if it is an ethnic, no specific youth is mentioned. On the whole it is better to take Karystios as a proper name like Kolchos, Lydos, Sikelos, Skythes, Syrakosios, Thrax, etc.

138. Kephisios kalos.

Klein, 86; Neugebauer, *Führer durch das Antiquarium,* p. 87, 2273 (illustrated in Cook, *Zeus,* I, p. 216, fig. 159). A white-ground lekythos, supposed to be in the Museo Civico (1446), Bologna, and having this love-name is not yet given in the *C. V. A.*

I. G., I, 338, mentions a Kephisios who was prytanis in 408/7 B. C. from the tribe Erechtheis. *I. G.,* I (Suppl.), p. 111, 462 d, col. II, 24, is a grave-stone with this name; it dates around the end of the fifth century.

---

[48] *I. G.,* I, 277.

139. Kephisodoros kalos (*v. sub* Leagros, and cf. Chapter III, p. 58, no. 49).

139A. Kephisophon kalos.

Klein, 105; Beazley, *A. V.*, p. 166, no. 8 (*Cabinet des Médailles* in Paris, Hartwig, *Meisterschalen,* pls. 15, 16 with three other love-names, Leagros, Dorotheos and Olympiodoros). White-ground lekythos of little-lion shape in New York in the Gallatin collection representing a goddess mounting a chariot. Kephisophon and *pais kalos* retrograde. Cf. Haspels, *Attic Black-Figured Lekythoi,* 1936, pp. 117-118, 230 (by companion of Sappho and Diosphos Painters, 500-490 B. C.). *I. G.*, I, 124, 129, 130, 150, give a person of this name, who was γραμματεὺς ταμιῶν τῆς θεοῦ in 426/5 B. C. A Kephisophon was sent to Sparta with Meletos in 403 (Xen., *Hell.,* II, 4, 36). Kirchner 8416 mentions a Kephisophon who was γραμματεὺς τῆς βουλῆς in 403/2 B. C. *I. G.,* I, 448, col. I, 21, is a grave-stone which may record the death of one of these (or they may all be the same person) at the end of the fifth century.

140. Kineas kalos.

Klein, 59; Hoppin, *Handb. R. F.,* II, p. 260, no. 41, Louvre G 18. Early fifth century; contemporary with the fair Memnon on vases. Under *Phrinos kalos* are cited passages which mention a sumptuary decree, forbidding excessive elegance on the part of the Athenian ephebes; the decree was moved by Phrinos and Kineas. Phrinos appears on vases at just about the same time as this Kineas of ours, and it is an interesting possibility that both these favourites of the early fifth century, when age had deprived them of their beauty and popularity, peevishly declaimed against the ways of those younger than they and still enjoying the attentions that were once theirs. Cf. Phrinos below, p. 173.

141. Kleinias kalos.

Beazley, *A. V.,* p. 296, no. 3, by Alkimachos Painter; p. 372, nos. 4, 5, 10, and p. 375, no. 50 by the Achilles Painter on vases of the "Meletos group." Klein [49] chronicles five vases with the name *Klenias* or *Kleinias*, four of them Nolan amphorai, and described in Beazley's [50] article on "The Achilles Painter." There are two more vases, not in Klein: one formerly in the Rogers collection, also a Nolan amphora (Beazley, *A. V.*, p. 372, 5: a woman running with a jug and phiale, Κλινίας καλός): the other, a Syracuse lekythos, published in *J. H. S.*, XXXIV, 1914, p. 198, p 203, figure 20 (Artemis and a woman girding herself; inscription: Κλενίας καλὸς Γήδιος).

The Syracuse lekythos rather invalidates the attempt to relate Kleinias to the great Alkibiades (Kirchner, *Pros. Att.*, I, 8510). Kleinias, father of Alkibiades, fell at Koroneia in 447,[51] but this Kleinias is specifically introduced as "son of Pedieus" on the lekythos, and Beazley thinks it likely that all these vases reflect admiration for the same Kleinias. Pedieus, the father of Kleinias, was himself *kalos* on three vases [52] and may have been the archon of the year 449-448 B. C.[53] This would accord with the dates for Kleinias (Achilles Painter, 470-430), because, if we assume that Pedieus was about forty when he was archon in 449 and set his birth in 489, his marriage conjecturally at the age of thirty, Kleinias might have been born c. 459 and have flowered into a *pais kalos* in his fifteenth year in 444 B. C.

This Kleinias is probably the beloved of Kritoboulos;[54] Xenophon tells us what the quality of being *kalos* in one person inspired in another who looked at him. The Xenophon passage reads: " But if I am really fair, and if you feel what I feel when I look on Kleinias, I think that beauty is better worth having than all Persia. I would choose to be blind to

[49] *L. I.*, pp. 162 ff.
[50] *J. H. S.*, XXXIV, 1914, p. 195.
[51] Plut., *Alkib.*, 1; Plato, *Alkib.*, I, 112c.
[52] Klein, *L. I.*, pp. 68 ff.
[53] Diod., XII, 4; Kirchner, II, 11748.
[54] Xen., *Sym.*, IV, 10, 11, 12. Κλεινίαν ἥδιον θεῶμαι ἢ τἄλλα πάντα τὰ ἐν ἀνθρώποις καλά (i. e. τοὺς ἄλλους πάντας καλοὺς ἀνθρώπους).

everybody else if I could see Kleinias, and I hate the night because it robs me of his sight. I would rather be the slave of Kleinias than live without him; I would rather toil and suffer danger for his sake than live alone at ease and in safety; I would go through fire with him, as you would with me. In my soul I carry an image of him better made than any sculptor could fashion." And Kritoboulos, the speaker, was a newly-married man!

142. Kleitagoras kalos.

Klein, 86, one red-figured vase with the name of Labotos accompanying.

143. Kleitarchos kalos.

Klein, 34, a black-figured vase vase by Taleides; Hoppin, *Handb. B. F.*, p. 344, no. 6.

144. Kleobis kalos.

Klein, 38; a black-figured fragment from Naukratis (*Cat. of Vases in the Brit. Mus.*, II, p. 273, B 601-9).

145. Kleomelos kalos.

Klein, 87; Beazley, *A. V.*, p. 52, 2, by Epidromos Painter. Cf. Graef-Langlotz, *Vasen von der Akropolis,* II, p. 65, no. 703.

146. Kleophon kalos.

Klein, 130; Hoppin, *Handb. R. F.*, II, p. 134, no. 10. A person with this name is mentioned as a λυροποιός by Andokides (I, 146) and Aristotle (*Ath. Pol.*, XXVIII, 3); he became the demagogue cited by Diodoros (XIII, 53, 2). This same person, probably, is slandered as a *kinaidos* by Aristophanes (cf. scholiast to *Thesm.*, 805). Some of the other spoiled pleasure-boys, the παῖδες καλοί of Athens, passed from a brilliant youth to a licentious later career.

147. Kleophonia kale.

Klein, 135; one red-figured vase, fragments in Braunschweig, published once in the *Arch. Zeit.*, XXXIX, 1881, pl. 15.

147A. Korone kale.

Lekythos in Lyons (75), near the style of the Sappho Painter. Cf. Haspels, *Attic Black-Figured Lekythoi*, p. 229.

148. Krates kalos.

Klein, 90; Beazley, *A. V.*, pp. 42, 167. Diog. Laert., IV, 23, mentions a Krates who was a poet of the old comedy at Athens (c. 451/0 B. C.). Krates kalos is one of the early fifth century favourites, and it is chronologically possible that he later developed into the poet. Diodoros, XII, 35, cites an archon of this name from the year 434/3 B. C., and this identification, too, is possible.

149. Kritias kalos (cf. Ch. III, no. 54).

A black-figured hydria, British Museum B 323 (*C. V. A., Brit. Mus.*, fasc. 6, III H e, pl. 84, 3), belonging to the Leagros group of hydriai (Beazley, *Attic Black-Figure*, p. 44, no. 26), has this name. The vase is dated by Beazley in the last second or third decade of the sixth century. An interesting identification is possible with the Kritias (Kirchner, 8791) with whom Anakreon fell violently in love when he was visiting Athens in 522 B. C., just about the time when the handsome stripling was celebrated on our vase. This would put his birth sometime around the year 540. The "golden-haired" Kritias is rebuked in an extant poem of Solon for being fractious (Hudson-Williams, *Early Gk. Elegy*, p. 67, 22):

Εἰπέμεναι Κριτίῃ ξανθότριχι πατρὸς ἀκούειν.
οὐ γὰρ ἁμαρτινόῳ πείσεται ἡγεμόνι.

Plato (*Charmides*, 157 E) has Sokrates say to Charmides, who is the grandson of our Kritias, son of Dropides: ἥ τε γὰρ πατρῴα ὑμῖν οἰκία, Κριτίου τοῦ Δρωπίδου, καὶ ὑπ' Ἀνακρέοντος καὶ ὑπὸ Σόλωνος καὶ ὑπ' ἄλλων πολλῶν ποιητῶν ἐγκεκωμιασμένη παραδέδοται ἡμῖν, ὡς διαφέρουσα κάλλει τε καὶ ἀρετῇ καὶ τῇ ἄλλῃ λεγομένῃ εὐδαιμονίᾳ. The scholiast to Aischylos, *Prometheus*, 130 adds this: ὁ ῥυθμὸς Ἀνακρεόντειός ἐστι κεκλασμένος πρὸς τὸ θρηνητικόν.

ἐπεδήμησε γὰρ τῇ 'Αττικῇ Κριτίου ἐρῶν καὶ ἡρέσθη λίαν τοῖς μέλεσι τοῦ τραγικοῦ. Cf. Bowra, *Greek Lyric Poetry*, pp. 307-309.

In passing, it may be noted that good-looks seem to have run in the family. Charmides was even more famous than his grandfather, Kritias, and Charmides' maternal uncle, Pyrilampes, was known as the handsomest man in Greece (Plato, *Charm.*, 158 A). This Pyrilampes was named ὀρνιθοτρόφος, because of the peacocks which he brought from Persia. His son, Demos, was later the toast of the town and especially of Kallikles; in the *Gorgias* (481 D) of Plato, Sokrates says to Kallikles, " We two are in love, each with two persons; I with Alkibiades and Philosophy; you with Demos, the son of Pyrilampes, and Demos, the Athenian people." His father, Pyrilampes, had been a friend of Perikles; he himself was trierarch later, and received a golden goblet from the King of Persia for friendship. He was called the Athenian Apollo. The inscription, *Demos kalos*, on a fragment from Kertch with a palaistra scene (*Arch. Anz.*, IX, 1894, p. 181) probably refers to this popular Demos. Hesychius (on Aristophanes, *Wasps*, 97) assures us that the Demos mentioned in the passage was a person: Δῆμος, ὄνομα κύριον, τὴν ὥραν κάλλιστος. The lines of Aristophanes play on the sound of the name:

> καὶ νὴ Δί' ἦν ἴδῃ γέ που γεγραμμένον
> υἱὸν Πυριλάμπους ἐν θύρᾳ Δῆμον καλόν,
> ἰὼν παρέγραψε πλησίον: " Κημὸς καλός."

From this one family, then, four members were celebrated on Attic vases for their beauty: Antiphon, Kritias, Charmides, and Demos; and the fifth, Pyrilampes, found his way into literature. (For Antiphon, the father of Pyrilampes, cf. Antiphon kalos, p. 84, no. 30).

150. Kynippos kalos.

Klein, 52, a black-figured lekythos in Oxford (251), but not yet given in the *C. V. A.* Haspels, *Attic Black-Figured Lekythoi*, p. 161, by the Athena Painter. Cf. Philon kalos.

I. G., I, 450 is a grave-stone from the second half of the fifth century which mentions a Kynippos from the tribe Antiochis.

151. Labotos kalos.

Klein, 86. A contemporary of Kleitagoras on red-figured ware.

152. Laches kalos (*v.* sub Lysis).

Klein, 95; Beazley, *A. V.,* pp. 233-235. The name Lacheas occurs on a krater in Boston by the Tyszkiewicz Painter, *ibid.,* p. 113.

153. Ladamas kalos.

Klein, 123; Hoppin, *Handb. R. F.,* I, p. 442, no. 19; *C. V. A., Brit. Mus.,* fasc. 3, III I c, pl. 3 (an amphora, E 256, with the name of Phayllos also). Cf. Phayllos below.

154. Lampon kalos.

This is probably the father of our Olympiodoros. His beauty is celebrated on a vase too (Klein, 57; Hoppin, *Handb. R. F.,* II, p. 259, no. 34), along with Memnon and A(i)schion. Beazley attributes the vase to Oltos, whose activity lay between 530 and 510 B. C. The name Memnon limits the vase to the decade 520-510, so that this may well be the father of Olympiodoros of Plataia. Cf. Dorotheos, p. 102, no. 73.

155. Leagros kalos. (Cf. Glaukon above.)

Beazley, *A. V.,* pp. 54, 59-61, 166-7, 228, gives the red-figured vases praising the beauty of Leagros. Klein (*L. I.,* p. 70) has counted forty-five vases of the transition period inscribed with his name; of these seven are on black figure. Cf. also Graef-Langlotz, *Vasen von der Akropolis,* II, nos. 176, 211, 862; Haspels, *Attic Black-Figured Lekythoi,* p. 49; *L'Antiquité Classique,* V, 1936, p. 31; *C. V. A., Robinson Coll.,* fasc. 2, III I, pl. 5; *C. V. A. Louvre,* fasc. 1, III I c, pl. 1, 3; pl. 4, 3; pl. 5, 2; fasc. 5, III I c, pl. 27, 8. Leagros, the center of an extensive chain of ephebes celebrated on common vases (Olympiodoros, Athenodotos, Epidromos,

Antiphon, Lykos, Ainias, Chares, Antias, Hipparchos, and Kephisophon) is, because of a successful identification, responsible for one of our most reliable chronologies for the appearance of red-figured ware in Athens and for the early history of its development. There is no doubt that the Leagros of vases is the strategos who fell in battle while commanding a fleet in Thrace on the Athenian expedition against the Edons in 465 B. C. (Her., IX, 75; Thuk., I, 51, Schol. Aisch., II, 31; Paus., I, 29, 5). He was a συνέφηβος and ἡλικιώτης of Themistokles (VIII Letter; cf. Hercher, *Epist. Gr.*, p. 747), who was born in 525 B. C. From that information we conclude that Leagros too must have been born c. 525, because he could have been only one year older or younger than Themistokles; the ephebic years were only two, from the eighteenth to the twentieth year of the boy. He was, then, sixty years old when he fell. His beautiful youth must have excited Athens in the last quarter of the sixth century; from the age of seven to fifteen years he was technically a *pais*, from fifteen to eighteen a *mellephebos*, and from eighteen to twenty an *ephebe*. His twentieth year, on which he officially must have entered his young manhood and become a *neos*, occurred still within the sixth century. But the vases with his name extend far past this limit and from this Langlotz (*Zur Zeitbestimmung der strengrotfigurigen Vasenmalerei und der gleichzeitigen Plastik*, pp. 51-54) has proved that Hartwig's theory (*Meisterschalen*, p. 8) of the restriction of the period in which one was *kalos* to within ten years is wrong. Indeed, the picture of Leagros, queasily returning from a symposion (Klein, *L. I.*, p. 77, fig. 16) for which he is still garlanded, is certainly that of a paunchy, bearded man who has lost the lissom lines of his youth. Since Langlotz sees no reasonable objection why many of these pictures should not refer to the one praised in the inscription, and, if we believe that this particular one shows Leagros in his riper years (but still prominent in the city), Hartwig's assumptions are of little value. Langlotz cites vases to follow Leagros through every period of his life. He is still a *pais* on an amphora in Leningrad (*Mon. dell' Inst.*, II, 24) and on a vase in Paris (Beazley, *V. A.*, p. 30, fig. 14), but an *ephebe* of eighteen or nineteen on the Geryon cup (*F. R.*, pl. 22, our pl. I, 3). The period between these and the signed vases must have been slight, as on the Antaios vase (*F. R.*, pl. 93) he is still a youth. But on the Louvre cup (Hartwig, *Meisterschalen*, pl. 9) with Leagros returning sick from a symposion we see him in his twenty-fifth year, Langlotz thinks. The famous hetairai psykter (F. R., pl. 63), the style of which seems to be later, is proved to be so by Smikra's τὶν τάνδε λατάσσω, Λέαγρε. If he was the lover of so magnificent an hetaira, it must have been a mature Leagros celebrated on this vase. He has a full-grown beard on a cup in Brussels (*C. V. A.*, fasc. 1, III I c, pl. 4, 5), where he can be anywhere from thirty to fifty; certainly this cup belongs to his fifth century years. We add to Langlotz's review of scenes from Leagros' biography a kylix (*Cat. of Vases in Br. Mus.*, III, p. 386, E 816) on which Leagros is a *wrinkled* old man! In or around his fortieth year he must have dedicated a statue base, found during the excavations of the Athenian Agora in 1934 (*Hesperia*, V, 1936, p. 358, illustration on p. 359). The base has four holes, probably for a bronze statue, and an inscription, possibly in dactylic hexameter in bad meter such as often occurs in inscriptions (cf. Allen, " On Greek Versification in Inscriptions," in *Papers Amer. School of Cl. Studies at Athens*, IV, 1888, pp. 35-204) Λ]έαγ|ρος ἀνέ|θεκεν. Γλαύκ| ονος | δόδεκα | θεοῖσιν. Theta with a circle in the middle, as in this inscription, occurs in the Hekatompedon and Marathon inscriptions, so this inscription dates about the year 485 B. C.

According to the Leagros chronology thus offered, the invention of red-figure must have been developed in Athens about fifty years before the Persian destruction, with which the archaic period generally is held to close; this would date it c. 530 B. C., for Leagros was fair earlier than the destruction of Miletos in 491 B. C. Other finds do not gainsay this; in the common grave at Marathon (Langlotz, *op. cit.*, p. 39) one of the earliest objects is a sherd of the type of cup occurring in the later Leagros period.

The interesting Leagros krater signed by Euphronios (*C. V. A., Louvre*, fasc. 1, III I c, pl. 4) has several noteworthy love-names, not so common as most of the other names of the Leagros coterie. On the one side of the vase a youth mounts a bema to give a musical performance before three other youths; all the boys are friends of Leagros in a familiar scene from everyday life. The inscriptions are: Λέαγρος καλός, Πολυκλές, Κεφισόδορος, -λας καλός. The vase dates 510-500 B. C.

For possible identifications of Kephisodoros cf. Kirchner, 8337, *I. G.*, I, 432 frag. a33, ἀπέθανε ἐπὶ Σιδείῳ c. 465 B. C.; 8338, *I. G.*, I, 432 frag. b4, dating c. 465; 8355, *I. G.*, I, 433, col. II, 53, an Erechtheid grave-stone of 459/8 B. C.

A Polykles dedicated an Akropolis inscription, which dates around the end of the sixth century: Πολυκλῆς ἀνέθεκεν ὁ κναφεὺς τἀθεναίᾳ (Lolling, Κατάλογος, p. 11, no XXXVI). This is probably the same Polykles as the one whose decease is marked in *I. G.*, I, 433, col. II, 14, of the year 459/8 and the tribe Erechtheis.

An even more comprehensive collection of Leagros contemporaries is found on the Euphronios kylix (510-500 B. C.) in the Cabinet des Médailles at Paris (De Ridder, *Cat. des Vases Peints de la Bibliothèque Nationale*, pp. 392-393). In its present state only a few of these are visible, but this is due to reckless restoration, and fortunately the older publication, while the kylix was still in the Museo Etrusco (1645), is very reliable in its list of the inscriptions. The inscriptions, as they exist today, are given by Klein, *L. I.*, pp. 105-6; in the older, more complete condition of the vase the full inscriptions are published by Hartwig (*Meisterschalen*, pp. 132 ff.; pl. 15, 2, and pl. 16) and by Klein (*op. cit.*, p. 106). Owing to the restorations almost all of the figures have been lost. Hoppin (*Handb. R. F.*, p. 427) publishes a bibliography of the kylix. The inscriptions are spread among the many ephebes and trainers participating in a palaistra scene. Hartwig (*Meisterschalen*, p. 136) believes that none of these is a real kalos inscription, but that the names of favourite men, youths and boys were sprinkled around on the vase, one for each figure; the only love-names, he says, are those on the shields. His argument centers on whether we wish to consider the figures as portraits of the names, but the decision on this point does not in any way interfere with the fact that these favourite men, youths and boys were favoured because of their renown in the matter of pulchritude. All the names, whether accompanied by an actual adjective of praise or not, can be regarded as those of real, historical personages of the period, and Hauser's argument, given under *Phayllos kalos* (no. 219 below), is valid here: namely, that the word *kalos* standing once on a vase can go with all the names on that vase. So all the inscriptions on this vase are given here for the sake of greater familiarity with the popular and good-looking people of Leagros' day. On the interior is a scene of two pancratists with their paedotribe: the two inscriptions, belonging to the youthful athletes are Ἀσοποκλῆς and Ἀντίμαχος (for the latter, cf. Antimachos kalos, no. 27 above); the name of the director is Εὐένορ. The first group on the exterior is of two boys, Λέαγρος καλός and Φοῖνιξ, and their trainer Κλείβουλος. The second group is of two boxers, Κλέον and Τίμον, and their referee Εὐαγόρας. Then follow two groups of wrestlers; Ἐπιχάρες (known elsewhere to be a *pais kalos,* cf. Chares) and Ἐρατοσθένες, and Βάτραχος and Φόρμος; the trainer for these athletes is Κλείσοφος. An additional paedotribe is named Ἀνβρόσιος. Other names on the shields and scattered throughout the scene are: Ἀντίας, Κεφίσοφον καλός, Δορόθεος καλός, Βάτραχος, Ὀλυμπιόδορος καλός.

156. Leokrates kalos.

The hydria and the epigram to the "fair Leokrates," doubtless referring to the same person, indicate that the vase-makers may have borrowed their "best-sellers" from the poets (Klein, p. 43, for the vase, a black-figured one in Munich, 7846; for the verses, Bergk, *Poetae Lyrici Graeci,* III, p. 499, no. 150).

Leokrates, the son of Stroibos (for the father, also a *kalos,* cf. *Stroibos*), made a dedication, and on this it ran:

Στροίβου παῖ, τόδ' ἄγαλμα, Λεώκρατες, εὖτ' ἀνέθηκας
Ἑρμῇ, καλλικόμους οὐκ ἔλαθες Χάριτας,
οὐδ' Ἀκαδήμειαν πολυγαθέα, τῆς ἐν ἀγοστῷ
σὴν εὐεργεσίην τῷ προσιόντι λέγω.

This may well be the Leokrates, son of Stroibos, who was a colleague of Aristeides at Plataia (Thuk., I, 105, 2; Diod., XI, 78, 5; Plut., *Aristeid.* 20) in 479, and a "strategos" again in 459/8 against the Aeginetans. (Tonks, *A. J. A.*, IX, 1905, p. 290, makes the identification.)

157. Lichas kalos (*v.* sub Diphilos, pp. 100-101 above;

Klein, 160; Beazley, *A. V.*, pp. 227, 477).

158. Liteus kalos.

Klein, 153. One red-figured vase, a lekythos in the Museo Nazionale, Palermo.

159. Lyandros kalos.

Klein, 157. On a red-figured vase, a lekythos in the Museo Civico, Bologna, though it is not yet published in the *C. V. A.* Cf. Pellegrini, *Cat.*, 1900, p .50, no. 297. It is found a second time on a kylix in Florence dating 460-450 B. C. For bibliography cf. Philippart, *L'Antiquité Classique*, V, 1936, pp. 69-71.

160. Lykis kalos.

Klein, 51. One black-figured vase in the Hermitage, Leningrad, 216.

161. Lykos I kalos.

Klein, 51: black-figure. Cf. Chapter II, p. 33 for Lykos, beloved of the poet Alkaios.

162. Lykos II kalos.

Klein, 111; Beazley, *A. V.*, p. 172, 2 and 3 by Onesimos; p. 232, 27 and 33 in "Antiphon group"; p. 235, 77. Kirchner

9245 refers to Lykos Sterieus, father of Thrasyboulos, at the end of the fifth century. Cf. Lysis. Cf. also *C. V. A., Louvre*, fasc. 1, III I c, pl. 6, 9; pl. 12, 3.

163. Lysikles kalos.

There is only one occurrence in Klein (p. 88) of this name; it is on a pyxis in Athens. Cf. also Heydemann, *Gr. Vasenbilder*, pl. IV, 2; Klein *Euphronios*[2], p. 313. It is also found on another pyxis (about 510 B. C.) in New York (*Bull. Met. Mus.*, May, 1925, p. 132; Beazley, *B. S. R.*, XI, 1929, pp. 16-17, note 3). It is now published by Miss Richter (*Red-Figured Vases in the Metropolitan Museum*, p. 19, no. 4, pl. 9). The name is there spelt Lisikles. Beazley thinks that the Metropolitan vase is by Epiktetos; certainly it is of the ripe archaic style. The scene shows a satyr sitting on his haunches; it and the inscription are on the lid of the pyxis.

Lysikles may be identified with the demagogue who became the first man of Athens upon the death of Perikles by marrying Aspasia (Kirchner, II, 9417). Plutarch (*Perikles*, 24) says that he was a sheep dealer and a man of low birth. The historian Thukydides says that he was made a commander of a squadron of revenue-collecting triremes, ἀργυρολόγους ναῦς and fell in battle with the Karians, near the river Maiandros about a year after the death of Perikles (Thuk., III, 19). Plutarch quotes a statement of Aischines that by means of his connection with Aspasia he managed ἐξ ἀγεννοῦς καὶ ταπεινοῦ τὴν φύσιν 'Αθηναίων γενέσθαι πρῶτον. But this is impossible; his civic career must have been completed before he married Aspasia; though possibly it may have been due to her influence that he obtained command of the revenue expedition in which he met his death, ἐπιθεμένων τῶν Καρῶν καὶ 'Αναιτῶν αὐτός τε διαφθείρεται (Thuk., III, 19). Rogers' note to Aristophanes, *Knights*, 765 says that Kleon was accustomed to call himself the foremost statesman of Athens μετὰ Περικλέα καὶ Κίμωνα καὶ Θεμιστοκλέα, and that Aristophanes parodies this vaunt by substituting a demagogue and two courtesans, so βέλτιστος ἀνὴρ μετὰ Λυσικλέα καὶ Κίνναν καὶ Σαλαβακχώ.

Kirchner, I, 9417, thinks that this may be the man who moved the decree concerning a temple of an unknown god, Zeus Soter, in *I. G.*, I, 68. The inscription dates shortly after 446, and deals with decorating and repairing the temple.

164. Lysippides kalos.

Beazley, *B. F.*, pp. 39, 41. *C. V. A., Br Mus*, III H e, fasc. 4, pl. 49, 3a and b, black-figured amphora; also fasc. 6, III H e, pl. 92, 3, where are the names of Lysippides and Rodon.

165. Lysis kalos.

Beazley, *A. V.*, p. 228, 15, 16; p. 229, 21 (attributed to Colmar Painter); p. 260, 11 (Pistoxenos Painter). Cf. also Graef-Langlotz, *Vasen von der Akropolis,* II, no. 287. In Harrow-on-the-Hill School Museum is a kylix with ephebes, and on the stele is the inscription ΛVΣIΣ KALOΣ. This is mentioned by Philippart, *Collections de Céramique Grecque en Angleterre* (*l'Antiquité Classique,* IV, 1935, p. 215). Twelve vases (Beazley, *A. V.*, pp. 231-235) have been ascribed to a painter known only through the name he found " fair," the Lysis Painter. Lysis is probably identical with the pupil of Sokrates known to us through the dialogue of that name by Plato. On vases of the middle decades of the fifth century there are many names from the Platonic circles: Lysis, Laches, Charmides, Kallias, Alkibiades, etc. Vases with the compliment to Lysis belong to the early period of this master, whose style is related to the later works of Douris, though that painter never praised this youth. (The Lysis Painter's figures are more compact than those of Douris; sometimes they seem squat and heavy. The painter also shows a quick mind and a predilection for diversity; seldom does the same object appear on all sides of a vase.) Hoppin finds a whole series of vases with the love-names of Lykos, Lysis, and Laches so very homogeneous as to preclude attempts at separating them, and Beazley (*A. V., loc. cit.*) prefers to call them the "Antiphon group."

For Lykos [55] Langlotz (*op. cit.*, p. 43) finds a celebration on vases throughout a period of fully twenty-five years separating an unsigned Euphronios krater (Beazley, *A. V.*, p. 61, 1) from the later Dresden cup by the " Pferdemeister " (*Arch. Anz.*, XIII, 1898, p. 135). During this interval he is praised on other cups such as that of Onesimos (Hartwig, *Meisterschalen,* pl. 53; Beazley, *A. V.*, 172, 2 and 3) and a hydria in Boston (*Annual Report,* 1898, p. 71, no. 45), so that two bearers of the same name are improbable. Seven vases from the " Antiphon group " have this name too.

Charmides and Lysis belong to a type of young man like Phaidros. Modest and retiring (Plato, *Lysis*, 207), prone to blush when disconcerted (Plato, *Charmides,* 158 C), rich and aristocratic (*Charmides,* 157 E, 158; *Lysis*, 205 C), beautiful in form and pure in heart (*Charmides,* 157d; *Lysis*, 207), their fresh and very buoyant dispositions enliven the pages of Plato with their grace.[56] Charmides had also some skill in poetry and was athletic enough to train for the Nemean games,[57] and he may have lost his fortune in sports, as he jokes about his poverty.[58] Sokrates urged him to enter public life [59] to overcome a timidity which continued even into manhood. When he did this, it was in the aristocratic party; he was made one of the committee of Ten who ruled the Peiraieus under the Thirty and was slain with Kritias while defending the cause [60] in 403, ἀπέθανον . . . τῶν δὲ ἐν Πειραιεῖ δέκα ἀρχόντων Χαρμίδης ὁ Γλαύκωνος.[61] Of the twenty vases Klein [62] chronicles with the name Charmides, the last several have the symbolical Eros in flight mentioned earlier.

---

[55] Klein, *L. I.*, p. 111.

[56] Xenophon, *Sym.*, VIII, 2, says of Charmides: Χαρμίδην δὲ τόνδε οἶδα πολλοὺς μὲν ἐραστὰς κτησάμενον. Here Hesychius says ἐραστής = φίλος.

[57] Plato, *Theages*, 128 E.   [59] *Mem.*, III, 7.
[58] Xen., *Sym.*, IV, 30 ff.   [60] Xen., *Hell.*, II, 4, 19.

[61] In battle at Munychia; cf. Kirchner, *Pros. Att.*, II, 15512, where all literary references to him are collected.

[62] *L. I.*, p. 142. Cf. sub Charmides above.

Lysis [63] is younger than his companions, and his conversation is full of boyish frankness and naïveté. His frequent oaths and his mischievous desire to see his saucy cousin discomfited are evidences of his youth. We know nothing further of Lysis or of Hippothales, his sentimental lover, who wearies his friends with his poems and eulogies. The end of this charming life may be marked by the inscription containing lists of members of the Attic tribes who died sometime between 446 and 403.[64]

Laches [65] was a leader of the aristocratic party and had great influence in the state; we know that a Laches led an expedition to Sicily in 427 B. C., when the Athenians undertook to aid the people of Leontini,[66] served as a hoplite at Delion, where he is mentioned along with Sokrates on the retreat from territory disputed by the Athenians and Boeotians in 424; "I particularly observed how superior he (Sokrates) was to Laches in presence of mind." [67] This Laches was also associated with Nikias in negotiating the peace of 421,[68] and fell at Mantineia in 413 B. C., along with Nikostratos (cf. no. 202 below), another strategos (*Thuk.*, V, 61, 74). If the Laches identification is correct, this Nikostratos may be the one on vases, as he appears on a vase with Laches in Boston (Hartwig, *Meisterschalen*, p. 567). But Hartwig doubts (*op. cit.*, p. 568) this identification of Laches on the ground that he and Nikostratos must have been 40 years of age when strategoi in 427 B. C.; therefore, he says, they must have been born between 470 and 465, and so would have been " paides kaloi " around the year 450. But the vase in question is of an earlier date, and he considers the identification not tenable. However, strategoi need not have been 40 years old, as we know that Alkibiades was only 32

---

[63] *L. I.*, p. 113.

[64] *I. G.*, I, 447, col. 1, 12.

[65] Klein, *L. I.*, p. 95; Beazley, *A. V.*, pp. 233-5, seven vases from "Antiphon group."

[66] Thuk., III, 90, 103, 115.

[67] Plato, *Sym.*, 221 A.   [68] Thuk., V, 43.

(cf. no. 13 above), so that Hartwig's objection becomes no better than the suggested identification. Kirchner, *Pros. Att.,* II, 9019 (Laches, son of Melanopos), collects all references to this name; we know that he was older than Sokrates,[69] hence born before 469.

In answer to a question of Sokrates at the opening of Plato's *Charmides* frequenters of the palaistra tell him that he will soon see the most beautiful boy in Athens.[70] "All the world seemed to be enamoured of him; amazement and confusion reigned when he entered; and a troop of lovers followed him. That grown-up men like ourselves should have been affected in this way was not surprising, but I observed that there was the same feeling among the boys; all of them, down to the very least child, turned and looked at him as if he had been a statue." Then comes the amazing picture of "everyone pushing with might and main at his neighbor to make a place for him next to themselves, until at the two ends of the row one had to get up and the other was rolled over sideways." And then he "caught sight of the inwards of his garment and took the flame."

In just such a scene Lysis is "standing with the other boys and youths, having a crown upon his head, like a fair vision, and not less worthy of praise for his goodness than for his beauty."[71]

These scenes are all in the palaistra, that incubus of these philosophic loves, of which Cicero says:[72] "Mihi quidem haec in Graecorum gymnasiis nata consuetudo videtur: in quibus isti liberi et concessi sunt amores."

166. Marikados, probably a genitive of Marikas.

The name, Marikados, appears on the bottom of a skyphos, published by Graef-Langlotz (*Die Antiken Vasen von der Akropolis,* II, 3, 1512, p. 127). Graef includes it under the *Lieblingsnamen* in the *Inschriften-Register* at the end of his text, but in the text itself it is classed under *Besitzerin-*

---

[69] Plato, *Laches,* 186 C.
[70] Jowett, transl., 154-5.
[71] *Lysis,* 207.
[72] *Tusc. Disp.,* IV, 70.

schriften, as indeed the genitive case in which the name appears would suggest. Under *Marikas* Pape-Benseler (*Griechische Eigennamen*) says that Μαρικᾶς is a barbaric word which signifies a lewd man or a *kinaidos* (according to Hesychius). Under this name Eupolis attacked Hyperbolos. The statement of Hesychius, Μαρικᾶν, κίναιδον, οἱ δὲ ὑποκόρισμα παιδίου ἄρρενος βαρβαρικοῦ, is appropriate to Hyperbolos on account of his supposed foreign origin (Schol. Aristoph. *Wasps,* 1007). The word is of barbarous, probably Persian source, but has an Attic termination. Zielinski (*Quaest. Com.,* pp. 41 ff.) suggests that Marikas was an actor, one of the *Phallophoroi,* and for its obscene sense compares Hesychius' βάρυκα. αἰδοῖον παρὰ Ταραντίνοις (Kaibel, *Comicorum Graecorum Fragmenta,* p. 206, no. 86) whence he emends the gloss of Hesychius: ἄρρενος ἀπὸ τοῦ μορίου τοῦ μαρικοῦ (= phalli). Aristophanes, *Clouds,* 553 (Starkie), says: "But my rivals, if once Hyperbolos has given them a hold, never cease pulling the rim out of (κολετρῶσ' = " trample on ") the poor wretch, him and his mother too. Eupolis first and foremost, having damnably mauled my 'Knights,' dragged upon the boards his 'Marikas.' " The *Marikas* of Eupolis was played in 420 B. C., while Hyperbolos was still living. Of Hyperbolos' reputation Plutarch (*Alkib.* 13, 3) says: ἦν δέ τις Ὑπέρβολος . . . οὗ μέμνηται μὲν ὡς ἀνθρώπου πονηροῦ καὶ Θουκυδίδης. He was the leading demagogue after Kleon's death, and Thukydides (VIII 73) too speaks badly of him: μοχθηρὸν ἄνθρωπον, ὠστρακισμένον οὐ διὰ δυνάμεως καὶ ἀξιώματος φόβον ἀλλὰ διὰ πονηρίαν καὶ αἰσχύνην τῆς πόλεως. The name is very rare, apart from this known instance and literary reference. Surely it is permissible to connect the name on the vase with these references.

167. Megakles I kalos (Glaukytes kalos).

These names are on an Akropolis pinax: Graef-Langlotz, *op. cit.,* II, 1037; Jones, *J. H. S.,* XII, 1891, p. 380; Casson, *Cat. of the Akropolis Museum,* II, p. 306; *Jahrb.,* II, 1887, p. 229 (Winter); Ἀρχ. Ἐφ., 1887, p. 115 (Benndorf); *Jahrb.,* II, 1887, pp. 149-161 (Studniczka).

The painting is done by an artist of the Epiktetan cycle, and probably dates from early decades of the fifth century. The manner of wearing the chlamys around the hips is a favourite style shortly before 500 B. C.

Casson says, " The inscription is of the usual kalos type found on vases, but the name inscribed to the left of the warrior's helmet hȧs been partially obliterated and a new name has been inscribed, some of the letters of the old name being used in the new name. This second inscription has, in turn, been partially erased."

First: Μεγα.λ.ς
Second: Γλα.υ.ες

Hoppin (*Euthymides and His Fellows*, p. 90) attributes the pinax to Euthymides. On page 91 he says: " The Akropolis pinax is certainly a work of some artist of the Epiktetan cycle whether vase-painter or not. Further, the use of the name Megakles narrows the execution of the pinax down to the first decade of the fifth century, and Phintias and Euthymides are the only vase painters who have used that name. As far as the style of the figure is concerned, it shows certain resemblances to the work of both artists. The warrior is to all intents a duplicate of that on E 14 (kylix Berlin 2304, Hoppin, *op. cit.*, p. 82, fig. 14), especially for the helmet and the drapery, as was pointed out by Benndorf. Further, the shield device is a duplicate of that on the shield of Thorykion on E 11 (Vienna pelike, *Id.* p. 77). In view of these facts it is certainly easier to consider Euthymides as the artist than not."

This Megakles I of vase fame (*Klein, L. I.*, p. 120; Beazley, *A. V.*, pp. 58, 64) is the friend of Kallias and Simonides and the patron of Pindar, the Megakles of Alopeke mentioned by Pindar in the seventh Pythian ode (486 B. C.). Studniczka identifies him with the son of Hippokrates, uncle of Perikles and grandfather of Alkibiades (Kirchner, *Pros. Att.*, II, 9695). Aristotle (*Ath. Pol.*, XXII, 5) says that he was ostracized in the archonship of Telesinos, 486 B. C. It is probably the same Megakles who appears on vases by Phintias and Euthymides. Many vase painters were attached to particular, wealthy houses; that Euthymides was patronized by the Alkmaionids may be shown in the crab (the emblem of that house) on the shield of the young soldier on the amphora of Euthymides in the British Museum (Beazley, *A. V.,* p. 65; Hoppin, *Euthymides,* pl. VIII; Bowra, *Greek Lyric Poetry,* p. 422, n. 1). Miss Swindler (*Ancient Painting,* pp. 153-4) dates the Akropolis pinax in the end of the sixth century, and Buschor too connects it with the Megakles banished in 486 and worthy of this praise some twenty-five years earlier. The sherd with the ostracism is pictured in Benndorf, *Gr. und Sic. Vasenb.,* pl. XXIX, 10, p. 50. Three additional sherds with votes against him were found in the Athenian Agora (*Hesperia,* II, 1933, p. 460), and several more in 1935. The name Glaukytes, the name superimposed on the erasure of Megakles, occurs as the name of a potter on vases in Berlin and London (Furtwaengler, *Beschreibung,* 1761; Hoppin, *Handb. B. F.,* pp. 113-117). But the potter can scarcely be the one on the pinax celebrated for his beauty, as the substitution of this *kalos* name for the earlier one ought not to have occurred before it was necessitated by the banishment of 486. The nearest we can come to an identification of this Glaukytes is in Kirchner 2951 (all instances in Kirchner spelled Glauketes), a strategos at Samos in 441/0 B. C. (*F. H. G.,* IV, 645; Schol. Aristid., III, 485 Ddf.), which would accord chronologically. Kirchner 2944 quotes a Glauketes celebrated as a glutton by Aristophanes (*Peace,* 1008, *Thesm.,* 1033).

168. Megakles II kalos.

Klein, 130; Beazley, *A. V.,* p. 420; *C. V. A. Louvre,* fasc. 4, III I d, pl. 23, 9. He appears on the same vases as Smikythos, Kleophon, and Philon. He is probably the same as the Megakles in Kirchner, 9697: Megakles, son of Megakles of Alopeke (*I. G.,* I, 122, 123, 149). In 436 he won in the charriot race at Olympia (Schollast to Pindar, *Pyth.,* VII).

The inscriptions mention him as the secretary of the treasures of the goddess in 428/7 B. C. That the expulsion of the Alkmaionidai, to which line our Megakles belonged, was not a lasting one, we know from Thukydides, I, 126, 12: καὶ τὸ γένος αὐτῶν ἔστιν ἔτι ἐν τῇ πόλει.

169. Meletos kalos.

Klein, 167; Beazley, *A. V.*, p. 372, 9, by Achilles Painter. Pausanias the periegete tells (I, 30) the love-story of Meletos and Timagoras, a story very popular in Athenian tradition. Timagoras, it seems, was a foreign potter at work in Athens; he was the "pursuer" of the young Meles (or Meletos according to Suidas, *s. v.*), who, rejecting his suit, bade him cast himself from the Akropolis rock; when Timagoras had complied out of his love, the wilful youth was so seized with remorse that he leaped from the same rock. Timagoras, the potter, is to be identified with the suicide who was a foreign resident of Athens (Seltman, *B. S. A.*, XXVI, 1923-25, p. 101). "The potter, it would seem, affected the vices which were fashionable in the tyrant's court, and it is possible to conceive of him as first the admirer of the youthful Andokides, perhaps another 'metoikos,' and later, as he rose in the social scale, seeking the favour of Meles, a young Athenian noble at whose behest he met his end" (Seltman, *loc. cit.*, p. 103). The Andokides referred to is the one on a blackfigured hydria of Timagoras (Hoppin, *Handb. B. F.*, p. 358; *Wiener Vorlegeblätter,* 1889, Taf. V, 3) with the inscription: Ἀνδοκίδες καλὸς δοκεῖ Τιμαγόρᾳ. Suidas (sub *Meletos*) reverses the positions of the characters: Meletos becomes the pursuer and Timagoras, the fair pursued. Changing the tale, he goes on to say that the petulant youth, repenting his judgment, took in his arms two singing birds, presents which the "metoikos" had given him, ran in the other's tracks, and hurled himself too from the Akropolis; and that, on that very spot, people set up a statue of a beautiful naked youth, holding two pedigreed cocks in his arms, in memory of the tragedy. Seltman says that the tale later became linked with the altar of Anteros (Love-Returned), and that the statue on the

Akropolis of a handsome boy holding a pair of cocks was not of Meles, as Suidas would suggest, but of Eros. In any case, " the tragic death of so prominent and so prosperous a tradesman, and the sequel of the favorite's suicide, so greatly impressed the Athenian imagination that it became for all time one of the stock stories concerning the Akropolis." (Seltman, *loc. cit.*).

The names, according to Pausanias, probably in the correct position there, can be identified with persons known to us from vase inscriptions. Timagoras, the potter and later the suicide, was a contemporary of Exekias, whose pupil and younger contemporary was Andokides, hence his floruit was 550-520 B. C. This ties in with the chronology of the Suidas story; the altar of Anteros Seltman identifies with the altar to Eros, erected between 546 and 510 B. C. by an Athenian noble, Charmos, father-in-law of the tyrant Hippias (Kleidemos, in Müller, *F. H. G.*, I, p. 364, 20; quoted by Athenaeus XIII, 609 d). The altar, set up at the entrance to the Academy, had a statue and an inscription running:

ποικιλομήχαν' Ἔρως, σοὶ τόνδ' ἱδρύσατο βωμὸν
Χάρμος ἐπὶ σκιεροῖς τέρμασι γυμνασίου.

Timagoras, a potter (some have taken the name to be feminine, Τιμαγόρα) is also the dedicator of the Akropolis inscription (Lolling, Κατάλογος, p. 12, no. XLII): Τιμαγόρα μ' ἀ[ν]έθεκεν τἀθεναίαι. Andokides is the co-dedicator along with the potter, Mnesiades, of the offering, *I. G.*, I, Suppl., p. 101, no. 373[215]. Another Meletos appears much later, on vases by the Achilles Painter, as a love name on Attic vases (Klein, 167, from the first half of the fifth century). A Meletos was indicted by Andromachos for the profanation of the mysteries in 415 B. C. (Andok., I, 12, 13) and by Teukros for mutilating the herms (Andok., I, 35, 63). Many of our *kalos* names were connected with this event, as we have seen. This same Meletos was sent to Sparta with Kephisophon in 403 to make peace (Xen., *Hell.*, II, 4, 36). Another Meletos is mentioned by Athenaeus (XIII, 605 e) as a tragic poet. This Meletos was the father of the Meletos who in 399 B. C. was the accuser of Sokrates. The Meletos of the legend given above may well have been an ancestor of this Meletos of vase-fame.

170. Melieus kalos.

Klein, 129; Hoppin, *Handb. R. F.*, I, p. 451, no. 5. One red-figured vase.

171. Melitta or Melete kale.

Klein, 135; Hoppin, *Handb. R. F.*, I, p. 345, 1, by Painter of Eretria Epinetron; I, p. 372, 22, attributed to Euergides; II, p. 95, 42, by Makron; II, p. 153, 2, by Kodros Painter; II, p. 192, 47, by Meidias; *J. H. S.*, XIV, 1894, p. 194; *C. V. A.*, *Bologna, Museo Civico*, fasc. 1, III I c, pl. 19, B.

172. Memnon kalos.

On page 54 of Klein's work are listed thirty-five vases with this name (Beazley, *A. V.*, pp. 12-17). Nearly all of them are by the hand of Oltos, who worked for Euxitheos and Pamphaios. This is the name of the legendary hero in Homer famed for his beauty. Murray (*Designs from Greek Vases*, p. 6) regards it as "highly improbable that any family in Athens would have adopted this name for one of its sons." Of its significance Walters (*Br. Mus. Cat. of Vases*, vol. II, pp. 45-46, Introd.) says: "*Kalos* inscriptions in many cases refer to certain popular characters of the day. . . . At the same time the frequent recurrence of 'Memnon kalos' reminds us of the line of the Odyssey where Memnon is cited as a type of the highest beauty, and suggests that the idea of personal beauty was generally associated with these names." The line from the Odyssey is from Book XI, 522: κεῖνον δὴ κάλλιστον ἴδον μετὰ Μέμνονα δῖον. It is probable, therefore, that this Memnon was simply a favourite character from their past for the Greek vase-makers. There was no objection to it in the lower classes as a name for a son, however, or among slaves. The grosser comic poets mention a Memnon associated with Panaitios and Hippokrates, calling all three "sons of pigs." The name is also used to popularize the vases of Chelis and Chachrylion; it must belong to the earliest wares in the new technique. If it belongs to an Athenian of the great age, it must refer to one who passed his ephebic years c. 520-510. He was a contemporary of Leagros. Cf. also Graef-Langlotz, *Vasen von der Akropolis,* II, 44.

173. Menandros kalos.

Stamnos. Louvre, N 3413. Severe style III I c, first half of fifth century. *C. V. A., Louvre,* fasc. I, group pl. 6, nos. 1 and 4. (A) Women pouring a libation into a phiale held by a young hoplite accompanied by a dog; inscription Menandros kalos. (B) A Seilen with an oinochoe approaches Dionysos who holds a kantharos and a large vine-shoot.

Kirchner, *Prosopographia Attica,* II, 9856: in a list of seven treasurers on an Akropolis inscription dealing with expenses for the chryselephantine statue of the Athena Parthenos, Menandros is mentioned as a ταμίας τῆς θεοῦ. The inscription is dated in the third year of the eighty-fifth Olympiad, 438/7 B. C.; the Σ used is after 446, though the Ionic alphabet has not yet superseded the Attic; it must be before 421, as -ῃσι (ἐπιστάτῃσι) has not yet given way to the later -αις. The inscription is published in *B. C. H.,* XIII, 1889, pp. 171-172, *I. G.,* I, suppl., p. 146, no. 298; *I. G.,* I², 355.

Kirchner, II, 9865. A votive tablet dating before 446. It was dedicated by Menandros, son of Demetrios, of the deme Aigilia, who beseeches his goddess to make him prosperous in return for this favour to her.[73]

πότνι', ἀπαρχὴν τήνδε Μένανδρο[ς
εὐχωλὴν τελέσας, σοὶ χάριν ἀντι[διδούς,
Αἰγιλιεύς, υἱὸς Δημητρίου, ὥ[ι πολὺν ὄλβον
σῷζε, Διὸς θύγατερ, τῶνδε χάρ[ιν θεμένη.

The Menandros, who was sent with Euthydemos as praetor

---

[73] *I. G.,* I, 397; and Kaibel, *Epigrammata Graeca ex Lapidibus Conlecta,* no. 753.

to Nikias [74] in the winter of 414 was also praetor in 405/4 B. C. at Aigospotamoi [75] and so is probably a later one, though it is not impossible that the youth who made the prayer to Athena for prosperity and was " fair " enough to be celebrated on vases in the first half of the century, later became a treasurer, and still later in his maturity was elected strategos while he was in Sicily with Nikias. In Thukydides, VII, 69, 4, " Demosthenes, Menandros and Euthydemos " took command of the Athenian fleet, wishing to force their way out of the harbor of Syracuse which was blockaded. Plutarch (*Nikias,* 20) says that " Menandros and Euthydemos, who were just commencing their new command, prompted by a feeling of rivalry . . . were eager to prove themselves superior to Nikias " and forced him to an unsuccessful sea fight with the enemy. While in *Alkibiades,* 36, Plutarch again says that Tydeus, Menandros, and Adeimantos were the new generals at Aigospotamoi who insultingly disregarded Alkibiades' suggestion that their position was open to the enemy's assaults, Xenophon [76] records that Menandros told Alkibiades to be gone, when he had come with his suggestions, and that he was in command, not Alkibiades. All these brief but deft indications of the headlong character of Menandros in his adult years, both at Syracuse and Aigospotamoi, suggest the youth who prayed the goddess to make him rich; we can follow him from his ephebic years through his ambitious dedication and rise to office of treasurer of Athena, to his strategic posts of later years. Though it is only a word or two here and there, the essential traits of character point always to this one Menandros.

174. Menis kalos.

This love-name appears on a cup of the Transitional Period in Munich, 2582,[77] black-figured inside, red-figured outside,

---

[74] Thuk., VII, 16, 1; Plut., *Nik.,* 20.

[75] Xen., *Hell.,* II, 1, 16-26; Plut., *Alkib.,* 36.

[76] *Hell.,* II, 1, 26.

[77] Beazley, *A. J. A.,* XXXI, 1927, p. 346.

by Pheidippos. Klein [78] restores it incorrectly as Memnon. Pape [79] lists a number of foreigners (non-Attic) of this name: a Theban, a man from Antioch, a Chian, an Ephesian, an old king of Egypt. None of these men can be our man. A metic so named was one of the workmen on the Erechtheion.[80] On a marble columella of the second century [81] we read: Μύστα Μήνιδος Αἰγινῆτις, Δημητρίου ἐκ Κολωνοῦ γυνή; and Conze, *Die Attischen Grabreliefs,* III, p. 125, addendum to 1785, and D. M. Robinson, *A. J. P.,* XXVII, 1906, p. 276 cite a gravestone with Μενίσκος Μήνιδος Σινωπεύς. These are not Athenian names, though we have noted several other such foreign ones, celebrated for their exotic beauty perhaps, on Attic vases.

175. Menon kalos.

Klein, 102; Hoppin, *Handb. R. F.,* I, p. 455, 5, by Foundry Painter. *I. G.,* I, 459, 5 is the sepulchral monument of a Menon, who was a trierarch in the second half of the fifth century. Cf. Chapter III, no. 61. For the " Menon kalos," beloved of Alkaios, the poet, cf. above, p. 61.

176. Mikion kalos.

This name occurs on a black-figured alabastron in Berlin (Klein, p. 52) and on two red-figured vases listed by Klein, p. 136, and also on an oinochoe from the middle of the fifth century, published by H. Philippart (*Collections de Céramique Grecque en Italie,* 1933, II, p. 86). This new vase, which certainly refers to the same Mikion as the other two, has the inscription: καλὸς φίλος Μικι. . . . For φίλος, " dear," compare the black figured Munich vase inscribed in a quatrain, and listed under *Dorotheos* above, p. 102. An interesting inscription found on the Athenian Akropolis (Dittenberger, *Sylloge*³, 1266; *B. C. H.,* XII, 1888, p. 336; *I. G.,* I (Suppl.), p. 191, no. 561), and of which Dittenberger says:

---

[78] *L. l.,* p. 54, no. 3.
[79] *Wörterbuch der Gr. Eigennamen,* sub nomine.
[80] *I. G.,* I², 374, 39.
[81] Hondius, *Supplementum Epigr. Gr.,* III, 1929, p. 43, no. 175.

"Puerorum amoris et nobilioris et volgaris testimonia in rupibus et lapidibus exstant et inter ea antiquissima Therae," most likely refers to the same Mikion of our vases, as it is a sentimental inscription of exactly the same type as the *kalos* ones, and is to be dated, Kirchhoff insists, before the middle of the fifth century, in spite of the Ionic omega (which, after all, is used also on the vases with this same name). The inscription reads: Λυσίθεος Μικίωνα φιλ[ε]ῖν φεσι μάλισ⟨σ⟩τα τὸν ἐν τεῖ πόλει· ἀνδρεῖος γάρ ἐστι.

This affectionate display reminds us of the fragment of the cup-kotyle from Naukratis in Oxford, G 141-48, Attic work, but dating from the fourth century. The graffito on the foot here reads:

Γοργίας φιλ[εῖ Τά]μυνιν
καὶ Τάμυνις Γοργίαν φιλ[εῖ],

and Beazley (*A. J. A.*, XXXI, 1927, p. 352) imagines an interesting scene between Gorgias and his little Egyptian friend, Tamynis.

Kirchner, 10174, quotes a Mikion from a sepulchral monument (*I. G.*, I, 438, 2), which may, however, be a little premature as a notice of our Mikion's decease, since it dates before the middle of the fifth century. Diodoros, XIV, 17, cites an archon of Olympiad 94, 3 (402/1 B. C.), whom other writers call Mikon. This may be the Mikion of our vases, or also the like-named person mentioned in Isaios, V, 22-24 (389 B. C.).

For Lysitheos, the lover of Mikion, there is the possibility that this was the archon of Olympiad 78, 4 (465/4 B. C.), cited by Diodorus, XI, 69. Kirchner 9405 is a Lysitheos who was a *hellenotamias* in 407/6, though this is perhaps a little late for the one in our inscription.

177. Mikon kalos.

Klein, 154, a red-figured lekythos in Schliemann's collection. Though only the first two letters of the name are preserved, there is space for only three more (*Ath. Mitt.*, XVII, 1892, pp. 434 ff., pl. 1).

178. Mikros kalos.

On a kylix (21.88.174) of early archaic style (530-500) in the Metropolitan Museum; attributed to Oltos (Beazley, *A. V.*, p. 15, no. 46; Luce, *A. J. A.*, XXXII, 1928, p. 441, though neither gives the inscription). The inscription is written on the outside, ΚΑΛΟΣ behind the standing boy and ΜΙΚΡΟΣ in front of him. Under the horse is the unknown name, ΛΕΚΕΣ. In the interior Μ(Ε)ΜΝΟΝΚΑΛΟΣΕΙ. The name, not occuring elsewhere so far as we know, is not listed in Kirchner, though there are many examples of Smikros: *I. G.*, I (Suppl.), p. 197, 373[12c], a votive inscription of the sixth century; *I. G.*, I (Suppl.), p. 91, 373[106], another votive inscription from a statue base of white marble on the Akropolis, also from the sixth century; *I. G.*, I (Suppl.), p. 103, 373[224], another sixth century dedication, this one telling us that Smikros was a "tanner of hides"; *I. G.*, I, 432, col. I, 17, is a sepulchral monument of the year 465 with the name Smikros. May the vase Mikros be this Smikros?

179. Milon kalos.

Klein, 66; Beazley, *A. V.*, p. 16. One red-figured vase.

180. Miltiades kalos.

Miltiades on vases (Klein, p. 87) is probably the later hero of Marathon. The scene on the famous plate in the Oxford Ashmolean Museum (*C. V. A., Oxford,* fasc. 1, III I, pl. I, 5) may be the Miltiades in Eastern garb or may not be, but the question of whether we have here a portrait of Miltiades or not does not interfere with the identification. The plate dates 520-510 B. C. (Langlotz, *op. cit.*, pp. 58-60), and as Miltiades was at least forty-five when he commanded at Marathon in 490—Alkibiades' age was unusually early for the same responsibility given him to Syracuse—he would have been about twenty years old in 515 B. C., a good age to be celebrated for beauty on an Attic vase. Cf. also Bowra, *Greek Lyric Poetry,* p. 130.

181. Mnesilla kale (cf. no. 58 above).

Black figure. Lysippides Painter, Munich, 1575. Klein, 46; Beazley, *B. F.*, p. 39, no. 7. Also B 330, a hydria in *C. V. A., Brit. Mus.*, III H e, pl. 88, 2. Possibly also on a Panathenaic vase, Graef-Langlotz, *Vasen von der Akropolis*, I, 921.

182. Moryllos (v. sub Karystios).

183. Myllos kalos.

This otherwise un-noted *kalos* name is given by Graef-Langlotz, *Die Antiken Vasen von der Akropolis*, II, 1497 (not in index). It is on the foot of a black-figured skyphos. Pape-Benseler, *sub nomine*, mentions a Myllos, who was a poet of the old comedy in Athens in Olympiad 73 (488-484 B. C.). We owe the information to Eustathius' Commentary to the *Odyssey*, XX, 106. Under *Epicharmos* Suidas says: ἦν δὲ πρὸ τῶν Περσικῶν ἔτη ἓξ διδάσκων ἐν Συρακούσαις. Ἐν δὲ Ἀθήναις Εὐέτης καὶ Εὐξενίδης καὶ Μύλλος ἐπεδείκνυντο. The proverb, Μύλλος πάντα ἀκούει, meaning one who represents himself as deaf but really hears everything, was originated by him, but was used by Kratinos according to Zenobius (V, 14) in Leutsch-Schneidewin, *Paroemiographi Graeci*, 1839, I, p. 122. Hesychius, sub Μύλλον, has these words: καὶ παροιμία ἐπὶ τῶν ἀκουόντων καὶ κωφότητα προσποιουμένων. ἔστι δὲ καὶ κωμῳδιῶν ποιητὴς οὕτω καλούμενος. Diogenianus (*Prov.* VI, 40) adds to this: ὃς μὴ ἀκούειν ὑπεκρίνετο. The Eustathius passage, ad Odyss. 1885, 21, reads: Μύλλος, ὅ πέρ ἐστι κύριον ὑποκριτοῦ παλαιοῦ, ὃς μιλτωτοῖς, φασί, προσωπείοις ἐχρήσατο.

184. Mynnichos.

Klein, 36. One black-figured vase, *C. V. A., Oxford,* fasc. 2, III H, pl. 8, 5-6. Klein spells it incorrectly with only one " n." Late sixth century.

185. Myrrhiniske kale.

Klein, 135; Hoppin, *Handb. R. F.*, II, p. 188, 32 by the Meidias Painter.

186. Myrtale kale.

Klein, 44; Langlotz, *Gr. Vasen in Würzburg*, p. 55, 304, pl. 94. On black-figure with Anthylla, Rodon, Mnesilla.

187. Mys kalos.

Klein, 39; *Cat. of Vases in Br. Mus.*, II, p. 246, B 507 (not in *C. V. A.*). This inscription on a black-figured vase reads: ὁ Μῦς καλὸς δοκεῖ ναί. Athenaeus (XI, 782 B) mentions Mys, a worker in relief, who was the artisan of the Heracleot bowl with a scene from the sack of Troy, the design by Parrhasios, the work by Mys.

188. Myte kale.

Klein, 47, a black-figured hydria in Naples with the name of Rodopis and the inscription. Μύτε καλὲ ναίχι.

189. Naukleia kale.

Klein, 104; Hoppin, *Handb. R. F.*, II, p. 68, 18, a kylix in New York by Makron, signed by the potter Hieron. Cf. Miss Richter, *Red-Figured Vases in the Metropolitan Museum*, p. 73, no. 52, pl. 52 (about 490-480 B. C.).

190. Nausistratos kalos.

Klein, 52; *C. V. A., Oxford*, fasc. 1, III I, pl. 49, 15. The inscription reads: Ναυσίστρατος καλὸς ναί. The vase is a black-figured one. Nausistratos, son of Euthymachos, is the dedicator of the sixth century inscription, *I. G.*, I (Suppl.), 477 1, p. 113.

191. Neokleides kalos.

Klein, 39. Black-figured oinochoe in the Louvre, Pottier, *Vases Antiques*, Salles E-G, p. 130, F 340; *Hoppin, Handb. B. F.*, pp. 343, 346 (three vases). An Akropolis dedication was made by a Neokleides, *I. G.*, I (Suppl.), 373[80], p. 86. The vases praising him are by Taleides.

192. Nereus kalos.

This name is on an unpublished red-figured krater in Boston, acc. 95.23, with scenes of Zeus pursuing Aigina on one side, and of Asopos, father of Aigina, receiving the news from a maiden hastening with extended hands on the other. Between an altar and a palm tree is the inscription.

The name Nereus recalls the hero of the *Iliad,* the handsomest man next to Achilles to have come to Ilion (II, 673):

Νιρεύς, ὃς κάλλιστος ἀνὴρ ὑπὸ Ἴλιον ἦλθεν
τῶν ἄλλων Δαναῶν μετ' ἀμύμονα Πηλεΐωνα.

It may, of course, refer to a fifth century Athenian (cf. Pape, *Griechische Eigennamen,* Nereus, 4, an Athenian, *C. I. G.,* I, 192), son of Alexandros and a late archon; cf. also the cook from Chios by this name, Athenaeus, IX, 379 e.

193. Nikesippos kalos.

Klein, 41; a black-figured hydria, *C. V. A., Louvre,* fasc. 6, III H e, pl. 72, 2.

194. Nikias kalos.

Klein, 43; *C. V. A., Madrid,* fasc. 1, III H e, pl. 8, 2, a black-figured hydria. Teles and Paris also appear as kalosnames. *I. G.,* I, 433, col. I, 47, the Erechtheid grave-stone of 459/8 mentions a Nikias.

195. Nikodemos kalos.

Klein, 124; Beazley, *A. V.,* p. 392. An archon of this name from the year 483/2 is mentioned by Aristotle (*Ath. Pol.* 22). The third oration of Isaios is directed against the morals of a Nikodemos, and there is a fragment of a speech by Lysias against Nikodemos and Kritoboulos. A Nikodemos of Aiantis is cited on a sepulchral monument of the Athenians who fell at Byzantion in 440/39 B. C. (Tod, *Gk. Historical Inscriptions,* p. 100, no. 48).

196. Nikomas kalos.

New York bell krater by Polygnotos, acc. 21.88.73, 450-440 B. C.; *A. J. A.,* XXVII, 1923, pp. 283-285; cf. Beazley,

A. V., p. 392, no. 13 (he neglects to give *kalos* here or in the list at the end). Attributed to Polygnotos, cf. Panofka, *Bilder Antiken Lebens,* plates 4-6, and Miss Richter, *Red-Figured Vases in the Metropolitan Museum,* p. 159, no. 126, pl. 125.

Kitharist playing before a group of three men. On reverse are three mantled figures. Above the seated man on first side is inscription, a single echo of the vanished beauty of Nikomas. Beazley chronicles (*loc. cit.*) four signed vases by Polygnotos, around which he groups twenty-six stylistically corresponding ones. Of these thirty vases there is only one with a *kalos* inscription, and that to Nikodemos (Beazley, *A. V.,* p. 392, 4) of which this name Nikomas is conceivably a reduction. But more probably it is a *Kosename* for Nikomachos. Cf. Bechtel, *Abhandlungen der kön. Ges. der Wiss. zu Göttingen,* XXXIV, 1887, p. 60; Pape, *Gr. Eigennamen,* s. v. Νικομᾶς, of Roman date, however.

197. Nikon kalos.

Beazley, *A. V.,* pp. 131-2, all by Nikon Painter, who uses names of Heras, Glaukon, Kallias, and Charmides as well as that of Nikon. Some have interpreted this as a general praise, ὁ νικῶν καλός, but it is conclusive that it is another love-name. Klein (p. 138) lists five vases with it; all have scenes of Nike or of conflicts from which victory might be courted. This has suggested the celebration of a *kalos* person because of prowess, athletic or military; Archinos, Hippon, and Kallikles are praised on vases with the same motif. Charmides is celebrated on twenty vases (Klein, 142) with scenes such as: Eros in flight carrying a burning torch or two rabbits, gifts to ephebes (*J. H. S.,* IV, 1883, p. 96). There is, however, a preponderance of this epinician element on Nolan amphorai and lekythoi, but that certainly does not preclude the possibility of identifying the love-names with known historical persons in other cases (such as those names already mentioned in this paragraph), and there is no reason to assume that our Nikon was not a real person. Beazley has named an anonymous painter after him ("Nikon Painter," *A. V.,* p. 131), and groups other names around Nikon; Glaukon, Kallias, Charmides, and Heras *kale*. All are contemporary; *Timoxenos kalos* has been added to the coterie (*C. V. A., Providence,* fasc. 1, p. 24, no. 1, pl. 15). All the vases with praise of Nikon are not by the same hand, however (Beazley, *V. A.,* p. 138 footnote). Add also the kylix signed by Hieron (Richter, *Red-Figured Athenian Vases in the Metropolitan Museum,* p. 73) with the name Nikon without *kalos*; a mixed petting party with all the participants named. The springtime of Nikon's popularity and beauty is fixed in the midfifth century or the decade preceding. Kirchner 11092 and 11099 are probably too early to be his funeral monuments, as the first (*I. G.,* I, Suppl. 462 b, p. 110) dates before 446, and the second is the familiar Erechtheid inscription of 459/8 B. C. (*I. G.,* I, 433, col. II, 60). Whether the archon of 379/8 B. C. (Diod. XV, 24; Dionys. Hal., *Lys.* 12) is our Nikon is also conjectural. A catalogue from the beginning of the fourth century mentions a Nikon Potamios as *prytanis* (*I. G.,* II, 864), which can hardly be our Nikon, grown to position and prominence as so many of our "younger set" of παῖδες καλοί did.

198. Nikondas.

Klein, 158. One red-figured vase, an amphora in Karlsruhe, 204, Winnefeld, *Beschreibung der Vasensammlung,* 1887, p. 48.

199. Nikophile.

Klein, 116; *Catalogue of Vases in Br. Mus.,* III, p. 91, E 68. Red-figured kylix with names of Diphilos, Smikythos, and Philon. It is not yet published in *C. V. A.*

200. Nikosthenes kalos.

Black-figured cup in Vienna, inv. 1870, lid missing, published by Buschor, *Jahrb.,* XXX, 1915, p. 40, fig. 2 on p. 39. The vase dates from the period in which red and black-figured wares were contemporaneous. Scene: four youths;

two standing facing each other at the left on a bema, one
playing a flute; another figure seated, a kitharist; fourth
figure dances off to right. On bema, inscription. Buschor,[82]
in the article in which he conclusively settles the Skythes-
Epilykos controversy, disclaims Rizzo's assumption [83]—that
this is a praise of the vase-artisan, Nikosthenes—and paral-
lels the Louvre krater by Euphronios,[84] where the name on the
bema labels the youth standing on it, to give strength to his
opinion that one of the two youths on the bema in this case
is introduced by the *Nikosthenes kalos* inscription. This may
be the same Nikosthenes, recalled but without the *kalos*
(which he outgrew by the time of this vase) on a kylix
in New York (12.231.1) signed by Hieron (490-480 B.
C.).[85] Nikosthenes here is leaning on a stick and having
his chin coaxed by a woman. The Vienna vase is too late,
Buschor thinks, to mean that the youth celebrated on it had
already painted amphorai in the period of Exekias and Amasis,
though it can date during the lifetime of the potter, and so
may refer to him (but the later date of the Hieron vase and
the youthful appearance of the Nikosthenes on the Vienna
one suggest that this was not the potter meant).

The potter Tleson cannot be Tleson kalos;[86] though the latter dates c. 465, the former is stylistically contemporary with
Exekias and Amasis. Also Andokides kalos (Klein, p. 40)
need not be the potter. Hermogenes (cited) is not the potter
of the same name, who belongs to the time of Exekias, while
the καλός Hermogenes is still a παῖς on the Douris vase [87] on
which Langlotz [88] says he must be such because of the obscenity of the scene. So Nikosthenes is not the potter of
that name.

---

[82] *Jahrb.*, loc. cit.

[83] *Mon. Piot.*, XX, 1913, p. 149.

[84] F. R., pl. 93.

[85] Richter, *Red-Figured Athenian Vases in the Metropolitan Museum*, p. 73.

[86] Klein, *L. I.*, p. 66.

[87] *Wien. Vorl.*, VI, 7.   [88] Zeitbestimmung, p. 48

201. Nikostratos kalos.

Klein, 35; Beazley, *A. V.*, p. 82. Nikostratos I, 550-500 B. C., *I. G.*, I (Suppl.), 446 a, col. II, 5, p. 109, is an Erechtheid sepulchral monument from 438 B. C. *I. G.*, I, 21, a decree from the middle of the fifth century, gives a Nikostratos of Leontis, ἐπιστάτης πρυτανέων.

202. Nikostratos II, 500-450 B. C.

Klein, 126; Beazley, *A. V.*, p. 235. An apt identification here is possible with the Nikostratos who fell on the side of the Thirty at Acharnai in 404/3 B. C., and of whom Xenophon (*Hell.*, II, 4, 6) says τῶν δέ ἱππέων Νικόστρατον τε τὸν καλὸν ἐπικαλούμενον. A patronymic is not given in the Xenophon passage or on the vase. Under Lysis (no. 165 above) was discussed the probability that this Nikostratos may have been the strategos of 427 B. C., whom Thukydides calls the son of Diitrephes (III, 75) and who with Laches commanded an expedition to the Argives in 418 (Thuk., V, 61). But this Nikostratos fell at Mantineia in 413 with Laches, and perhaps it is better to prefer the Xenophon passage for identification with the fair Nikostratos of vase-fame. This latter seems a more reasonable identification, and the relationship between *Nikostratos kalos* of both vases and literature is surely an attractive one.

203. Nikoxenos kalos.

Klein, 120; Beazley, *A. V.*, p. 91. The inscription is on an amphora formerly in the Straganoff collection at Leningrad, now in Baltimore in the collection of D. M. Robinson. Cf. *C. V. A., Robinson Coll.*, fasc. 2, III I, pls. XXIV, 1 and XXV and references there.

204. Oinanthe kale.

Klein, 129. One red-figured vase, *C. V. A., Br. Mus.*, fasc. 6, III I c, pl. 85, 1. The inscription is read Οἰνάνθε by Beazley, *A. V.*, p. 252, no. 4, who created an Oinanthe Painter.

204A. Oionokles kalos. Cf. p. 97, no. 69 above, Dionokles.

205. Olympichos kalos.

Klein, 149. On a white-ground lekythos in Berlin, F 2252, Neugebauer, *Führer durch das Antiquarium,* p. 61, pl. 55 (Zahn, *Die Antike,* I, 1925, pls. 30 and 31). *I. G.,* I, 443 is a grave-stone from the year 430 B. C. with the name of Olympichos of Hippothontis. Cf. Diphilos.

206. Olympiodoros kalos.

This name, of the Leagros circle (Klein, 105; Beazley, *Black-Figure,* p. 45), was very popular with Euthymides, along with those of the fair Leagros and Antias. Olympiodoros may be identified with the son of Lampon of that name, who with three hundred Athenians defended a dangerous out-post before Plataia at Erythrai (Her., IX 21; Busolt, *Gr. Gesch.,* II, p. 727). A vase in the Cabinet des Médailles (Hartwig, *Meisterschalen,* pl. 15, 2; Beazley, *A. V.,* p. 166, 8) with the names of Leagros, Dorotheos, Kephisophon, and Olympiodoros coincides in date with the youth of Olympiodoros, if he was a general at Plataia. Cf. on Olympiodoros, Hoppin, *Euthymides and his Fellows,* pp. 18 ff., 31-32; Graef-Langlotz, *Vasen von der Akropolis,* II, 636.

207. Onetor kalos.

Klein, 34; Hoppin, *Handb. B. F.,* p. 109, 12-13 by Exekias. Lolling, Κατάλογος, I, p. 98, no. 189, is a votive inscription from the Akropolis, dedicated by Onetor and dating from the fifth century.

208. Onetorides kalos.

Klein, 33; *C. V. A., Br. Mus.,* fasc. 4, III H e, pl. 49, 2a and b. Exekias praises Onetorides three times, on a Berlin Herakles-amphora, on the Vatican Dioskouroi-amphora, and on the London one just cited, cf. Technau, *Exekias,* pp. 8-10, pls. 1, 2; 20, 21; 25.

209. Orthagoras kalos.

Klein, 38. One black-figured vase, Langlotz, *Gr. Vasen in Würzburg,* p. 36, no. 205.

210. Palos kalos.

This love-name, besides being found on the vases listed under *Euthymos* (no. 103 above), occurs on the hydrias E 161 and E 168 in the British Museum. The first vase (*C. V. A., Br. Mus.*, fasc. 5, III I c, pl. 71, 1) has the inscription: καλὸς ὁ Πάλος ὁ παῖς. The second (*C. V. A., Br. Mus.*, fasc. 5, III I c, pl. 73, 3) has ὁ Πάλος καλός, ὁ παῖς καλός. There is a third vase with this name inscribed (Graef-Langlotz, *op. cit.*, II, 1, no. 284, p. 23, pl. 15) has Πάλο[ς] καλὸ[ς], which Peek (*Epigraphische Nachtraege, Akrop. Vas.* II, 3, p. 130) reads as meaning πάλ[λ]ō καλō[ς]. These three vases stand close in time: the British Museum ones are assigned to the Syriskos Painter by Beazley (*A. V.*, p. 159); the Athens one is dated as "near the Antiphon Painter." It is generally assumed that the *Palos* of the inscription refers to the thrust or dart of a spear or sword, and, indeed, the three vases mentioned here have scenes that would fit such an explanation: British Museum E 161 shows Menelaos pursuing Helen with a drawn sword; E 168 shows Herakles busied over the Nemean lion, while the Athens vase has a picture of a youth with a spear in one hand, the other on his hips, looking at a companion with a large shield. It is possible to argue, however, that, since the *Dexios* coupled with the word or name *Palos* has been shown to be a proper name, the case is the same with *Palos,* who then must be the "pretty boy" referred to by the inscriptions, which are independent of the scenes on the British Museum vases, and that all that is meant by the inscription on the Athens vase is the usual approbation of attractive youths in ancient Athens, here to be read "Palos is pretty." Diodoros Sic. II, 43, says that Palos was a Scythian after whom the Paloi, a Scythian folk, were named. Though we have only one case of Palos as a proper name in Athens, that is enough to establish it, even though the single case does not allow of identification with our Palos of the vases. On the base of the statue of the Moschophoros (*I. G.* I, Suppl., p. 198, no. 373[235]; Kirchner, *Imagines Inscriptionum Atticarum,* pl. 2, 5) is the inscription: (R)onbos, son of Palos.

In any case it is not advisable to take Πάλος on the British Museum vases as a mistake for παῖς as the *C. V. A* does.

211. Panaitios kalos.

Klein (p. 106) catalogues seventeen red-figured vases with this love-name. Cf. Richter, *Red-Figured Athenian Vases in the Metropolitan Museum,* pp. 32, 58, 59 (Colmar Painter kylix about 500 B. C.). Studniczka (*Jahrb.,* II, 1887, p. 164) thinks that this inscription, common to a ripe work of Euphronios, two works of Douris, and the output of an anonymous painter, called after him the Panaitios Painter (Beazley, *A. V.,* pp. 166-172, 473, twenty vases by him with this name; p. 201, no. 15 by Duris; p. 228, no. 8, by Colmar Painter), might be " ein patriotischer Bravoruf zu einer wichtigen Tat vor Salamis," and proceeds to suggest an identification with the Panaitios who conducted a trireme from Tenos out of the Persian fleet and over to the Greeks (Her., VIII 82). The identification can stand, but the inscription need not be considered a *Bravoruf,* as Panaitios appeared on vases considerably before the feat at Salamis. Rather we should consider him, too, as one of the favourite " pretty boys " of Athens, who, after reaching his manhood, continued to keep himself in the public eye, doubtless because he came from the stratum of Athenian society which brought its boys up into a more noteworthy class of duties and activities, to which they were entitled, when they had grown into manhood, because of their birth. For the Brussels kyathos A 2323 with Panaitios kalos cf. *C. V. A., Bruxelles,* II I, pl. 14, 18.

212. Pantoxena kale.

Klein, 129; Beazley, *A. V.,* p. 405 (Pantoxena Painter), nos. 1 and 2: Παντόξενα καλὰ Κορίνθοι.

212A. Paris kalos.

Cf. *C. V. A., Madrid,* fasc. 1, III H e, pl. 8, 2. Cf. no. 194 above.

213. Pasikles kalos.

Klein, 36. One black-figured vase. Langlotz, *Griechische Vasen in Würzburg*, p. 40, no. 220.

214. Pausimachos kalos.

Klein, 86. Red-figured. καλὸς ναίχι.

215. Pedieus kalos.

Klein, 68; Beazley, *A. V.*, p. 42, nos. 27-29, by Skythes. Perhaps he can be identified with the archon of 449/8 B. C. (Diodoros, XII, 4). His son, Kleinias, was also a favourite in Athens at a later day.

216. Perikleides.

Published by Langlotz, *Griechische Vasen in Würzburg*, 474. Vase dates c. 500 B. C. Cf. Aischines, *Against Timarchos*, 156 (c. 345 B. C.), in which Perikleides of Perithoidai is mentioned in a list of men who have had lovers and yet lived honourably. "I will recite to you the names of older and well-known men—some of whom have had many lovers because of their beauty, and some of whom, still in their prime, have lovers today" (Adams). May this have been the Perikleides of the vase inscription, his fame recalled by tradition 155 years later? He is a young warrior on the kylix in Würzburg and it is not certain that *kalos* ever was on the vase, though it might have been on the lost portion.

217. Phaidimos kalos.

Boston lekythos, .09. 69 (Fairbanks, *Athenian White Lekythoi*, VII, p. 253, 8 a, 480-430 B. C.), by the Thanatos-Painter. The scene shows a woman in profile, an alabastron in her extended right hand; at the right stands a youth "en face," a cane in his lowered right hand. To the left of the top of the stele we see the inscription to Phaidimos, a debut on vases for this youth.

Kirchner, *Pros. Att.*, II, 13937, says that Phaidimos was one of the Thirty Tyrants (404 B. C.) mentioned by Demosthenes[89] as the father of Xenophon and one of the Thirty; Xenophon[90] calls him Phaidrias in his list of Tyrants, but this is certainly the same man of the tribe Leontis as the one mentioned by Demosthenes. The son Ξενόφρονα τὸν υἱὸν τοῦ Φαιδίμου, τοῦ τῶν τριάκοντα is also of versatile name, as in Aischines, 2, 157, he is called Ξενόδοκος τῶν ἑταίρων τις τῶν Φιλίππου (cf. Xenodotos kalos, sub Xenodoke, no. 279 below).

Fairbanks[91] says of the group in general (class VI, series C) to which this lekythos belongs that the scene is always located at the grave, the stele is always present, women are usually bringing offerings, and that "one figure, usually the figure at the right, seems to represent the dead person himself." So that the youth "en face" on the vase may be the dead one, though the inscription here, as in other cases, is certainly independent of the action, for, according to the passages cited, one Phaidimos was still very much alive in 404, and it can easily be assumed that the one who in his maturity was prominent enough to be selected one of the Thirty, in his youth was a "radiant" Phaidimos of beauty enough to star on a vase. The vase must date c. 450, and the youth of fifteen to twenty-five so remarkable for his comeliness, in 404 would have been the Tyrant of sixty-one to seventy-one years. And, if there were variations in the name, it is certainly the significant *Phaidimos* form that is happiest to perpetuate the glory of the limbs "shining" with oil or the hair "sleek" with the unguent of one's favourite. For his presence on this funerary urn it might be conjectured that he was a friend of the deceased, one of his συνέφηβοι who dropped by the wayside, for, while in cases of vases less restricted in use or of less defined purposes than lekythoi, it is possible that the haphazard placement of love-names indicates serving the pleasure of the purchaser, here the ultimate destination of a tomb should rather suggest a closer relation.

---

[89] XIX, 196.
[90] *Hell.*, II, 3, 2.
[91] *Athenian Lekythoi, Univ. of Michigan Humanistic Studies*, VI, p. 280.

218. Phainippos kalos.

Red-figured lekythos in the Fogg Art Museum at Harvard University, and published by Dow in *Harvard Studies in Classical Philology*, XLI, 1930, p. 63. The scene is of a woman in rapid motion, carrying a mirror and a tainia, on the latter of which the name is inscribed. The vase dates between 470 and 450 B. C., the latter date being more probable.

Kirchner, *Pros. Att.*, 13979, cites Phainippos, son of Phrynichos, mentioned by Thukydides, IV 118, 11, as *grammateus* in connection with a psephisma of 424/3 B. C. The sources for this identification are: (1) *I. G.*, I², 57, a decree of the year 424; (2) *I. G.*, I², 70, 5, a decree of the people resolving to praise Potamodoros the Erchomenian, and his son, Eurytion, written by Phainippos as *grammateus*; (3) Thukydides (*loc. cit.*) quotes a decree concerning the Lakedaimonians and their allies, mentioning Phainippos as scribe.

From these three inscriptions we know that Phainippos was scribe in 424/3 B. C.; he was γραμματεὺς κατὰ πρυτανείαν (this officer changed each prytany and in the pre-Eukleidian period was responsible for the engraving of the decrees).

There is also Phainippos Paionides, a λογιστής, *I. G.*, I², 304, line 68, or "auditor" in year 407-406, at which time this Phainippos, if the one of the vase and therefore born c. 465, would be fifty-eight years of age.

Dow (*loc. cit.*, p. 72) suggests: "May it not have been that Phainippos died after the vase was made, that some admirer selected it as an offering, appropriate for its design, had the name written on it, and made it his poor offering?" But to offer a man still living in 424 or even 407 B. C. a vase made in 450 at the latest, when he had died sometime after either of these dates, would have been to offer a gift too uncomplimentarily *démodé* in an age when vase-styles were developing to greater beauties almost over night; another discordant element in his assumption is that, quite apart from such ephemeral things as style, Phainippos could certainly not have been *kalos* when he died, at an age at least advanced enough to be entrusted with political office. Much more probably was this inscription put on when the vase was made and not a few decades later, and that Phainippos was then one of the many handsome young-bloods exciting Athens and of prominence enough to be capable of his secretarial office later in his life.

And if this lekythos must be classified among those with funereal scenes, the mirror which Dow quotes from Fairbanks as along with the fan and the kalathos " characteristic of the daily life of the person who carries them " (just as the jewel box in the hands of dead ladies on grave stelai) must refer to the dead and certainly to a woman, so that it is more plausible to assume that the lekythos with this scene of feminine appointments was a gift to a deceased lady, who may have been a friend of the youth Phainippos c. 450 B. C.

Miss Richter [92] has proved that vases were fired only once, against the earlier notion that inscriptions were put on after the first firing and that then the vases were fired a second time. Certainly this name, then, was put on when the vase was made, in 450, and referred to a youth resplendent with life, and not to a dead and aged man.

218A. Phaon kalos.

Klein, 137; F. R., pl. 59; Robinson, *Sappho and her Influences*, pl. 5. This is probably not a real kalos name but a reference to the mythical beautiful Phaon. But it shows the use of kalos names.

219. Phayllos kalos.

This love-name is listed by Klein, p. 123. The important vase with this name is a psykter, listed under *Sostratos,* no. 4, p. 123 by Klein; it was formerly in the Bourguignon collection at Naples, but is now in Boston (Hoppin, *Handb. R. F.,* II, p. 365, no. 11). Hoppin has attributed it to Phintias; its best publication is in the *Antike Denkmaeler,* II, 2, pl. 20. The two vases with Phayllos' name are in Hoppin's *Euthy-*

---

[96] *Craft of Athenian Pottery,* pp. 106-107.

mides and His Fellows, E II, p. 13, pl. 2; and E IV, pp. 18 and 31, pl. 4. Hauser (*Jahrb.* X, 1895, p. 110) suggests that this is the Phayllos, the celebrated athlete of Kroton. Gardiner (*J. H. S.,* XXIV, 1904, pp. 70 ff.) has written a long and informative article on *Phayllos and His Record Jump,* from which we extract the sections relating to our identification.

Herodotos (VII 48) says that the people of Kroton were the only Greeks beyond the sea who sent help to the Greeks at Salamis, and that the help came in the form of a single ship commanded by Phayllos. Plutarch (*Alex.,* 34) adds that Phayllos fitted out this ship at his own expense, and that later Alexander, in recognition of his spirit and courage, sent a portion of his Asiatic spoils to the Krotoniates. Pausanias (X, 9) saw the statue of Phayllos at Delphi, and adds that Phayllos won no victory at Olympia, but was victorious once in the stadium race and twice in the pentathlon at Delphi. Aristophanes twice alludes to one Phayllos as a noted runner (*Achar.,* 213; *Wasps,* 1203), and, as Dikaiopolis in the *Acharnians* is speaking of the days of his youth, the Persian wars, it seems certain that he is thinking of Phayllos of Kroton; the identification of the Phayllos in the *Wasps,* however, is not so certain. The following epigram is found composed to a Phayllos (*Anth. Pal.,* App. 297):

> Πέντ' ἐπὶ πεντήκοντα πόδας πήδησε Φάϋλλος,
> δίσκευσεν δ' ἑκατὸν πέντ' ἀπολειπομένων.

The references up to, but not including, the epigram, are all we know [93] at first hand of Phayllos. We hear nothing of the record jump or of the epigram in them—an omission certainly remarkable in Pausanias' case. Late references to the athlete are: Scholiast to Plato, *Kratyl.* 413 A; Schol. Lucian, *Somn.*

---

[93] To Gardiner's list add: *I. G.,* I (Suppl.), p. 203, 373[258]; Hoffmann, *Syll. Ep. Gr.,* no. 364:

- - - σι Φάϋλ[λο - - - -;
- - νι]κῶν τρὶς - - - -
- - - Πυθοῖ κα - - -
- - - ας 'Ασὶς - ι - - -

s. Gall. 6; Zenobius VI, 23; Eustathius; and Suidas. Now, Phayllos lived a century before Plato, we do not know how many before the scholiasts, and fifteen centuries before Eustathius and Suidas (the latter of whom preserves a tradition that, in breaking the record with his fifty-five foot jump, he also broke his leg!). Gardiner believes that the authority of the epigram is absolutely worthless, and such as no historian would think of recognizing. The style of the epigram itself, so different from that of actual inscriptions, makes it improbable that it was written till centuries after the incident recorded. The silence of Herodotos and Pausanias on the affair of the jump makes it likely that for reliable information about our Phayllos we can believe everything except the fifty-five foot jump, the authority for which, after all, rests only on the rhetorical epigram and a doubtful reading in Sextus Julius Africanus:

'Ολ. κθ'. Χίονις Λάκων στάδιον· οὗ τὸ ἄλμα νβ'· ποδῶν.

Even with the aid of *halteres* the performance has been rightly questioned as physically impossible. Perhaps νβ' should be κβ' (22 feet). The diskos-throw we need not question.

Apart from the chronological agreement of vase and person, Hauser thinks that his case is strengthened by the fact that Phayllos is the only one of all the athletes represented on this vase, who, like the four paidotribai, is distinguished by a leaf-crown; the other boys wear a simple fillet. " Diese Ausnahme lässt erkennen, dass der Maler sich bei diesem Kranz etwas dachte, dass er also seinen Phayllos auszeichnen wollte " (*loc. cit.*, p. 110). This vase (*Ant. Denkm.*, II, 2, pl. 20) has a scene in the palaistra; Phayllos is only one of the twelve persons pictured. Though his name on this vase is written without the *kalos,* it appears on the other vase (Klein, p. 123; *C. V. A., Brit. Mus.,* fasc. 3, III I c, pl. 3, 2) with the adjective, and so he has been identified as a " favourite." Now several of the other youths named by the inscriptions on this vase also appear on other vases with the adjectives calling them " pretty "; Hauser has assumed, rightly, that all the names inscribed can be understood as those of favourite boys. I quote his arguments (*Jahrb.*, X, 1895, pp. 108 and 111): " Der Maler suchte das Interesse an der Darstellung zu steigern, idem er seine Figuren für bestimmte Personen ausgab, und dadurch gewinnt in der That auch für uns noch sein Werk an Bedeutung. . . . Die Namen der dargestellten Personen, welche man nicht ohne Weiteres als Lieblingsinschriften bezeichnen kann, haben dennoch für uns den gleichen Werth wie diese, das Fehlen des Zusatzes macht in diesem Fall keinen Unterschied. Wenn der Meister diese Namen Epheben beischrieb, denen er alle Reize seiner Kunst verlieh, so rechnete er nicht damit, dass seine Malerei in die Hand von Menschen kommt, welche einem solchen Epheben das Prädikat καλός verweigern." He goes on to plead for identifications of all the named figures on the basis of their being *kalos* names. The inscriptions read:

Σίμον	Φίλον	Ἐτέαρχος	Γτοιόδορος
Σότρατος	Ε(ὐ)κράτες	Ἐλιοας	Εὔδεμος
Σόσρατος	Ἐπίλυκ··	Χσένο.	Φάϋλο.
Εοπποκι			

Two of them are not names at all: ελιοας εοπποκι. For the rest it is legitimate to try to find identifications, wherever possible. Hauser himself suggests identifying the paidotribe Ptoiodoros with the member of the famous athletic family from Corinth, celebrated by Pindar as a victor in the Isthmian games (Pind. *Ol.* XIII, 58; cf. Boeckh, *Pindar* I, p. 422). We add as a possibility the Theban exile of this name, who arranged to betray his country into the hands of the Athenians under Demosthenes and Hippokrates because he wanted a revolutionary change in government (Thuk., IV, 76).

For Simon there are the following references: *I. G.*, I (Suppl.), 373 F, p. 42, a dedication by Simon ὁ κναφεύς, probably of the sixth century; Aristophanes, *Clouds,* 351, cf. 399, calls a Simon ἅρπαξ τῶν δημοσίων; Eupolis, frag. 218, whence the proverb Σίμωνος ἁρπακτικώτερος, cf. also Suidas, *s. v.*, Simon and Aristoph., *Knights,* 242 with Scholia.

There is a sepulchral monument of the tribe Leontis from 438 B. C. (*I. G.*, I, Suppl., 446 a, col. II, 34, p. 109) with the name Eudemos.

Etearchos is mentioned as γραμματεὺς ἐπιστατῶν in the year 409/8 (*I. G.*, I, 322).

For Eukrates there are the following possibilities for identification from which to choose: *I. G.*, I, 432, frag. c 11, a gravestone from 465 B. C.; *I. G.*, I, 446, 47, from 425 B. C.; an inscription from the year 438 B. C. (*I. G.*, I, Supplement, 446 a, col. I, 30, p. 109), Kirchner 5747; Kirchner 5759, Eukrates Meliteus, demagogue after death of Perikles, and called κάπρος, "boar" Aristoph. frag. 143; στυππειοπώλης, Aristoph. *Knights* 129 and Scholia. This Eukrates is probably the same as *I. G.*, I (Suppl.), 179 Aa, p. 161: Εὐκρά[της . . . στρατηγὸς εἰς Μακ]εδονίαν in 432/1 B. C.; Kolbe, *Hermes,* XXXIV, 1899, 381 ff. Philon, Sostratos, Epilykos, Xenon are identified under other headings. Philon appears on a vase with Smikythos (Klein, 116-117) another of the Euthymidean ephebes.

220. Pheidiades.

Klein, 126. Beazley, *A. V.*, p. 62, no. 3. London, E 438: *C. V. A., Br. Mus.*, fasc. 3, III I c, pl. 19, 2. On vase signed by Smikros. Name of Antias kalos accompanies. The only identification is with Pheidiades who dedicated two early fifth century inscriptions found on the Akropolis (Lolling, Κατάλογος, p. 13, no. XLIII; *J. H. S.*, XIII, 1892, pl. VII, no. 57).

221. Pheidon kalos.

Klein, 66; *Cat. of Vases in Br. Mus.*, III, p. 45, E 9. One of the Thirty Tyrants was named Pheidon (Lys. XII, 54, 55; Xen., *Hell.*, II, 3, 2).

222. Philliades kalos.

Hoppin, *Handb. R. F.*, I, p. 406 reads the inscription on the vase in Arezzo Φιλλιάδες and not Φειδιάδες, as Klein (*L. I.*, sub. nom., 126) gives it. Beazley agrees (*A. V.*, p. 59), and includes the new love-name in his list at the end of *Attische Vasenmaler*. There was a Philliades who was the author of the grave inscription for the Thespians fallen in the Persian Wars (Eust., *ad Iliad*, II, p. 201, 40). Chronologically this is acceptable for our identification.

223. Philon kalos.

Klein, 116, also a black-figured lekythos in Oxford, 1889 (251), having the names, Philon and Kynippos, and dating c. 500 B. C. Cf. Klein, 52; Haspels, *Attic Black-Figured Lekythoi*, p. 161 (Athena Painter). *I. G.*, I, 293, mentions a Philon Probalisios, γραμματεὺς ἐπιστατῶν around the year 448 B. C. *I. G.*, I, 439, 26, and 447, col. III, 61 are gravestones with this name, and both date in the second half of the fifth century. For additional material see under Antimenes, p. 83, footnote 17.

224. Phrinos kalos.

This inscription is found on a white-ground kylix, excavated by the Americans in the Agora in Athens, and published in *Hesperia*, II, 1933, p. 229. The kylix was found in the Stoa formerly called the "Royal Stoa" but now held by Homer Thompson to be also the Stoa of Zeus in a stratum dating before the Persian burning of 479 B. C. The scene is of an ephebe with a lyre. Only four letters of the name are preserved, but at a regular space ahead of the "R" a chip is out of the vase, just where a "phi" might have been. The name Phrynos or Phrinos is a common enough one, and, as there are no cases in Fick-Bechtel, Pape-Benseler, or Kirchner of a proper name formed from the word ῥινός for "hide" (or "tanner"), the ample evidence that Phrynos was a good Attic name at the time of our vase inclines to an identification with the known persons of that name. That Phrynos was sometimes written Phrinos we know from the scholiast to Aristophanes' *Knights* 580, where we are told of a sumptuary law forbidding the over-elegant fashions of the youth of the day. The law was introduced by Kineas and Phrinos, and is otherwise unknown. The scholiast says: κομῶσι: τρυφῶσι, πλουτοῦσι · Κινέας γὰρ καὶ Φρῖνος εἰσηγήσαντο μεταστῆναι τοὺς νέους, νόμον γράψαντες μηκέτι ἁβροδιαίτους εἶναι, ὃν τρόπον τὸ πάλαι, μηδὲ κομᾶν, ἢ ἀπεξεσμένοις καὶ ἐπανήκουσιν ἀπὸ ἀλείμματος. The passage in Aristophanes to which this has been added reads (Rogers' translation) : " Grudge us not our flowing ringlets, grudge us not our baths and oil." Our ephebe of c. 480 B. C. would have been an old man in his seventies, protesting against the luxury and softnesses of the young men at the time of the play, which was produced at the Lenaian Festival in 424 B. C. By this time he was either resentful of his own lost youth and peevishly out of sympathy with the fashions of the young. This is a better supposition (not mentioned in *Hesperia*), than to identify him with the Phrynos of Erechtheis who died in 459/8 B. C. (*I. G.*², I, 929).

Kirchner 15025 concerns a Phrynos named on a votive tablet from the early fifth century as a co-dedicator along with Aristogeiton, but this is more probably the Phrynos, famed as a Little-Master potter and working about the middle of the sixth century (Tonks, *A. J. A.*, IX, 1905, 288 ff.), or the Phrynos named on a base for ceramic votives from c. 500 B. C. as the father of the otherwise un-named dedicator (Graef-Langlotz, *op. cit.*, II, 3, no. 1300, pl. 92). From it we can assume that the dedicator was the son of a famous father, who may well have been the potter Phrynos or Kirchner's 15025 or both, though all these references are doubtless too early in date to be identified with the Phrynos of the vase-fragment from the Agora.

The scholiast passage, then, and the fact that other cases are known of the change from *u* to *i* (cf. *Euriptolemos* on vase in Klein, *L. I.*, p. 105, 2) can be taken as good evidence that the name on the kylix was Phrynos, though Beazley (*A. J. A.*, XXXIX, 1935, p. 482) suggests further that the original may have been Ἐρινός or Ἡρινός, the masculine counterpart of the woman's name Ἡρινή. Cf. above p. 105, no. 84.

225. Pithon kale.

On a pseudo-Panathenaic red-figured amphora of severe style in Boston. Published by Chase, *Harvard Studies in Classical Philology,* XVII, 1906, pp. 143 ff. On both sides is the figure of Athena, whose shield on the obverse is inscribed *Pithon kale* and has a Pegasus; on the reverse her shield has an ivy-wreath and *Nike kale.*

The name Pithon has not been noted before as a *kalos* name, though it appears in inscriptions and in literature, being confused in MSS. with Πύθων and Πείθων (two of Alexander's generals were of this name). Chase (*loc. cit.*) thinks that the form of the adjective may be a careless mistake, influenced by the *kale* for *Nike* on the other side, but perhaps we can regard it much more probably as intentional, especially in view of the parallel, contemporary case of the "womanishly fair" Hippodamas, a *confrère* of Pithon (cf. *Hippodamas*), and the similar perversion of the usual formula in the debut of Euphiletos (cf. above pp. 110-111). It has also been regarded as a vocative (so Beazley regards the Euantete of the Oxford Xanthes cup), somewhat like "Pithon, thou fair one," though this, too, is unprecedented. Cf. below p. 189.

Pithon is probably the member of the tribe Erechtheis who fell in the year 459/8 B. C.[94] We can therefore assume that Pithon was still a middle-aged man at this time and that his youth must have been unfolding c. 490, a date to which this vase may reasonably be assigned. His name is also found in a list of about the same date: *I. G.,* I, 434, line 16.

Cf. Pindar, *Pyth.* II, 72: καλός τοι πίθων παρὰ παισίν, αἰεί καλός ... "the monkey is a pretty thing to children."—This vase inscription may possibly have been added by an admirer of Pindar's verse.

226. Polemainetos kalos.

Klein, 128, a red-figured stamnos in Munich, 349 (8045). *I. G.,* I (Suppl.), 53b, p. 165 is a decree from 413 B. C. mentioning a person of this name as ἐπιστάτης πρυτανέων.

---

[94] *I. G.,* I, 433.

227. Polyeuktos kalos.

Klein, 133, a red-figured kantharos in Altenburg with the name Sophanes. A fragment of an oration of Antiphon against Polyeuktos survives (Blass, frag. 47). Andokides, I, 35, cites a Polyeuktos indicted by Teukros for the mutilation of the herms in 415 B. C.

228. Polykles (v. sub Leagros).

229. Polyphrassmon kalos.

Klein, 117; Beazley, *A. V.,* p. 207, no. 107, by Douris. There was a tragic poet of this name, and he was the son of Phrynichos (Suidas, *v.* sub Phryn.). In 467 B. C. he contested with Aischylos (*Argum. Aischyl. Sept.*).

230. Pordax kalos.

This vulgar name (if we accept Beazley's interpretation) [95] occurs on a fragment of a black-figured amphora from Locri in Reggio and on a black-figured amphora in Munich, 1478. On the Munich vase it is Ποραδχς. Buschor [96] couples it with καλός, and supposes that it is an old-fashioned proper name. Beazley says, "Not otherwise known, perhaps because the family dropped it, one can understand why." If so, the name must be derived from πορδή, *crepitus ventris.*[97] On the Locri vase it appears mutilated: . . . ρδαχς καλ . . Both vases are from the same period and in the same style, the one in Munich being assigned to the Lysippides Painter by Beazley (*Attic Black-Figure,* p. 39, no. 5).

231. Praxiteles kalos.

Klein, 100; Beazley, *A. V.,* p. 218. Perhaps this Praxiteles is to be identified with the archon of 444/3 B. C. (Diodoros, XII, 23).

232. Proxenides kalos.

Graef-Langlotz, *op. cit.,* II, 2, no. 636, pls. 50 and 51. The vase dates 510-500 B. C., and has this inscription 'Ολυπιό-

---

[95] *A. J. A.,* XXXI, 1927, p. 346.
[96] F. R., III, p. 220.   [97] Aristophanes, *Clouds,* 394.

[δωρος] κα[λός] · [Πρ]οξσενίδε[ς κα]⟨λ⟩λός · ho παῖς καλός. Klein (*L. I.*, pp. 82, 83) mentions only the first line and the name of Olympiodoros, omitting the second line which Peek (*Epigr. Nachtr.*) reads [Πρ]οξενίδης καλός. Cf. Aristophanes, *Birds,* 1126; *Wasps,* 325: Proxenides is καπνὸς καὶ κομπαστής ("the Braggadocian," an invented deme). The *Birds* dates 414 B. C., and Προξενίδης ὁ Κομπασεύς is a needy braggart perpetually boasting of his wealth.

233. Proxenos kalos.

This name, in its single occurrence, appears on a lekythos from the end of the sixth century (Graef-Langlotz, *op. cit.*, II, 3, no. 1081, p. 99, pl. 84). It was a very common name in Athens, but most of the known cases of persons so-called, are a little too late in date to be our Proxenos. Kirchner, 12268, Proxenos III of Aphidna, is the only one dating from the end of the sixth century, and nothing further is known of him. He is connected, however, with the line of Harmodios, the tyrrannicide, as Kirchner 12267, is another Proxenos of Aphidna, 429 B. C., father of Dikaiogenes (Isaios, V, 6, 15, 46, 47), and in 410/9 was Hellenotamias. This Proxenos is probably the next generation after our Proxenos of vase-fame.

234. Ptoiodoros (*v.* sub Phayllos).

235. Pyles kalos.

Klein, 36; *C. V. A., Br. Mus.,* fasc. 3, III H e, pl. 39, 2a and b. One black-figured vase.

236. Pythaios kalos.

This love-name is on a lekythos by Douris (510-460 B. C.) in Syrakuse, mentioned by Beazley, *A. V.*, p. 209, no. 131 (*Mon. Linc.,* XIX, Beilage, 128, fig. 12). With this spelling there is no such name in Kirchner; Pape says it is a *Beiname* of Apollo, for Pythios, but as there are no instances of its having been used as a proper name in this guise, we can suggest that it be a version of Πυθέας, of which there are many cases in Kirchner. He can hardly, however, be the

Pytheas mentioned in fragment 232 of Lysias (floruit 411) as the lover of Teisis: Ἔστιν οὖν Πυθέας ἐραστὴς μὲν τοῦ μειρακίου ἐπίτροπος δὲ ὑπὸ τοῦ πατρὸς καταλελειμμένος.

In a list of θιασῶται of a cult to Herakles (*I. G.*, II, 2, Addenda, 986b, p. 539) of the early fourth century is the name, Πυθαῖος.

237. Pythodelos kalos.

Klein, 134; Hoppin, *Handb. R. F.*, I, p. 29, no. 15, by Ambrosios Painter.

238. Pythodoros kalos.

This is a love-name hitherto unknown, and recently found on the inside of a partly glazed krater in the Agora at Athens (*Hesperia*, V, 1936, p. 348, no. 3, fig. 17). Cf. the owner's Πυθοδόρο εἰμί on the foot of a black-glazed kylix also from Athens (Graef-Langlotz, *Die Antiken Vasen von der Akropolis zu Athen*, II, 1506). It was a common fifth century name: an archon of 432/1 had it (*I. G.*, I², p. 286), and it is possible that it was he who was celebrated on this vase, which was discarded around 460 B. C. The Leagros kalos of c. 500 was Leagros the general in the sixties, and so " we may reasonably assume that the same gap between youthful charm and political distinction, or responsible office, pertained later in the century " (Talcott, *Hesperia, loc. cit.* p. 352). Read Πυθόδωρος for Miss Talcott's Πυθώδορος.

239. Pythokles I kalos.

Klein, 34, a black-figured amphora in the British Museum (*C. V. A.*, fasc. 4, III H e, pl. 62, 4a and b) from the end of the sixth century.

240. Pythokles II kalos.

Klein, 120; Hoppin, *Handb. R. F.*, I, p. 276, no. 41 by Douris. Kirchner 12447 cites a person of this name, who was the father of Phaidros at the end of the fifth century. *I. G.*, I, 448, col. I 30 and II 1, grave-stones of the second half of the fifth century, mention a Pythokles.

241. Rodon kale (v. sub Euthymos; also Beazley, *Attic Black-Figure,* p. 41). Klein, 46; *C. V. A., Brit. Mus.,* fasc. 6, III H e, pl. 88, 2 (Lysippides Painter). Cf. no. 58 above.

242. Rhodopis kale.

Klein, 47, a black-figured hydria in Naples. Cf. also a black-figured hydria in London (*C. V. A., Brit. Mus.,* fasc. 6, III H e, pl. 88, 1). Also Miss Richter, *Red-Figured Athenian Vases in the Metropolitan Museum,* p. 75, no. 53. Rhodopis is the name of the hetaira loved by Charaxus, Sappho's brother, cf. Her. II, 134; D. M. Robinson, *Classical Philology,* XX, 1925, pp. 343-345; *Sappho and her Influence,* pp. 16, 17.

243. Sekline kale.

Klein, 123; Hoppin, *Handb. R. F.,* I, p. 404, no. 14 by Euphronios (F. R., pl. 63); p. 440, 11, by Euthymides. The name is not from σὲ κλῖνε but from Σηκλίνη = Σηκυλίνη. Cf. Hesychius, *s. v.* σηκύλλαι and Robert, *Hermes,* XL, 1905, p. 480.

244. Sikinos kalos.

Klein, p. 58, 23 (Hoppin, *Handb. R. F.,* II, p. 252, 7, by Oltos) p. 136, fig. 36; Neugebauer, *Führer durch das Antiquarium,* II, *Vasen, Berlin,* p. 123 (Inv. 3242), dating about 450 B. C. Contemporary with Memnon on vases. *I. G.,* I, 459, 8, a grave-stone from the end of the fifth century, mentions a Sikanos.

245. Sime kale.

Klein, 48, a black-figured hydria (*Cat. of Vases in Br. Mus.,* II, p. 196, B 336; *C. V. A., Br. Mus.,* fasc. 6, III H e, pl. 90, 4).

246. Simiades kalos.

Klein, 58; Beazley, *A. V.,* p. 14, no. 38 by Oltos. Memnon is an associate.

247. Simon (*v.* sub Phayllos).

248. Smikrion (*v.* sub Karystios).

249. Smikythos kalos.

Klein, 122; Hoppin, *Handb. R. F.,* I, p. 431, no. 1 by Euthymides; II, p. 258, no. 30 attributed to Oltos; II, p. 366, 14 by Phintias. Megakles and Philon are contemporaries. *I. G.,* I (Suppl.), 373 w8, p. 127 is a vase-dedication from the Akropolis by a Smikythos. *I. G.,* I, 130 gives a Smikythos as secretary of the treasures of the goddess in 425/4, though this man, also mentioned by Aristophanes (*Knights,* 969) is too late in date. The Erechtheid gravestone (*I. G.,* I, 433, col. II, 40) of 459/8 B. C. may be the handsome ephebe of our vases.

250. Sokrates kalos.

Klein, 124; Beazley, *A. V.,* p. 77, 6, by Berlin Painter; p. 82, 79 also by him. These are vases from the first half of the fifth century. A Sokrates was strategos in the Samian War of 441/0 (*F. H. G.,* IV, p. 645), and also in the naval expedition around the Peloponnesos in 432/1 (*Thuk.,* II 23, 2). *I. G.,* I, 454, 6 is a grave-stone with this name from the end of the fifth century.

251. Solon kalos.

Klein, 56; Hoppin, *Handb. R. F.,* II, p. 256, 26, attributed to Oltos. The name of Memnon accompanies.

252. Sophanes kalos.

Klein, 133, a red-figured kantharos in Altenburg having the name of Polyeuktos also. The Sophanes who fought on Aigina in 488/7 B. C. (Her., VI, 92), was valorous at Plataia in 479 (Her., IX, 73-75), and died while commanding in 465 B. C. may possibly be the one who was an ephebe on early fifth century cases.

253. Sositheos kalos.

C. V. A., Louvre, fasc. 5, III I c, pl. 28, nos. 5 and 6. Cf. Demostratos, p. 93, no. 61.

254. Sostratos kalos.

Cf. Hartwig, *Meisterschalen,* p. 257, 3. On this vase one of three revelling men sings Σοστράτο καλō εἰμί. This shows that the figures in the scenes on Greek vases can be meant to be those of the persons mentioned in the inscriptions. This particular vase, a black-figured amphora, is given in Klein (*L. I.,* p. 37) under the heading of Sostratos I. The same name is found on red-figured vases (*e. g.,* Graef-Langlotz, *op. cit.,* II, 3, no. 1294, p. 114, and 1295). Klein calls this one Sostratos II, but Hauser in his thorough and critical review of the second edition of Klein (*Berl. Phil. Woch.,* 1900, 1367) says that Sostratos I (Klein, p. 37) and Sostratos II (Klein, p. 122) are one and the same person. This was a very common name in Athens; Kirchner's numbers 13324 to 13374 give examples of the name. Of these only two can fit in date the person on our vases; they are 13339 (*I. G.,* I, 433, col. II, 28) from the year 459/8; and 13372, Sostratos, father of Autokleides. Autokleides was the secretary of the treasury of the goddess in 412/1 B. C. (*I. G.,* I, 134, 135, 152, 166, 167). All we know of this Sostratos is that he was the father of Autokleides and that he was called Phrearrios. On Sostratos in general on vases cf. Aristophanes, *Clouds,* 678, for a reflection on his effeminate ways (Sostrate instead of Sostratos). He appears on vases from the end of the sixth century.

255. Sotinos kalos (*v.* sub Demostratos).

256. Stesagoras kalos.

Helbig (*Mél. d'Arch. et d'Histoire,* IX, 1889, p. 25, pl. 1) says: " Le nom de Στεσαγόρας καλός est tout ce qu'il y a de plus aristocratique. Un petit bourgeois ou un métèque athénien, au moins avant l'époque hellénistique, n'aurait pas osé donner ce nom à un de ses fils. Le nom se rencontre à Athènes exclusivement dans une grande famille qui prétendait descendre d'Eaque, et dont les membres les plus célèbres étaient Miltiade, le vainqueur de Marathon, et son fils Cimon."

Only one vase, a red-figured cup (Klein, *L. I.,* p. 93, *C. V. A., Copenhague,* fasc. 3, III I, pl. 139) has this name; it dates about the middle of the fifth century. The known persons in the genealogy given by Helbig (*loc. cit.,* p. 26) do not date at the same time. Stesagoras I is anterior to Peisistratos and before the invention of red-figure; Stesagoras II was killed in 515 B. C. (Her., VI, 38, 39), and was a contemporary of Epiktetos, the oldest red-figured artist. Furthermore he, the second, could not have been an interesting person to the artisans of the Kerameikos, because he did not live in Athens but was brought up in the Chersonese by his uncle, Miltiades: Her., VI, 103, ὁ μὲν δὴ πρεσβύτερος τῶν παίδων τῷ Κίμωνι Στησαγόρης ἦν τηνικαῦτα παρὰ τῷ πάτρῳ Μιλτιάδῃ τρεφόμενος ἐν τῇ Χερσονήσῳ. Nevertheless, considering the typical way in which the same names repeat themselves in the important Athenian families, it is highly probable that the Stesagoras of our cup belonged to the same family as the two known Stesagorases. Helbig believes that if Hippokleides, archon in 563 (Her. VI, 127-130), of whose descendants we know nothing, had had children, it is probable that the name Stesagoras must have figured in this branch of the line, too. The family was very prominent in fifth century Athens; its politics were directed at that time by another member of that family, Kimon, son of the victor of Marathon.

259. Stesias kalos.

Hoppin, *Handb. B. F.,* p. 100, 6, by Exekias (*C. V. A., Louvre,* fasc. 3, III H e, pl. 19, 1); p. 108, 11 (Neugebauer, *Führer durch das Antiquarium,* II, *Vasen, Berlin,* p. 41, F 1698), attributed to Exekias. This love-name, one of the earliest of its kind on black-figured vases of the period of Exekias (Klein, p. 33; on three vases), helps show the close relation between the poets and these inscriptions at the very inception of the latter. It is through an identification that this relation becomes apparent. After having been celebrated on vases for a beautiful youth, our Stesias was mourned by a poet again for having died "too soon." The distych on his sepulchral monument (*I. G.*, I, 479, sixth century) reads:

> Σῆμα φίλου παιδὸς τόδε ... κατέθηκεν
> Στησίου, ὃν θάνατος δακρυόεις καθέχει.

It is to be dated in the time of Exekias, soon after the middle of the century (cf. the quatrain with Memnon, Dorotheos, and others, p. 102 above), so that, while still in the flower of his youth, our Stesias must have died.

258. Stesileos kalos.

Klein, 40; Neugebauer, *Führer durch das Antiquarium*, p. 44, no. 3274; p. 78, no. 1906 (Lücken, *Gr. Vasenbilder*, pl. II). Kirchner thinks that he is the "vir in armis exercitatus, de quo res ridicula Lachete duce facta narratur" in Sicily in 427 B. C. (*Pros. Att.*, 12905). A strategos of this name fell at Marathon (Her., VI, 114). Cf. the *Stesileos kalos*, no. 76 in Chapter III, who may be the youth meant on vases.

259. Stroibos kalos.

Hoppin, *Handb. B. F.*, p. 116, 6-8 by Glaukytes; Klein, p. 49, lists four black-figured vases with this name. Tonks (*A. J. A.*, IX, 1905, p. 290) gives the vases with the praise of Stroibos to Phrynos, the Little Master potter and artist, and also suggests that this is the same Stroibos as the one who was the father of the Leokrates who commanded at Plataia (*v.* no. 156 above).

260. Teisias kalos.

Klein, 145, 16; Beazley, *A. V.*, p. 130, 10; *C. V. A., Louvre*, fasc. 6, III I c, pl. 50, 6. The name of Charmides accompanies. A Teisias was strategos in 417/6 B. C. and went to Melos in 416 (*Thuk.*, V, 84, 1-4). In Lysias frag. 232 (cf. no. 236 above) there is a Teisis the beloved of Pytheas. The name is found as that of a potter even in the sixth century. Cf. Robinson, *Greek Vases at Toronto,* pp. 150-151.

261. Telenikos kalos.

Klein, 52, a black-figured lekythos formerly in the Van Branteghem collection, and published with illustration in *Gaz. Arch.,* 1888, pl. 29. Cf. Haspels, *Attic Black-Figured Lekythoi,* p. 228, 50 bis, by Sappho Painter. Andokides (I, 35) says that a Telenikos was indicted by Teukros for mutilating the herms in 415 B. C., and, as many of our *paides kaloi* seem to have been mixed up in this escapade, it is possible that this is the Telenikos meant.

262. Teles kalos.

Klein, 41, one black-figured vase, a hydria: *C. V. A., Madrid,* fasc. 1, III H e, pl. 8, 2. The names of Nikias and Paris also occur as *kalos* names.

263. Thaliarchos kalos.

Klein, 88, fig. 23, an early fifth-century pyxis in Paris. *I. G.,* I (Suppl.), 299a, p. 147, mentions a treasurer of the goddess from the mid-fifth century, who had this name. Beazley groups two pyxides (one in Athens, Graef-Langlotz, *Akrop. Vas.* II, p. 53, no. 574, pl. 44; and the one in Paris in Petit Palais, Klein, p. 88) with this *kalos* name along with two pyxides mentioned above (*s. v.* Lysikles) and assigns them all to Epiktetos about 510 B. C. Cf. *B. S. R.,* XI, 1929, p. 17 note.

264. Theodoros kalos.

Klein, 65; Beazley, *A. V.,* p. 42, 1-2. The names of Isarchos and Epileios accompany both times. *I. G.,* I, Suppl., pp. 88 and 181, 373,[90] is a dedication by Theodoros, the son of Onesimos. Diodoros (XII, 31) and the scholiast to Aristophanes' *Acharnians,* 67, mention a Theodoros who was archon in 438/7 B. C. Cf. the Theodoros, no. 77 in Chapter III.

265. Theognis kalos.

Theognis, instrumental figure that he was in the broadcast of the *pais kalos* sentiment throughout Greece (as we have seen), himself appears forcefully celebrated in an inscription with *kalos*—the very adjective that he first struck so deep into the Greek consciousness in this specialized sense. The *kalos* is heightened in the case of the lip-cup from Selinus (*Beazley, J. H. S.*, LII, 1932, pp. 194 and 176, footnote 19) with the inscription for him: Θεόγνις: καλὸς νὴ Δία. Beazley says, " Theognis does not occur elsewhere as a love-name; and I suppose that this is our earliest authority for the expression νὴ Δία, as the cup cannot be later than 550 B. C." The floruit of the poet was in Olympiad 59 (544-540 B. C.), and so the cup undoubtedly refers to him, whether his personal appearance justified the intensity of the praise or not. Possibly on a visit to Athens his youthful charm impressed the society there. Certainly the other known instances of this name in Attic history (*I. G.*, I, 456, 11, a grave-stone; and *I. G.*, I, Suppl., 462d, p. 111, line 11, also a grave-stone) are too late in date to refer so neatly to the Theognis of the vase as the poet himself.

266. Therikles kalos.

This name, hitherto unknown as a love-name, was found on the floor of a partly glazed krater discarded c. 460 B. C. and unearthed in the Athenian Agora (*Hesperia*, V, 1936, p. 350, no. 6, fig. 21). *Kalos* inscriptions are incised, the inscriptions being with the invocation θεοί (cf. Smith, *Cat. of Vases in Br. Mus.*, III, p. 213, E 291). The inscriptions read: Θερικλῆς καλός · Τιμόξενος καλός. Χαρμίδης καλός, Therikles is otherwise unknown on vases. Here he is a contemporary of Timoxenos and Charmides. The *Classical Journal*, XXX, 1935, p. 573, speaks of him as " doubtless the famous Corinthian-Athenian potter, inventor of the highly prized Theriklean cups." Even though he was a contemporary of Aristophanes, the Therikles on the Agora vase may be the same. (Cf. on Therikles, *T. A. P. A.*, vol. LII, 1921, pp. 119 ff.).

267. Thero kale.

Klein, 85. Hoppin, *Handb. R. F.,* II, p. 250, 2, by Oltos; I, p. 409, 25, by Euphronios.

268. Thespieus kalos.

A graffito on the underside of the foot of a skyphos of Corinthian type mentions this new love-name (*Hesperia,* V, 1936, p. 348, no. 2, fig. 16). Is it a proper name or an *ethnikon,* " the boy from Thespiae? " The vase was discarded c. 460 B. C. Cf. Appendix A, below.

269. Thessalos' Son is Fair.

This inscription is on the base of a red-figured fragment from Athens (Graef-Langlotz, *op. cit.,* II, 2, no. 863, p. 81, pl. 75). Peek (*Epigr. Nachtr.,* II, 3, p. 131) reads it: Κ[αλ]ὸς ὑὸς Θεσ[σ]άλο, and says that the four-barred sigma in ὑός can be a mistake. The reading in the text proper, ΚΑΛΟϞ ΕΚ . . . ΟϞLΟΜΘ does not spell out anything sensible after the *kalos,* and Peek's interpretation is one that can be followed. What would the inscription, then, say? " The son of Thessalos is fair? " Or possibly, if an extra sigma has been left out, " Thessalos is a fair son "? In any case, the name Thessalos reminds us of Peisistratos' bastard son, Hegesistratos (Kirchner 7207), known as Thessalos when, after the death of his father, he returned to Athens and was received into citizenship. Before that he had been tyrant of Sigeion, appointed by Peisistratos (535-527 B. C.). But Thukydides (VI, 55, 1) says that he died childless: ἡ στήλη περὶ τῆς τῶν τυράννων ἀδικίας ἡ ἐν τῇ 'Αθηναίων ἀκροπόλει σταθεῖσα, ἐν ᾗ Θεσσαλοῦ μὲν οὐδ' Ἱππάρχου οὐδεὶς παῖς γέγραπται. Assuming that it is the famous and popular illegitimate son of the tyrant mentioned on our vase-fragment, either the name is in the genitive and there was a son, or it is in the nominative and it is Thessalos himself, who is praised for his attractions. The inscription on the vase fragment can hardly be interpreted as Peek seems to do, as " Kalos son of Thessalos."

There is no particular way of dating the fragment. Red-figure ware came into use at Athens at the time of Thessalos' return to Athens, and it could date from that time. If the fragment is later, it may refer to Thessalos, son of Kimon (Kirchner. 7208). This Thessalos was the accuser of Alkibiades in the affair over the violation of the mysteries (Plutarch, *Alkib.*, 19, 22; *Kimon*, 16; *Perikl.*, 29). He is of the family of Miltiades, hero of Marathon, and the nobility of his birth would recommend him to such a distinction.

270. Thrasykleides.

Klein, 102; Hoppin, *Handb. R. F.*, I, p. 206, 2, by the Diogenes Amphora Painter. *Diogenes kalos* accompanies. The dedicator of an Akropolis inscription (Lolling, Κατάλογος, XIX, p. 7; *J. H. S.*, XIII, 1892, pl. VI, no. 20) had this name. In the *C. V. A., Brit. Mus.*, fasc. 3, III I c, pl. 4, 2 a and b (E 261) καλός is taken separately but it might go with Thrasykleides or Diogenes.

271. Timarchos kalos.

Klein, 130; Beazley, *A. V.*, p. 159; *C. V. A., Villa Giulia*, fasc. 1, III I c, pl. 1. He is praised by the Syriskos Painter. Diodoros (XIII, 65, 1-3) cites a Timarchos who was strategos at Megara in 409/8 B. C. Cf. also *I. G.*, I, 181; Timarchos Hellenotamias.

272. Timodemos kalos.

Klein, 151, a red-figured alabastron in the Cabinet des Médailles. Kirchner's numbers 13668-71 are all grave-stones from the second half of the fifth century, all that we have in the way of identification for our Timodemos.

273. Timokrates kalos.

Klein, 148: two red-figured lekythoi, one in Oxford, 267, not yet published in *C. V. A.*, the other in Terranuova, Russo collection. Thukydides (V, 19, 2 and 24) says that a Timokrates swore to the oath in the peace with the Spartans in the year 421 B. C.

274. Timonides kalos.

Klein, 149; Beazley, *A. V.*, p. 472, 29, by the Providence Painter. The president of the prytany in 428/7 B. C. was called Timonides (*I. G.*, I, 40).

275. Timotheos kalos.

Klein, 36: two black-figured vases, one in Corneto, the other in the market.

276. Timoxenos kalos.

Klein, 146. *C. V. A., Brit. Mus.*, fasc. 5, III I c, pl. 49, 2. A new appearance of this name is on a black-glazed kylix base, on the underside of which is inscribed the name (*Hesperia*, V, 1936, p. 348, no. 1, fig. 16; also on no. 6, fig. 21). Timoxenos is praised on two vases by the Charmides Painter, one having the praise of Charmides as well (Beazley, *A. V.*, p. 129, 3; p. 130, 5); he is also mentioned on a vase by the Nikon Painter (*C. V. A., Providence*, fasc. 1, pl. 15, 1, and p. 24). This name is known from a sepulchral monument from 425/4 B. C. (*I. G.*, I², 949). The president of the prytany, when the treaties with Rhegium and Leontini were proposed by Kallias in 433/2 (*I. G.*, I², 51, 52), also had this name.

277. Tleson kalos.

Klein, 66; *C. V. A., Brussels*, fasc. 1, III I c, pl. 4, 2. Probably not the potter, who is contemporary with Exekias, whereas this vase dates c. 465 B. C.

278. Xanthes kalos (cf. above *s. v.* Kallias).

A cup by the Ambrosios Painter in the Ashmolean Museum at Oxford (*C. V. A.*, fasc. 1, III I, pl. V, nos. 5 and 6; pl. 1, 6), dating c. 510 B. C., has this name. Twenty-seven or more vases are attributed to this painter (Beazley, *V. A.*, p. 20, n. 5 and *A. V.*, p. 38, no. 8), who is known to us from the name of the ephebe, Ambrosios (Klein, 90). Ambrosios does not occur in Kirchner, and Pape-Benseler calls the name late, giving a single reference to the *Anthology,* IX, 671, an anonymous piece to an "Ambrosios of Mylasa" (in Karia).

Xanthes may be one of the Athenian board of ecclesiastical commissioners for the management of the property of the Delian temple mentioned in *I. G.,* I², 377, 3. The same inscription quoted by Hicks and Hill (*Greek Historical Inscriptions,* 50) reads (N)eanthes or (Kl)eanthes, but in *I. G.* it is clearly Xanthes, and Tod (*Greek Historical Inscriptions,* no. 54) reads it the same. Beazley in the Oxford fascicule (*loc. cit.*) connects the name with the *I. G.* inscription. If the Xanthes who captured a part of Athens with his boyish beauty in 510 B. C. (then at the minimum orthodox age of fifteen, hence born c. 525) lived on to the year of this inscription, 434/2 B. C. he would then have been ninety-one, a not impossible but rather unusually tenacious age.

The name also appears on a red-figured Nolan amphora in the Hermitage,[98] where we are reminded inaccurately of a red-figured cup in the British Museum, E 19 (Klein, p. 56, no. 14, not p. 33 as the *Anzeiger* says) with a recension of names, among others being those of Memnon and *Xanthos.* Memnon was called *kalos* by admirers for a decade, 520-510, so associations with him would be a good thing for us to remember Xanthes by; also Xanthes was a good enough Attic name. But two occurrences on vases of the form *Xanthes* establish this reading quite as firmly as the more Attic *Xanthos.* However the forms quarrel, it is doubtless the same person meant.

The exterior of the Oxford cup (cf. *C. V. A.,* fasc. 1, III I, pl. 5, 5 and 6) has many interesting names, which though without an appended *kalos* are useful in chronological groupings. The scene is a kind of komos; a column krater stands on the ground in the middle of sides A and B, around which youths and men with beards carouse. On the right of side A a naked youth gambols up to the krater to fill (or refill) his oinochoe; a man in an himation follows with a drinking forn. To the

---

[98] *Arch. Anz.,* XLV, 1930, p. 32.

left a youth with a stick endeavours to elude the grasp of a man who has him by the wrist. The names are: Ναύβιος, Ἀντίμαχος, Διόδορος and the man catching the youth . . . ντετε (which may or may not be taken as a vocative, whether preceded by χαῖρε or not, says Beazley). What seems more probable to us, in consideration of the evidence, is that this is a case of decadent feminization, and that the name was to be read Euantete in the sense of the Κλεωνύμη for Κλεώνυμος (Aristophanes, *Clouds*, 680) and the Σωστράτη instead of Σώστρατος (Aristoph., *op. cit.*, 678). The meaning of Euantete, "Easy-to-meet," also suggests the trade-name or *nom de guerre* of a *kinaidos*.

The names on side B of this cup are Kallaischros and Hipponikos. The Antimachos on this side is known on several cups of this period.[99] This must have been a coterie of *enfants terribles* who indulged in many pranks. The Diodoros also on this side is recalled on a psykter by Smikros, Louvre G 58, illustrated on the frontispiece of Emmanuel's *Essai sur L'Orchestique Grecque*, on which piece there is yet another feminization: *Mosokle* for *Mosokles*, which is also found on a black-figured amphora of the same period in Munich.[100] Hipponikos is a name known in the family of Kallias; Kallaischros[101] in that of Kritias, who was leader of the radical faction of the thirty in 404 B. C. Roughly speaking, the persons celebrated on archaic vases are the ancestors of the Sokratic and Platonic circle.

For the boy arrested at the krater compare the cup by the Epileios Painter in Munich, cf. F. R., pl. 155.

The vase in the Hermitage cited above (Inventory 5577) is said to be stylistically analogous to the work of the Provi-

---

[99] Klein, *L. I.*, pp. 67 and 105; add Munich cup 2591. In Klein cf. especially p. 67, no. 3 with Kleonymos; Kraiker, *Die Rotfigurigen Attischen Vasen Heidelbergs*, p. 14, no. 32.

[100] Lau, *Gr. Vasen*, pl. 12, 1.

[101] One Kallaischros, who was the father of the Kritias mentioned above as leader of the Thirty, poet and orator, was himself a leader of the Four Hundred in 411 B. C. This Kallaischros may have been the grandson of the one on our vase.

dence Painter (480-470). This presents an interesting point, for it means that Xanthes must have been forty-five when he was still called *kalos* on a vase dating from the time of the Providence Painter (assuming that he was born in 525 to be at least fifteen in 510 B. C., the time of the Oxford vase). This cripples the old theory that *kalos* on vases belongs only to ephebes of fifteen to twenty-five years, and supports the observations which Langlotz has made on vases showing Leagros a mature, rather paunchy man in the later, riper years of his life. So on the Oxford cup Xanthes is remembered not perhaps for his haughty lineage, as Leagros was, but rather for a notorious whirl-top youth, if the scene on the Ambrosios cup gives an indication of the character of his younger years, spent in wanton company.

279. Xenodoke kale.

Klein, 39; *Cat. of Vases in Br. Mus.*, II, p. 288, B 631, a black-figured oinochoe with white ground and the inscription Ξενοδόκη [μοι δοκε]ῖ παῖς καλή. The vase is a plastic one by Charinos from the second half of the sixth century. Klein doubts the δοκεῖ and Wernicke (*Arch. Zeit.*, XLIII, 1885, p. 252) once read the name as Ξενόδοτος καλός, but in his monograph on love-names (1889) he corrects his reading to Xenodoke. There are two huge gaps in the inscription, but Wernicke and Walters follow Cecil Smith's restoration of a δοκεῖ, which Klein rejected. Nicole is the only one still to read Xenodotos. The kappa is missing in the extant inscription, but Klein and Walters read a clear and definite epsilon at the end of the name and after that a clear *kale*.

280. Xenon I kalos.

Klein, 123; Beazley, *A. V.*, p. 59, n. 4, by Euphronios. A contemporary of Pheidiades and Sostratos.

281. Xenon II kalos.

Klein, 118; Beazley, *A. V.*, p. 426, n. 16 (London E 94), by the Kodros Painter. *I. G.*, I, 448, col. II, 26, is a sepulchral stone from the end of the fifth century, and may refer to the demise of Xenon II.

282. Xenophon kalos.

Klein, 61; Hoppin, *Handb. R. F.*, II, p. 366, 11, attributed to Phintias (here it is the name of an athlete in the scene); I, p. 144, 2, by the Kerberos Plate Painter, and having the name of Dorotheos as well. This may be the Xenophon who was strategos at Samos in 441/0 B. C. (Androtion, *F. H. G.*, IV, p. 645), who fell at Spartolos in 429 (*Thuk.*, II, 79, 1-7), and who was satirized by Kratinos (Kock, *Com. Att. Frag.*, I, p. 28, 53) for his καταπυγοσύνην, a familiar charge against several of our *paides kaloi*; cf. Alkaios and Antimachos, above.

283. Zephyria kale.

Klein, 149, one red-figured vase, a lekythos in a private London collection.

APPENDIX

A. Boeotian vases with *kalos* inscriptions

Klein (*L. I.*, p. 53) gives three Boeotian vases with *kalos* names inscribed on them. The names are: Sibon, Kleiergos, and Abaiodoros. The first is in the Ionic alphabet, and comes from Abae; it is considerably later than the others (publ. *Ath. Mitt.*, XIV, 1889, p. 151). The second (Berlin 2116) may not be a *kalos* inscription at all, as Collitz (*Sammlung Gr. Dialekt-Inschriften*, I, 793; *I. G.*, A., 206a) reads it Κλείεργος Καλόκει, though we incline to read καλὸς εἶ, an inscription of the type we are considering; the inscription is incised, as most of the non-Attic ones. The third, Abaiodoros kalos, in the National Museum at Athens, comes from the Kabeirion, is early Boeotian and incised also. In adding a fourth *kalos* name to the list of Boeotian vases, Ure (*J. H. S.*, XXIX, 1909, pp. 315, 320, 342) questions whether these vases were incised in a Boeotian shop or later by a Boeotian owner, or whether perhaps imported from Attica. The last possibility is unlikely, as it is not probable that a Boeotian, if he had had a *kalos*-vase made for him in an Attic shop, would have chosen so plain a vase for it, or that an Attic shopman would have gratified his taste for Boeotian lettering. He concludes that they were Boeotian-made, and that Teisias may have introduced to Boeotia the *kalos*-vase as the latest thing from Athens. The fourth vase, which he adds to Klein's three, is a plain, black-glaze kantharos from Rhitsona and now in the Museum at Thebes. The inscription on it is " Anticharos kalos," Ἀντίχαρος καλός. It is incised on the main body of the vase, and obviously meant to be seen. Ure says, "The provenance of our black-glaze ware is uncertain, but the V for X is Boeotian or Chalcidian. We have no example of a *kalos* vase from Chalkis, and we may reasonably leave it out of the question. Our choice is probably between Boeotia itself and Athens." We have already chosen in favor of the latter. Now the vase was found in a burial, and Ure, basing his speculations on his acceptance of Klein's erroneous statement (*L. I.*, p. 24) that *kalos* names are not found on white-ground sepulchral lekythoi, thinks that " a *kalos* inscription written on the spot, and not a work of art from the outside, would surely be out of place at a funeral unless it had special appropriateness to the present or the past." And so, who was Anticharos? A friend of the past whose name the dead man had once written on a vase and then kept it? Or was he a mourner giving back a gift, as in II Samuel, 1, 23? Ure suggests an identification with an Antichares mentioned by Herodotos, V, 43 (also in *I. G.*, VII, 2385, 2916, 3191), who was old and important enough in 511 B. C. to give advice to Dorieus, the Spartan prince. When the vase was buried he must have been a young man, not improbably a young aristocrat of the familiar *kalos* type. Antichares, Herodotos says, lived at Heleon, which is only four miles away from Rhitsona, where the vase was found buried.

As further evidence that the statement in Walters-Birch (*History of Ancient Pottery,* II, p. 266) must be rejected, that *kalos* inscriptions "occur exclusively on Attic vases," we add two more, published by Ure (*Sixth and Fifth Century Pottery from Rhitsona,* pp. 29, 103): Κόμαρχος καλός and Θέστιος καλός. The publisher makes no attempt at reading or identifying them. The former, it is interesting to note, also appears on Attic vases of the Ambrosios Painter and Euthymides (Hoppin, *Hand, R. F.,* sub Ambrosios, p. 29, no. 15; *Euthymides,* p. 12). For this name, see *I. G.* (I, 134-135, 165, 167), where we have Leukaios, son of Komarchos of Aphidna, mentioned as the secretary for the treasures of the goddess in 413/412 B. C. This would date Komarchos around the second quarter of the fifth century, and accord well enough with the vase chronology.

The reading of the second of these two names is somewhat more problematical. If it is Thespios, that would be usual enough in Boeotia, as that is the name of the founder and king of Thespiai in Boeotia (Diod. Sic., IV, 29, 68; V, 15; Paus., IX, 26, 6). But the letters fit better the name Thestios.

We add to those already mentioned here still another Boeotian *kalos*-vase with the name of Gorginos [1] or Gorginis, if Gorginios is a genitive as it should be. The inscription reads: Γοργίνιός ἐμι, ὁ κότυλος καλὸς καλō. The vase was found in Thisbe. Rolfe [2] translates: "I am the kotylos of Gorginos; the beautiful cup of a beautiful owner." The name of the owner is in the nominative case, and its form is that of a proper adjective; but the writer of the inscription thought of it as equivalent to the usual genitive, as is shown by the καλὸς καλοῦ which follows. The letters are in the Boeotian alphabet. The Ionic letter-forms were not introduced into Boeotia until c. 360 B. C., but the general appearance of both the cup and the inscription is much earlier. Rolfe (*loc. cit.*, p. 100, note 4) says: "Our vase might belong to the fifth century." Pape-Benseler gives instances of Γοργίδας, Γοργίων, and Γόργοινος as proper names. There was an Argive by the name of Γόργιλος, as we know from Aristotle (*Ath. Pol.*, 17) where the father of the second wife of Peisistratos is so called.

B. Φιλτῶς ἠμὶ τᾶς καλᾶς ἁ κύλιξ ἁ ποικίλα. Published *J. H. S.*, VI, 1885, pp. 371 ff. The inscription is on a rough black-figured kylix from Rhodes, and is of a Doric character, as can be seen in ἠμί and the genitive termination. The vase is now in the British Museum. The inscription reads:

"Philto's fairest of the fair;
Philto's painted cup am I."

The cup has a scene of a bearded figure with a chelys on the interior; on the exterior is a quadriga with Maenads riding on mules. The statement in the *J. H. S.*, *loc. cit.*, p. 372, is:

---

[1] Cf. Simonides, frag. 156: Μίλωνος τόδ' ἄγαλμα καλοῦ καλόν; and Rhianus, *Anth. Pal.*, VI, 278: παῖς 'Ασκληπιάδεω καλῶι καλὸν εἴσατο Φοίβωι.

[2] Kretschmer, *Vaseninschriften*, p. 4, n. 3; *Classical Review*, IV, 1890, p. 383; *Harvard Studies*, II, p. 89; Beazley, *J. H. S.*, LII, 1932, p. 178, n. 21.

"It is curious that the beautiful Philto or her admirer should have taken so much pains to identify as her property a cup which is intrinsically of so little value. May it not be that painted fictile ware was seldom or never in antiquity applied to daily use, but was reserved, as *editions de luxe* of the shapes of metal or common crockery, for presents, or for temple or funeral service? In that case the meanest painted vase would for the ancients have had its own peculiar interest." Though Miss Richter [3] has definitely disproved such an assumption as this latter, it is an interesting fact that the inscription in this case is on such a crudely drawn vase. The idea or fashion for a *kalos* inscription had doubtless strayed down to Rhodes, where this vase seems certainly to have been made, and this particular dedication to the beauty of Philto suggests that it, like its Attic equivalents, was inscribed at the order of the purchaser. Certainly, such a rough work was much more probably the property of an individual than a dedication. The strong Doric character of the inscription makes the origin of the cup most probably Rhodian.

The name Philto is feminine. Rolfe [4] says: "In the *J. H. S.* the form Φιλτῶς is given, but according to Professor F. D. Allen, *Greek Versification in Inscriptions* (as cited p. 134), p. 70, it should be Φιλτός, a Doric genitive."

C. καλ[ὸς] Παντέλεος, τὰ ποτήρια καλά.

This inscription is on a black-figured skyphos found in Opuntian Lorkis, Kretschmer, *Vaseninschriften,* p. 4, n. 3. Cf. *B. C. H.,* II, 1878, p. 588, pl. XXVI, 27. Kirchner, 11600, cites a Pantaleon, son of Kleagoras, mentioned by Aischines (*Against Timarchos,* 156) as κάλλιστος γεγενημένος καὶ πλείστων καὶ σωφρονεστάτων τυχὼν ἐραστῶν. There is also a Pantaleon on the Erechtheid monument for those fallen in the foreign wars of 459/8 B. C. (*I. G.,* I, 433, col. I, 7). Of a poet Panteleios we know from Stobaeus, *Florilegium,* VII, 62, περὶ ἀνδρείας;

---

[3] *Craft of Athenian Pottery,* p. 108.
[4] *Harvard Studies,* II, p. 92, n. 6.

in speaking of the valour of the Athenians against the Persians at Marathon Stobaeus adds nine lines which he says were written about this event by him. It is difficult to know how to read our inscription, whether as a genitive of Panteleus or a nominative, Panteleios. The name is a variant of Pantaleon perhaps but Pantaleon is probably a different person.

D. South Italian Vases.

Klein, p. 170, lists two such vases with inscriptions to *Eupolis* and *Glyko*.

SELECTED BIBLIOGRAPHY

Beazley, J. D.: *Attische Vasenmaler des rotfigurigen Stils.* Tübingen, 1925 (second edition being prepared).
——— *Attic Red-Figured Vases in American Museums.* Cambridge, 1918.
——— *Attic Black-Figure.* London, 1928.
Bechtel, F.: *Die historischen Personennamen des griechischen bis zur Kaiserzeit.* Halle, 1927.
Becker: *Charikles. Bilder altgriechischer Sitte.* Leipzig, 1854. Second edition.
Bergk, T.: *Poetae Lyrici Graeci.* Teubner, 1882.
Bethe: "Die Dorische Knabenliebe," *Rheinisches Museum für Philologie,* LXII, 1907, pp. 438-475.
Bryant, A. A.: "Boyhood and Youth in the Days of Aristophanes," *Harvard Studies in Classical Philology,* XVIII, 1907, pp. 73-122.
Corpus Vasorum Antiquorum. Union Académique Internationale. Paris, 1922-.
Fick-Bechtel: *Die griechischen Personennamen.* Göttingen, 1894.
Furtwängler-Reichhold: *Griechische Vasenmalerei.* Munich, 1904- (continued by F. Hauser and E. Buschor).
Graef: *Die Antiken Vasen von der Akropolis zu Athen,* Unter Mitwirkung von Paul Hartwig, Paul Wolters, Robert Zahn. Band I, Berlin, 1909. Band II, Graef and Langlotz, Berlin, 1929-1933. Band I includes 4 Hefte of text and plates each; Band II is in 3 Hefte.
Hartwig, P.: *Die Griechischen Meisterschalen der Blütezeit des strengen rotfigurigen Stiles.* Berlin, 1893.
Haspels, C. H. E.: *Attic Black-Figured Lekythoi.* Paris, 1936.
Hoppin, C.: *Euthymides and His Fellows.* Cambridge, 1917.
——— *A Handbook of Greek Black-Figured Vases.* Paris, 1924.
——— *A Handbook of Attic Red-Figured Vases.* 2 vols. Cambridge, 1919.
Kirchner: *Prosopographia Attica.* 2 vols. Berlin, 1903. *Nachträge,* by J. Sundwall. Helsingfors, 1910.
Klein, W.: *Die Griechischen Vasen mit Lieblingsinschriften.* 2nd edition. Leipzig, 1898.
Kraiker: *Die Rotfigurigen Attischen Vasen Heidelbergs.* Berlin, 1931.
Kretschmer: *Die Griechischen Vaseninschriften.* Gütersloh, 1894.
Langlotz, E.: *Zur Zeitbestimmung der strengrotfigurigen Vasenmalerei und der gleichzeitigen Plastik.* Leipzig, 1920.
——— *Griechische Vasen in Würzburg.* Munich, 1932.

Licht, H.: *Sittengeschichte Griechenlands.* Zwei Bände und ein Ergänzungsband. Dresden, 1928.

Pape-Benseler: *Wörterbuch der griechischen Eigennamen.* 2 vols. 3rd edition, Braunschweig, 1875 and 1884.

Pottier, E.: *Vases Antiques du Louvre.* Paris, 1897-1922.

Richter, G. M. A.: *Red-Figured Athenian Vases in the Metropolitan Museum of Art.* 2 vols. New Haven, Yale University Press, 1936.

Studniczka, F.: "Antenor und Archaische Malerei," *Jahrbuch,* II, 1887, pp. 156-167.

Swindler, M. H.: *Ancient Painting.* New Haven, 1929.

Symonds, J. A.: *A Problem in Greek Ethics.* London, private, 1901.

Ure, P.: *Sixth and Fifth Century Pottery from Rhitsona.* Oxford, 1927.

Walters, H. B.: *Catalogue of the Greek and Etruscan Vases in the British Museum.* 4 vols. London, 1896-1925.

Wernicke: *Die griechischen Vasen mit Lieblingsnamen.* Halle, 1889.

ABBREVIATIONS

A. J. A.—*American Journal of Archaeology.*
Akrop. Vas—*Die Antiken Vasen von der Akropolis zu Athen*, Graef-Langlotz.
Arch. Anz.—*Archäologische Zeitung.*
Ath. Mitt.—*Mitteilungen des Deutschen Archäologischen Instituts, Athenische Abteilung.*
B. C. H.—*Bulletin de Correspondance Hellénique.*
Beazley, *A. V.*—*Attische Vasenmaler.*
   V. A.—*Attic Red-Figured Vases in American Museums.*
Berl. Phil. Woch.—*Berliner Philologische Wochenschrift.*
B. S. A.—*Annual of the British School at Athens.*
B. S. R.—*Papers of the British School at Rome.*
Cat. of Vases in Br. Mus.—*Catalogue of the Greek and Etruscan Vases in the British Museum.*
C. I. G.—*Corpus Inscriptionum Graecarum.*
C. V. A.—*Corpus Vasorum Antiquorum.*
F. H. G.—*Fragmenta Historicorum Graecorum*, Müller.
F. R.—Furtwängler-Reichhold, *Griechische Vasenmalerei.*
Hoppin, *Handb. B. F.*—*A Handbook of Greek Black-Figured Vases.*
   Handb. R. F.—*A Handbook of Attic Red-Figured Vases.*
I. G.—*Inscriptiones Graecae.*
Jahrb.—*Jahrbuch des Deutschen Archäologischen Instituts.*
J. H. S.—*Journal of Hellenic Studies.*
Klein, *L. I.*—*Die Griechischen Vasen mit Lieblingsinschriften.*
Rev. Arch.—*Revue Archéologique.*
Rev. Ét. Gr.—*Revue des Études Grecs.*
Rev. Ét. Anc.—*Revue des Études Anciennes.*

INDEX

Abaiodoros, 192.
Achilles, 48.
Agasias, 70.
Agasikles, 70.
Agathon, 70.
Agorakritos, 48.
Agrippa, 48.
Ainios, 72.
Aischines, orator, 24, 26, 39; *kalos*, 73.
Aischis, 74.
Aisimedes, 74.
Akestor, 75.
Akestorides, 75.
Aktaion, 49.
Alexander, 49.
Aleximachos, 75.
Alexis, 50.
Alexomenos, 76.
Alkaios, poet, 33, 61; *kalos*, 76.
Alkibiades, 26 (n. 44), 29 (n. 63), 76.
Alkides, 78.
Alkimachos, 78.
Alkimedes, 79.
Alkmeon, 79.
Alones, 81, 107.
Alphinoos, 50.
Amasis, 81.
Ambrosios, 81, 187.
Amphoe, 81.
Anakreon, 33.
Andokides, 81.
Andrias, 82.
Androxenos, 82.
Antheseos, 82.
Anthylla, 82.
Antias, 82.
Anticharos, 192.
Antigonos, 52.
Antileon, 51.
Antimachos, 83.
Antimenes, 83.
Antiochos, 51.
Antiphanes, 84, 96.
Antiphon, 84.
Antoxenos, 85.
Aphrodisia, 85.
Aphrodite, 10 (n. 38), 51.
Apollodoros, 85.
Archedike, 85.

Archestratos, 51.
Archias, 51, 86.
Archinos, 86.
Argilios, 51.
Aribazos, 52.
Aristagoras, 52, 86.
Aristarchos, 86.
Aristeides, 7, 86.
Aristokles, 52.
Aristoleon, 87.
Aristomenes, 87.
Aristophanes, 36-38, 91, 131.
Aristotle, 41, 43 (n. 112), 52.
Artemidos (?), 87.
Asopichos, 52.
Aster, 34.
Athenaia, 88.
Athenodotos, 88.
Autolykos, 52.
Automenes, 89.
Axiopeithes, 78-9, 89.

Bathyllos, 53.
Batrachos, 53, 136.
Brachas, 89.
Bryson, 53.

Chachrylion, 89.
Chairaia, 89.
Chairephon, 89.
Chairestratos, 89.
Chairias, 4, 90.
Chairippos, 90.
Chairis, 90.
Chares, 91.
Charidemos, 54.
Charmaios, 91.
Charmides, 91, 140, 142.
Charops, 92.
Chironeia, 92.
Choiros, 92.
Cicero, 25, 33, 59.
Crete, 20 ff.
Cyrus, 54.

Dailochos, 54.
Damas, 92.
Damon, 54.
Demetrios of Phaleron, 54.
Demokles, 54.
Demos, 10 (n. 37), 92, 131.

201

INDEX

Demostratos, 93.
Dexandros, 55.
Dexios, 93, 112-3.
Dikaios, 93.
Diodoros, 55, 96.
Diogenes, 97.
Diokles, 55, 97.
Diomnestos, 97.
Dion, 34, 97.
Dionokles, 97.
Dionysios, 55.
Diotimos, 98.
Dioxippos, 98.
Diphilos, 55, 98.
Dorotheos, 102.
Dositheos, 55.
Drakon, 55.
Dromippos, 100.

Echekles, 103.
Elita, 103.
Elpinikos, 103.
Epainetos, 104.
Epameinondas, 52.
Epeleios, 104.
Epidromos, 104.
Epikrates, 56.
Epilykos, 104.
Epimedes, 105.
Episthenes, 56.
Erasippos, 105.
Erinos, 105.
Eris, 106.
Erosantheo, 105.
Erothemis, 106.
Etearchos, 106, 170-1.
Euagra, 106.
Euainetos, 106.
Euaion, 101, 106.
Eualkides, 106.
Eualkes, 107-8.
Eualkos, 107.
Eubiotos, 56.
Eucharides, 108.
Eudemos, 170-1.
Eukleides, 96.
Eukrates, 170-1.
Eumares, 108.
Eumele, 110.
Euparitos, 110.
Euphamidas, 110.
Euphiletos, 110.
Euphragoras, 56.
Eupolis, 196.
Eurymachos, 112.

Euryptolemos, 112.
Euthydemos, 56, 59.
Euthymos, 112.
Eutychia, 10 (n. 38), 56.
Euxitheos, 56.

Ganymedes, 113.
Glaukon, 114.
Glaukytes, 114, 143-4.
Glyko, 196.
Gorgias, 152.
Gorginos (Gorginis?), 194.

Habrasia, 114.
Harmodios, 56.
harpagmos, 20.
Hediste, 114.
Hegeleos, 115.
Hegesilla, 115.
Herakleitos, 57.
Heras, 115.
Hermogenes, 11, 115.
Hesiod, 53.
Hestiaios, 115.
Hieron, 54.
Hiketas, 57.
Hiketes, 116.
Hilaros, 116.
Hipparchos, 117.
Hippeos, 57.
Hippias, 57.
Hippodamas, 119.
Hippokles, 120.
Hippokrates, 121.
Hippokritos, 121.
Hippolochos, 121.
Hippon, 121.
Hippoteles, 122.
Hippoxenos, 122.
Hygiainon, 98, 100, 122.

Iphis, 122.
Isarchos, 122.
Isokrates, 57.

Kalliades, 122.
Kallias, 6, 52, 122.
Kallides, 123.
Kallikles, 124.
Kallikrates, 124.
Kallipe, 124.
Kallippos, 124.
Kallistanthe, 124.
Kallisthenes, 124.
Kallisto, 124.

INDEX

Kalos Kothokides, 57.
Karton, 125.
Karystios, 125.
Kephisios, 126.
Kephisodoros, 58, 127, 135.
Kephisophon, 127.
Kineas, 127.
Kleander, 56, 58.
Kleiergos, 192.
Kleinias, 127.
Kleitagoras, 129.
Kleitarchos, 129.
Kleobis, 129.
Kleoboulos, 50, 58.
Kleomelos, 129.
Kleomenes, 58.
Kleonymos, 58.
Kleophon, 129.
Kleophonia, 129.
Komarchos, 193.
Korone, 130.
Krates, 130.
Kritias, 59, 130.
Kydias, 93, 94.
Kynippos, 131.

Labotos, 132.
Laches, 132, 141.
Ladamas, 132.
Lado, 59.
Lampon, 102, 132.
Leagros, 4, 114, 132-6.
Leokrates, 136.
Leon, 59.
Leptines, 60.
Lichas, 60, 100-1, 137.
Liteus, 137.
Lyandros, 137.
Lykis, 137.
Lykos, 33, 137.
Lysanias, 60.
Lysikles, 138.
Lysippides, 139.
Lysis, 139.
Lysitheos, 67, 152.

Marikas, 142-3.
Megabates, 60.
Megakles, 143-6.
Megistes, 60.
Meletos, 146-7.
Melieus, 148.
Melitta, 148.
Memnon, 148.
Menandros, 149-50.

Menis, 150-1.
Menon, 60, 151.
Mikion, 151.
Mikon, 152.
Mikros, 153.
Milon, 61, 153.
Miltiades, 153.
Mnesilla, 154.
Moryllos, 125-6, 154.
Mousa Paidike, 46.
Myiskos, 61.
Myllos, 154.
Mynnichos, 154.
Myrrhiniske, 154.
Myrtale, 155.
Mys, 155.
Myte, 155.

Naukleia, 155.
Nausistratos, 155.
Neokleides, 155.
Nereus, 156.
Nikesippos, 156.
Nikias, 156.
Nikodemos, 156.
Nikomas, 156.
Nikon, 157.
Nikondas, 158.
Nikophile, 158.
Nikosthenes, 158-9.
Nikostratos, 160.
Nikoxenos, 160.

Oinanthe, 160.
Oionokles, 97, 160.
Olympichos, 161.
Olympiodoros, 161.
Onetor, 161.
Onetorides, 1 (n. 2), 161.
Orthagoras, 161.

Paederasty, 10 f., 18 ff.
Paidikos, 2.
Palos, 162.
Panaitios, 163.
Pantarkes, 62.
Panteleos, 195.
Panteus, 58, 62.
Pantoxena, 163.
Paris, 163.
Pasikles, 164.
Pausanias, 51, 62.
Pausimachos, 164.
Pedieus, 164.
Periander, 62.

Perikleides, 164.
Phaidimos, 164-5.
Phaidros, 50, 63.
Phainippos, 166.
Phanokles, 35.
Phaon, 167.
Phayllos, 167-9.
Pheidiades, 171.
Pheidias, 48.
Pheidon, 171.
Philebos, 63.
Philliades, 171.
Philokles, 63.
Philon, 83 (n. 17), 172.
Philto, 194.
Phrinos, 172-3.
Pindar, 16, 72.
Pithon, 174.
Plato, 15, 17, 26 ff., 29, 34, 40, 63.
Polemainetos, 174.
Polyeuktos, 175.
Polykles, 135, 175.
Polykrates, 63.
Polyphrassmon, 175.
Pordax, 175.
Praxiteles, 175.
Protarchos, 63.
Proxenides, 175.
Proxenos, 176.
Ptoiodoros, 170, 176.
Pyles, 176.
Pythaios, 176.
Pythodelos, 177.
Pythodoros, 177.
Pythokles, 177.

Rhodopis, 178.

Sappho, 16.
Sekline, 178.
Sibon, 192.
Sikinos, 178.
Sime, 178.
Simiades, 178.
Simon, 170, 179.
Simonides, 53, 61, 65, 107.
Smerdis, 63.
Smikrion, 125-6.

Smikros, 153.
Smikythos, 179.
Sokrates, 64, 179.
Solon, 24, 39, 179.
Sophanes, 179.
Sosiades, 64.
Sositheos, 93, 180.
Sostratos, 180.
Sotinos, 93, 180.
Stesagoras, 180.
Stesias, 1 (n. 2), 181.
Stesileos, 64, 182.
Stroibos, 182.
Suidas, 15, 17.

Taleides, 1.
Tamynis, 152.
Teisias, 182.
Telenikos, 183.
Teles, 183.
Thaliarchos, 183.
Theodoros, 60, 65, 183.
Theognetos, 65.
Theognis, 21, 31-2, 184.
Theokritos, 34, 65.
Thera, 21-4.
Therikles, 184.
Thero, 185.
Theron, 65.
Thespieus, 185.
Thessalos, 185.
Thestios, 193.
Thrasykleides, 186.
Timarchos, 186.
Timodemos, 186.
Timokrates, 186.
Timonides, 187.
Timotheos, 187.
Timoxenos, 187.
Tleson, 187.

Xanthes, 187.
Xenodoke, 190.
Xenon, 190.
Xenophon, historian, 15, 17, 59, 64; kalos, 191.

Zeno, 52, 65.
Zephyria, 191.

MORALS AND LAW IN ANCIENT GREECE

An Arno Press Collection

Apffel, Helmut. **Die Verfassungsdebatte Bei Herodot (3,80-82)**, Wuest, Karl, **Politisches Denken Bei Herodot** and Bruns, Ivo, **Frauenemancipation in Athen.** Three vols. in one. 1957/1935/1900

Bevan, Edwyn. **Stoics and Sceptics.** 1913

Bolkestein, Hendrik. **Wohltaetigkeit und Armenpflege im Vorchristlichen Altertum.** 1939

Bolkestein, Johanna Christina. **Hosios En Eusebēs,** and Bolkestein, Hendrik, **Theophrastos' Charakter der Deisidaimonia als Religionsgeschichtliche Urkunde.** Two vols. in one. 1936/1929

Bonner, Robert J. **Evidence in Athenian Courts,** and Harrell, Hansen Carmine, **Public Arbitration in Athenian Law.** Two vols. in one. 1905/1936

Caillemer, Exupère. **Études Sur Les Antiquités Juridiques D'Athènes.** Ten parts in one. 1865-1872

Clerc, Michel. **Les Métèques Atheniens.** 1893

Fustel De Coulanges, [Numa Denis]. **Recherches Sur Le Droit De Propriété Chez Les Grecs** and **Recherches Sur Le Tirage Au Sort Appliqué À La Nomination Des Archontes Athéniens.** 1891

Croissant, Jeanne. **Aristote et Les Mystères.** 1932

Davidson, William L. **The Stoic Creed.** 1907

Demosthenes. **Demosthenes Against Midias.** With Critical and Explanatory Notes and an Appendix by William Watson Goodwin. 1906

Demosthenes. **Demosthenes on the Crown.** With Critical and Explanatory Notes; An Historical Sketch and Essays by William Watson Goodwin. 1901

Demosthenes. **Demosthenes Against Androtion and Against Timocrates.** With Introductions and English Notes by William Wayte. Second Edition. 1893

Demoulin, Hubert. **Épiménide De Crète.** 1901

Diogenes, Laertius. **La Vie De Pythagore De Diogène Laërce.** Édition Critique Avec Introduction et Commentaire par A[rmand] Delatte. 1922

Dyroff, Adolf. **Die Ethik Der Alten Stoa.** 1897

Egermann, Franz. **Vom Attischen Menschenbild** and **Arete und Tragisches Bewusstheit Bei Sophokles und Herodot.** Two vols. in one. [1952]/1957

Erdmann, Walter. **Die Ehe im Alten Griechenland.** 1934

Ferguson, John. **Moral Values in the Ancient World.** 1958

Forman, Ludovico Leaming, **Index Andocideus, Lycurgeus, Dinarcheus** and Preuss, Siegmund, **Index Aeschineus.** Two vols. in one. 1897/1896

Gernet, Louis. **Droit et Société Dans La Grèce Ancienne.** 1955

Gigante, Marcello. **Nomos Basileus.** 1956

Glotz, Gustave. **L'Ordalie Dans La Grèce Primitive.** 1904

Guiraud, Paul. **La Propriété Foncière En Grèce Jusqu'à La Conquête Romaine.** 1893

Haussoullier, B[ernard]. **La Vie Municipale En Attique.** 1883

Hemelrijk, Jacob. **Penia en Ploutos.** 1925

Hirzel, Rudolf. **Agraphos Nomos**, and Marg, Walter, **Der Charakter in Der Sprache Der Fruehgriechischen Dichtung.** Two vols. in one. 1900/1938

Hirzel, Rudolf. **Der Eid:** Ein Beitrag Zu Seiner Geschichte. 1902

Hitzig, Hermann Ferdinand. **Das Griechische Pfandrecht.** 1895

Hruza, Ernst. **Die Ehebegruendung Nach Attischem Rechte** *and* **Polygamie und Pellikat Nach Griechischem Rechte.** Two vols. in one. 1892/1894

Jost, Karl. **Das Beispiel Und Vorbild Der Vorfahren.** 1935

Kohler, Josef and Erich Ziebarth. **Das Stadtrecht Von Gortyn Und Seine Beziehungen Zum Gemeingriechischen Rechte.** 1912

Koestler, Rudolf. **Homerisches Recht** and Vos, Harm, **Themis.** Two vols. in one. 1950/1956

Kunsemueller, Otto. **Die Herkunft Der Platonischen Kardinaltugenden** and Wankel, Hermann, **Kalos Kai Agathos.** Two vols. in one. 1935/1961

Leisi, Ernst. **Der Zeuge Im Attischen Recht** and Schlesinger, Eilhard, **Die Griechische Asylie.** Two vols. in one. 1908/1933

Lotze, Detlef. **Metaxy Eleutherōn Kai Doulōn** and Hampl, Franz, **Die Lakedaemonischen Perioeken.** Two vols. in one. 1959/1937

Lofberg, John Oscar. **Sycophancy in Athens** and Barkan, Irving, **Capital Punishment in Ancient Athens** (Doctoral Dissertation, The University of Chicago, 1935). Two vols. in one. 1917/1935

Martin, Victor. **La Vie Internationale Dans La Grèce Des Cités.** 1940

Maschke, Richard. **Die Willenslehre Im Griechischen Recht.** 1926

Meier, Moritz Hermann Eduard and Georg Friedrich Schoemann. **Der Attische Process.** 1824

Menzel, Adolf. **Hellenika:** Gesammelte Kleine Schriften. 1938

Minar, Edwin L., Jr. **Early Pythagorean Politics in Practice and Theory.** 1942

Oliver, James H.. **Demokratia, The Gods, and The Free World.** 1960

Phillipson, Coleman. **The International Law and Custom of Ancient Greece and Rome.** Volume I. 1911

Pickard-Cambridge, A[rthur] W[allace]. **Demosthenes and the Last Days of Greek Freedom, 384-322 B.C.** 1914

Pringsheim, Fritz. **Der Kauf Mit Fremdem Geld.** 1916

Robinson, David M. and Edward J. Fluck. **A Study of the Greek Love-Names.** 1937

Romilly, Jacqueline De. **Thucydides and Athenian Imperialism.** Translated by Philip Thody. 1963

Schaefer, Arnold. **Demosthenes Und Seine Zeit.** Three vols. 1856/1856/1858

Schodorf, Konrad. **Beitraege Zur Genaueren Kenntnis Der Attischen Gerichtssprache Aus Den Zehn Rednern** and Demisch, Edwin, **Die Schuldenerbfolge Im Attischen Recht.** Two vols. in one. 1904/1910

Schulthess, Otto. **Vormundschaft Nach Attischem Recht.** 1886

[Shellens], Max Salomon. **Der Begriff Der Gerechtigkeit Bei Aristoteles.** 1937

Szanto, Emil. **Das Griechische Buergerrecht.** 1892

Toutain, Jules. **The Economic Life of the Ancient World.** Translated by M. R. Dobie. 1930

Voegelin, Walter. **Die Diabole Bei Lysias.** 1943

Vollgraff, [Carl] W[ilhelm]. **L'Oraison Funèbre De Gorgias.** 1952